AMERICA'S GROWTH STOCKS

Published by
Bob Adams, Inc.
260 Center Street
Holbrook, Massachusetts 02343

AMERICA'S GROWTH STOCKS

THE 169 STRONGEST PERFORMERS

THEODORE DREY

BOB ADAMS, INC.
PUBLISHERS
Holbrook, Massachusetts

*To my late uncle James Drey,
who introduced me to the stock market
and the Kirstein Business Library in Boston
when I was in high school.*

CONTENTS

INTRODUCTION

During the past decade and the turbulent eras preceding it, few stocks have shown as high a degree of relative stability as those of the growth stock group. Throughout the years, in peace and in war, in boom and in recession, under Democrats and under Republicans, growth stocks have, better than any other group, weathered the undulation of the business cycle.

The most reliable indicator of growth is consistent above-average gains in sales and earnings. Prominent among growth issues are business-forms manufacturers, consumer food-oriented companies, pharmaceutical companies, psychiatric hospital chains, and a number of regional banks. Growth industries are less vulnerable to recessions than cyclical ones such as steel, chemical, textile, and automobile companies. While growth companies may be found in a variety of industries, they have in common a number of characteristics, namely, strong profit margins, a commitment to research and development, an above average return on equity, modest dividend payouts, and expanding sales.

A number of parameters were used in selecting stocks for inclusion in this book. First, the stock must have a Standard & Poor's rating of A+, A, A-, B+, or B. Second, the corporation must have a minimum of at least $100 million in assets. This means that only established growth stocks are included. Third, the corporation must have a public track record of at least ten years. Fourth, the corporation must have experienced consistent long-term uptrends in assets, revenues, and operating earnings. Finally, and most important, the company must give indication that it can extend into the future its upward momentum in sales, earnings, and dividends.

INVESTMENT FUNDAMENTALS

The stock market is at the confluence of many forces, including economic, monetary, technical, political, and international influences. In almost no other art can performance be so objectively measured as in investing. Success in the market is heavily dependent upon what Robert Kirby, chairman of Capital Guardian Trust, calls "instinct," or knowing how.

There are basically two types of learning situations, namely, knowing *that* (knowing about something) and knowing *how*. Knowing about the stock market comes from studying books, magazine articles, newspapers, brokerage reports, etc. Knowing how to make money in the stock market comes from the ability to analyze the track record of a company and from actual experience in buying and selling. The successful investor should have a knowledge of both, but it is more often the latter "knowing how" that is lacking.

Franklin Roosevelt once remarked that "people don't eat in the long term." But investors do not achieve their objectives in the short term. History has established that the stock market moves in cycles. Money is made by individuals who single out a few undervalued rapid-growth stocks and stick with them over a long time.

Stock selection, then, is basically a search for value. And despite the emphasis on quantitative and technical analysis, successful investing remains more an art than a science.

The most difficult aspect of learning about the stock market or individual stocks is obtaining sound, objective information. While much is written about the market and individual stocks, most of the authors have some vested interest in what they write about. For example, many brokerage firms are either underwriting or making a market in the equities they are writing about. Many books about the stock market are written by the proprietors of investment advisory letters, whose objective is to prove their thesis of how to beat the market.

The most objective information about individual equities usually can be obtained from the financial review sections of their annual reports, the 10-K Forms filed with the Securities and Exchange Commission, and sources such as *Standard & Poor's*, *Moody's*, and *Value Line*. The most objective information about the *how* of the stock market is *Better Investing* and other publications of the National Association of Investment Clubs. The association's *Stock Selection Guide* format is indispensable for someone interested in learning how to evaluate the track record and intrinsic value of individual stocks. One does not need to be a member of an investment club to purchase these publications. Their association's address is P.O. Box 220, Royal Oak, MI 48068. In addition, for someone interested in investing as a profession, I would recommend the publications and correspondence of the New York Institute of Finance, 70 Pine Street, New York, NY 10270.

A corporation can raise capital in four ways:

- by borrowing it,

- by selling bonds, which yield a fixed rate of return either to call or to maturity,

- by issuing preferred stock with a fixed dividend and prior rights to dividends,

- by selling equities (common stock).

Frequently, a corporation opts for the equities route because it does not obligate the company to future payments for the use of capital. This is especially true if a company pays little or no dividend. However, equities cannot always be sold. In times of gloom, doom, recession, and low stock prices, it is almost impossible to market new issues of equities, so corporations choose to borrow, issue preferred stock, or sell bonds. In times of economic euphoria, prosperity, and cheap money, corporations usually sell equities to raise capital.

When a corporation decides to take the equity route, it usually sells shares wholesale to an investment banker or a group of investment bankers (also usually brokers). The investment bankers then retail the shares at a predetermined price. Very often, new issues include some shares of insider stockholders, who purchased them for a few cents and are unloading them to the public for considerable profit.

If the new issue involves an established major company, the broker can often sell the shares to institutions or substantial customers. On the other hand, if the new issue is an unseasoned, new or fledgling company, the broker must sell the shares to the "gullible" public, knowing full well

16

that institutional investors will not touch them with a ten-foot pole. For example, if the new issue is a fledgling cosmetic firm, the broker sends a prospectus and research report to potential customers. The research report contains a narrative about the industry and statistics concerning the company. The narrative is likely to focus on the bright prospects for the cosmetics industry without mentioning that the new firm will be competing with such giants as Proctor & Gamble, Revlon, Colgate Palmolive, and Alberto Culver. Whether they represent substantial or fledgling corporations, new issues usually come to market during a period of price euphoria and are, historically, overpriced.

It is possible to prove almost *any* investment thesis either by citing specific examples or by using a carefully chosen time span. For example, one could establish that low price-earnings ratio is the key to investment success by citing a variety of low-priced earnings ratio issues that have substantially appreciated. One could also establish that new issues are the key to investment success by considering a time range favorable to new issues. During the early seventies, it was almost impossible to establish any thesis except perhaps the virtues of short selling. Most growth stocks, during the early seventies, continued to increase earnings and assets, but their prices declined from those of the astronomical sixties. Basically, what happened was that interest rates began a long historic climb, making fixed-income investments, such as bonds, more attractive, and thus placing a lower price-earnings value on equities.

The automobile industry was a rapid-growth industry for more than fifty years. There were as many as three hundred and fifty automobile companies in the United States at one time or another, yet only a handful survived. Most went bankrupt, and some were merged. In order to have made money in automobile equities, one would have to have invested in General Motors or Chrysler or one of the companies which amalgamated with them. (Ford was not a public company until the 1950s.) The high-tech industry will be an expanding and developing industry for the next twenty-five or more years. However, I can't help but feel that, ultimately, only a small number of high-tech firms will survive. Rest assured that IBM, AT & T, and Raytheon will be among them.

The wild inflationary boom of the twenties ended in a massive bust and long-term depression largely because the Federal Reserve, instead of putting on the brakes slowly, jammed them on suddenly. In 1929, the Federal Reserve not only tightened money but also raised bank reserve requirements, forcing the banks to call in loans. That meant that construction firms immediately owed money, which they could not pay, to the bank. The construction firms went bankrupt and laid off workers; the

17

banks ended up owning partially completed homes and other projects, which they could not sell. Idle construction workers and engineers were the first domino that lead to an unemployment rate that reached as high as 25%. The debacle of 1929 was followed by the 1930 Hawley-Smoot Tariff Act, a protectionist measure, which raised U.S. tariff rates almost 50% and effectively stifled world trade.

During the twenties, banks and brokers sold securities on a low (10%) margin, and on that fateful day when the Federal Reserve increased bank reserve requirements, millions of stockholders ended up owing more than they owned. The Glass-Steagall Act (1933) highly regulated banks and effectively put them out of the stock brokerage business. Now, almost sixty years later, under the guise of deregulation, the banks may once again get into the brokerage business.

Could a 1929 style economic collapse occur again? The answer is yes, but probably for entirely different reasons. Like all big busts, it will occur completely unheralded. For example, a collapse of the world banking system or the bombing of American cities could trigger a massive collapse. While the Federal Deposit Insurance Corporation (FDIC) insurance on bank deposits can cover problems here and there, it could never sustain a massive run on banks. The banking system is based on confidence, and no bank, however financially sound, could sustain a large run on its deposits. Increasing banks' mandated reserves for real and imagined losses and increasing capital requirements, when banks are weak, are just the ways to erode confidence. The moral of the story is, don't buy stocks on margin or buy equities with money that you can't afford to lose. (In passing, let me note that in the opinion of many observers, the so-called meltdown on October 19, 1987, was basically technical rather than economic.)

Now a word about those old reliable investment advisors, who consistently make more money dispensing advice then their clients make following it. Most market forecasters are correct, only their timing is off. The question is not whether the market will go up or down, but when? The flamboyant Joseph Granville is an excellent technician, but in 1982, when he became very specific in urging his clients to sell out, he lost face with the investment community. Investment letters often score more winners than their clients, because they recommend a large number of stocks. An investor can usually own between five and twenty individual securities at a time, whereas many market letters recommend anywhere from ten to twenty a month. Market letters often proclaim their success by using favorable time periods. For example, if the market has just jumped 20%, the letter advertises how its recommended stocks did during that period of increase, ignoring how they may have done the year before, when prices were declining. A number of market letters recommend stocks only superficially, by providing a list of stocks expected to increase earnings next year or a list of stocks selling below $25.00. The well-known advisory letters usually discuss large companies with wide investment appeal and active trading. The smaller, lesser-known advisory letters often concentrate on small companies with a small float (number of shares available for trading) and high betas (that is, strong leverage on the upside and little resistance on the down side). In choosing a market letter, one should know the basic philosophy of its author. Most market letters recommend stocks as trading vehicles; very few are recommending stocks for long-term holding, such as five, ten, or twenty-five years.

The analysts in large brokerage firms tend to specialize in certain industries. While they recommend what they believe to be the best buys in their appointed industry, the individual investor is usually interested in acquiring the best value, irrespective of industry. The best investment letters or advisory services are probably those which are long on information and short on recommendations.

The stock market closely parallels money-rate fluctuations and anticipates future business trends by about six or nine months. There are basically two types of market analysts:

- the technician, who bases his or her decisions on the reading and interpretation of statistics and charts,

- the fundamentalist, who bases his or her decisions upon such factors as economic conditions, level of interest rates, earnings history, dividends, supply and demand, management, labor problems, and the product itself.

While technicians claim to be more objective, the interpretation of charts and other technical data is highly subjective.

Many macroeconomic factors affect the price of an individual stock. Some such factors are interest rates, the money supply, the availability of commercial bank loans, general economic conditions for business as a whole and specific industries in particular, the short-sale ratio, margin requirements, and the strength of the dollar. Interest rates are one of the more important macroeconomic factors. As interest rates rise, they tend to cause money to flow out of stocks into more attractive, higher-yielding investments such as bonds and bank certificates of deposits. This results in stocks being valued at a lower price-earnings ratio and a lower price.

Conversely, a decrease in interest rates causes money to flow out of bonds and other fixed-income securities into equities, and thus results in a rise in the stock market. The direction of interest rates can be determined by observing the average maturity of money fund loans. When the average maturity of money-fund loans lengthens, interest rates are headed lower, and conversely when the average maturity of money-fund loans shortens, interest rates are headed higher.

When commercial bank loans rise rapidly, the Federal Reserve tends to tighten the money supply (sells securities). On the other hand, when commercial bank loans rapidly decrease, the Federal Reserve moves to increase the money supply (buys securities). These actions by the Federal Reserve tend to dampen an overheated market and to stimulate a depressed market. A high short-sale ratio in the market as a whole or in a particular stock creates buying power because, ultimately, the shorts must "cover" by buying stock. The increase and decrease of margin requirements contribute, likewise, to the ebb and flow of the market. If the dollar is weak, currency translation expands the foreign earnings of American companies. Conversely, if the dollar is strong, currency translation contracts the foreign profits of American companies.

Some microeconomic factors affecting the price of individual equities are management, earnings, dividends, the ratio of current assets to current liabilities, the float, institutional ownership, and funded debt. The history of the earnings of a company determines whether a company is fast growth, moderate growth, slow growth, or cyclical. A high dividend yield on a stock usually indicates that it has little growth or is cyclical. Growing companies tend to have low dividend yields and comparatively higher price-earnings ratios. The ratio of current assets to liabilities is a major determinant of the financial soundness of a company. For small and medium-sized companies (under $1 billion in assets) the ratio should be at least two to one. In large companies (over $1 billion in assets) the ratio should be at least one to one. The float is the number of shares actually available for public trading. A large float aids price stability; a small float tends to accentuate price movements, both up and down. Institutional ownership can be both good and bad. Purchases of large blocks of a particular equity by institutions move the price per share up. Conversely, if institutions sour on an issue, massive blocks of an equity suddenly go on sale, depressing its market price. The debt of a company determines to what extent the profits of a company will be divided (first to the debtor and second to the common stockholder).

In analyzing individual stocks, historical track record and value are paramount. The investor should study the earnings and price movements for at least the prior ten years and should especially note the earnings and price performance during the most recent recession. Note that traditional growth stocks such as those of drug and publishing companies sell at higher comparative price-earnings ratios than other usually cyclical stocks such as those in the paper, metals, and housing industries. While a history of long-term increases in earnings and dividends is a chronicle of the past, it is the single most reliable prelude to the future, particularly if earnings and dividends have increased during the previous recession. However, there must be sound reasons for growth to continue.

The hallmarks of a quality company are:

- a small amount of debt as a percentage of total capitalization,
- a good current ratio,
- a high return on equity,
- a high profit margin,
- a low break-even point, and
- a consistent pattern of growth.

While the quality of a company is not directly related to its stock's price, there are many more lemons available at $10.00 per share than are available at $40.00 per share. While there are many excellent stocks selling at low prices, the risks of selection are much greater as price per share decreases.

The quantitative analysis of stock-market trends began early in the twentieth century through the writings of Charles H. Dow and William Peter Hamilton in their evolutionary development of the Dow Theory. The Dow Industrials in its present form is much more of an index than an average. Quantitative analysis came to fruition in the writings of Benjamin Graham: *Security Analysis* (1934) and *The Intelligent Investor* (1949). Today, technical analysis of the market utilizes many indicators such as the cash holdings of mutual funds, the odd-lot short-sale ratio, moving averages, the high-low differential, volume momentum, and many others. What one tends to get from an analysis of indicators is plenty of positives and plenty of negatives. Also, the indicators do not carry equal weightings in all market cycles. Picking tops and bottoms, with any degree of consistency, has eluded the technical experts. This, however, is not very important, because the tops and bottoms of specific industries and equities rarely coincide with the indicators. For example, when the Dow Industrial Average hits bottom, many stocks have already hit bottom and are on the way up; conversely, many individual equities have yet to hit bottom. In short, while many indicators such as the short-sale ratio and cash in brokers' accounts are valuable tools for interpreting the market, no one indicator or group of indicators rings a bell when the market hits a high or a low.

Because this book includes several regional banks, which one must analyze quite differently than industrial companies, a discussion of them is imperative. Many regional banks afford excellent growth at relatively low price-earnings ratios. Because regional banks are often local in both operation and ownership, with a small float, the prices of their stocks rarely will be bid up too high, expanding price-earnings ratios. In singling out individual growth banks, the investor must guard against so-called innovative bankers such as Parsons of Bank of the Commonwealth (now merged with Comerica). Basically, what Parsons did was perfectly legitimate but unsound. In the mid-sixties, when interest rates began to rise, Parsons locked up its assets in long-term bonds. He thought that long-term interest rates would fall, but instead they continued to rise, depressing the value of the bank's assets, making the bank highly illiquid and ultimately insolvent.

A quality bank is distinguished by an aggressive marketing policy and a conservative credit policy. A consistent positive return on assets is the single most important indicator of a bank's performance, preferably at least 1% for a small bank and slightly less for a large bank. (A return on assets of 1% means that the bank earned $1.00 for each $100.00 of assets.) It is also preferable that the bank have a high ratio of consumer assets to total liabilities. The deposits of individual consumers are considered more stable than those of businesses or large depositors, who will flee more quickly for higher rates. The key financial figures to look for in a bank's statement are, first, the ratio of capital to assets. The federal government requires 7%, but the higher the better. Second in importance is the ratio of delinquent loans to assets, preferably below 2%, but the lower the better. A potentially excellent bank stock is one with a good price-earnings ratio, selling at or below book value, with a consistently above-average return on assets. *Bank Quarterly Rating & Analysis*, published by Sheshunoff Information Services, 505 Barton Springs Road, Austin, TX 78711, represents a good summary of statistical information on the nation's banking companies.

Property and casualty insurance companies, likewise, do not lend themselves to easy analysis. Not many property and casualty companies qualify as growth equities, because their earnings are subject to the fluctuations of the underwriting cycle. Long-term success can be obtained by restricting investment to those companies that consistently demonstrate loss and expense ratios lower than those of their competitors. Best's *Property & Casualty Insurance, Life Insurance* directories are the bibles of the insurance industry and can be very helpful in evaluating choices in this area.

INTELLIGENT INVESTING

There are no universal rules, systems, or formulae for investment success. Equity market movement is a composite of many diverse internal and external forces. Rather than trying to forecast the highs and lows of the market, it is more important to distinguish values among individual equities. Investment management consists of three elements:

- learning about individual issues,

- relating values to the market, and

- recognizing one's own goals and limitations.

Moreover, it is important to remember that no one is right all the time.

The investor must be aware that both the market and groups within the market move in cycles. Every cycle has a beginning and an end. It is when the public becomes convinced of the evolutionary character of a cycle that it collapses. Witness the boom in energy issues in the late seventies and their subsequent collapse in the early eighties. Every decade has at least one triumph and one washout. Clearly there are times when security prices are too high and, conversely, times when they are too low. The investor should be willing to wait for the bargain even if it takes several years.

A growth stock should have a proven record of earnings, be a well-seasoned equity, and operate in an industry of above-average potential. The investor should focus on long-term investments in companies whose management's performance indicates that they will be worth substantially more in five or ten years. Robert Kirby, chairman of Capital Guardian Trust, stated in the "Money Manager" discussion in the *Wall Street Transcript* (June 4, 1984) that "people get rich not by anticipating interim market swings, but by investing in the right companies and staying there. You rarely see a large fortune that arose out of trading. Fortunes come from a few holdings in the right companies held over a long period of time. We think selection is 95% of successful investing and market timing is 5%."

The more an investor concentrates on short-term expectations, the more likely he or she is to insulate himself or herself from long-term appreciation. The ideal growth stock is a very successful company with more than $100 million but under $1 billion in assets with a long history of consecutive increases in earnings and dividends. Companies such as John H. Harland, Dun & Bradstreet, and Wallace Computer Services come to mind.

The problem with most so-called emerging growth stocks is that most of them never emerge. Most of them are characterized by the greater fool theory; one buys them with the expectation that a greater fool will take them off one's hands at a higher price. Emerging growth stocks are often mere concepts, underpinned with negligible assets, yielding marginal earnings and selling at prices that discount the future. To say that a stock has compounded earnings at 35% annually for the past five years, when earnings have gone from 5¢ to 22¢, doesn't signify much. Therefore, the claims for substantial percentage earnings gains in emerging growth stocks, while they may be accurate, are not very meaningful. The fledgling investor, who can least afford to lose money, is usually the market for these issues.

The best opportunities in growth stocks arise when the market is temporarily depressed. Fear and greed are the greatest obstacles to market success. While one should not put all one's eggs in a single basket, it is also a mistake to put them in too many baskets. Diversification is good up to a point. While wide diversification protects the investor against staggering losses, it also insulates him from dramatic gains. Try to invest when you believe the long-term market is turning upward. Search for stocks that are about to have explosive earnings growth but whose prices have not yet discounted that growth. Investigate and then invest—do not, as so many do, invest and then investigate. Condition your emotions to make mistakes and take losses. Many investors cling to a falling stock as an inexperienced parachute jumper clings to a falling airplane.

It is often stated that America's enormous industrial complex was built with risk dollars. While the statement is true, it is certainly not a justification for risk taking when the risk-reward ratio is not realistic. Trying to find the next superstock should be reserved for the investor with extensive market experience, and even then it is an extremely difficult task. Many brokerage firms and mutual funds hire electronics engineers to evaluate high-tech firms and while the engineers are usually long on technical expertise, they are more often short on market expertise.

Unfortunately, many neophyte investors begin their investment career trying to pick the next Xerox. This inevitably leads to unmitigated investment disaster. An intelligent approach to picking the next super-stock would be to work over lists of securities selected by analysts, who specialize in this pursuit. Investors seeking maximum long-term capital appreciation might take a look at Diagnostic Products Corporation, First Financial Management, and Policy Management Systems Corporation, all highlighted in this book.

Predicting the future direction of the market is fraught with danger. There are dozens, even hundreds of financial variables that fluctuate daily and influence on the market direction. The market tends to over-reach itself, going too high on the upside and too low on the downside. The longer a bull market extends, the more it discounts the possibility of picking up sound values and ultimate capital gains. Many investors buy too early and sell too late.

Traditionally, there is a three-point spread between interest rates and inflation. When there is a divergence, either one or the other will eventually give way. When interest rates are high and inflation is low, inflationary expectation is high. When interest rates rise, investors capitalize earnings at a lower multiple and, conversely, when interest rates fall, investors capitalize earnings at a higher multiple. What usually aborts a recovery is excess build-up in inventory and capital spending.

A rising (bull) market raises all ships; conversely a falling (bear) market lowers all ships. Every bull market creates a host of new so-called market experts, but only a handful of them, such as John Marks Templeton, Warren Buffett, Peter Lynch, the late T. Rowe Price, and the late Ralph Coleman, withstand the test of time. When such men retire or pass on, they are usually succeeded by technocrats with accounting, computer, and assorted MBA degrees. These successors can rarely continue in the footsteps of their mentors, many of whom had little or no formal business education.

No two bull or bear markets are exactly alike. The various indicators in a bull market top or a bear market bottom yield different and diverse weightings in the historical pattern of market movements. This is the principle reason why it is almost impossible to pinpoint objectively the exact market tops and bottoms. Tops and bottoms are a composite of numerous indicators, evidencing a variety of quantitative strengths and weaknesses at market turns. The experienced can reasonably identify market highs and lows, when such a composite of indicators is in evidence. Investing in growth stocks, in a down market, when price-earnings ratios are low, should provide a minimum of portfolio turnover.

The market is basically manic-depressive, fluctuating between moods of euphoria and gloom. A market high is generally discernible when the number of Big Board stocks hitting new highs has dried up, price-earnings ratios are high by historical standards, institutional cash reserves (including those of mutual funds) are low, Big Board short-interest ratio is low, market sentiment is euphoric with economists predicting that the millennium has arrived, and a surging number of new issues and concept stocks are coming to market, many being underwritten by brokerage firms with repeated regulatory problems.

The characteristics of a bear-market low are discernible when the market is hitting new lows, yet the number of individual new lows on the Big Board has dried up; the market fails to yield much on the downside to gloomy economic news; institutional cash reserves (including those of mutual funds) are surging; the Big Board short-interest ratio is high; negative sentiment is extremely high; and there is a dearth of new issues and concept stocks.

While individual stocks should be bought on the basis of track record and value rather than chart formations, certain technical indicators are excellent for following market trends. When the price-earnings ratio for the Dow Jones Industrials is below 9, the market is on the low side, and when it is above 19, it is getting high. At market highs, the Dow Industrials tend to have dividend yields below 3.2%; at market lows, 5% or above. Over the years the market has generally seen its highs when the Dow Industrials have sold above 1.9 times book value and its lows when the same average has sold at 1.2 times book value. The cash position of mutual funds usually hovers around 3% to 4% at market tops and around 9% to 10% at market bottoms. The Big Board short-sales ratio is a major technical factor: when it reaches 8.5% of all transactions on the Big Board, it is reasonably safe to buy, and when it falls below 6.5%, the market is ready for a sale. Another valid indicator is the ratio of specialists' shorts to public shorts. When it runs over 3½ to 1, it is bearish; conversely when it runs under 2 to 1, it becomes bullish. A high short-interest ratio means that eventually the shorts will have to cover, thus creating buying power. The cash position of brokerage accounts tends to rise rapidly toward the termination of a bear market.

Much of the selling on the downside of a market is caused not only by disillusionment but also by the technical factor of margin calls, which adds to the cascade. The value of institutional cash holdings as a predictor of future market moves has been blunted by the fact that most large institutional investors now tend to convert cash to money-market funds and other short-term instruments. The advent of options trading and extensive arbitrage have also diminished the reliability of the short-interest indicator. The problem with many market indicators is that there is often a time lag between when they occur and when they are published. While statistics don't lie, inferences drawn from then often do. In short, it is much easier to ferret out undervalued equities than it is to predict future market trends.

The advantage of mutual funds are said to be diversification of risk, low start-up costs, professional management, freedom from bookkeeping, little emotional involvement, automatic reinvestment of dividends, and readily available information on fund records. Yet aside from a few outstanding funds such as the Templeton Growth Fund and the Magellan Fund, most funds have a lackluster long-term performance. The rating of a fund's performance can vary widely depending upon the time periods examined. Any comparative rating of fund performance is influenced by the time frame used. For example, the comparative rating of funds over an annual, five-year, or ten-year span often yields quite divergent results.

A number of mutual funds are specialized and perform in accordance with their speciality. For example, the performance of a fund which specializes in medical stocks or life insurance issues will parallel the performance of those industries. While having a large family of funds will enhance a management's chance for a winner, it will be a negative in management's overall performance, because mass phenomena tend toward stability, or average performance.

Mutual funds have a number of inbuilt problems. Their funds tend to be bought in small amounts by the masses of people (the public). These small investors usually buy funds in good times when they are flush with money and cash them in during a recession, when they need cash. The result is that mutual funds must purchase shares on a surging market and sell them on a falling market. A way to partially negate this problem is to invest in a fund which requires a high initial down payment.

Another problem is that both in mutual funds and in institutional investing, safety is often sacrificed on the high altar of performance. Money moves toward performance, so many fund managers, while they may be aware of market euphoria, cannot afford to lose that final 1% or 2% rise, so they get caught in the downturn.

Also, fund managers are often motivated to buy and sell stocks for a variety of reasons other than the prospects for an individual company. They might want to dress up the portfolio at the end of a quarter by selling a loser and buying a winner. They might want to increase or decrease capital gains distributions or might be motivated to sell a stock because an executive officer of a company refused to take phone calls or ignored their visit. It is also very difficult for a fund manager to stick with an undervalued stock that is not moving. In short, professional investment managers are often caught between the chasm of sound investment practices and a greedy get-rich-quick constituency.

Understanding the Financial Listings in a Newspaper

The accompanying chart shows a New York Stock Exchange listing from a recent newspaper.

52 Weeks Hi	Lo	Stock	Sym	Div	Yld %	PE	Vol 100s	Hi	Lo	Close	Net Chg
				-A-A-A-							
27¼	25	ANR pf		2.67	10.3	...	10	26	25¾	26	+ ½
44¼	33⅛	ARCO Chm	RCM	2.50	6.6	20	513	38⅜	37⅞	38⅛	– ⅛
2⅝	**1**	**ARX**	**ARX**		...	...	**340**	**1¼**	**1**	**1¼**	**+ ⅛**
56	40½	ASA	ASA	3.00	6.4	...	548	48	47	47⅛	– ⅝
61⅜	39¼	AbbotLab	ABT	1.00	1.6	25	5809	60⅞	59⅝	60⅝	+1⅛
14⅝	9⅞	Abitibi g	ABY	.50	...	...	5	13⅛	13⅛	13⅛	...
6	3⅜	AcmeFlec	AC[illegible]				[illegible]	[illegible]			

Note that the companies are listed alphabetically. Find Abbott Laboratories, which is the first company profiled in this book. To the left of the Abbott name, under the columns "Hi" and "Lo," are two share prices. The number on the left, 61⅜, represents the high per share price for Abbott during the past 52 weeks, while the number on the right, 39¼, represents the low per share price for Abbott during the past 52 weeks.

Immediately to the right of the name AbbottLab is the symbol ABT. This is the symbol under which Abbott Laboratories shares trade on the New York Stock Exchange.

To the right of the symbol ABT, under the column "Div" is 1.00, which means that Abbott Laboratories currently pays a dividend of $1.00 per share on its common stock per year.

To the right of the dividend column is the "YLD %" column which shows 1.6. This means that based on the present per share price of Abbott (60⅜) and a dividend of $1.00, the shareholder receives a cash return of 1.6% on his investment. The figure is derived by dividing the cash dividend by the price per share of the stock. In other words, divide 1.00 by 60⅜.

To the right of this column is the column headed "PE" which shows the number 25. This is the price earnings ratio, a popular yardstick for evaluating market prices. It is derived by dividing the current price per share by the earnings per share for the most recent 52 weeks for which information is available. Growth stocks traditionally have higher price earnings per share ratios than income stocks. Earnings figures are not available in daily *Wall Street Journal* listings but are available in *Barron's Weekly* and a number of Standard & Poor's and Moody's publications.

The next column to the right is headed "Vol 100s" and furnishes the volume, or total number of shares (in hundreds), traded the previous day. In Abbott's case, the 5809 means that 580,900 shares were traded the previous day.

The next three figures headed "Hi," "Lo," and "Close" report the prices for the previous day's trading. In the Abbott transactions some investors paid a high of 60⅞, a low of 59⅜ and the last or closing sale was for 60⅜.

The last column headed "Net Chg" represents the net change in price from the closing price of the preceding day. In this case Abbott Labs gained 1⅛.

GROWTH COMPANIES

Key to Statistical Data on Company Profiles

Total assets

Assets represent the total amount of property belonging to a corporation, whereas liabilities represent the total amount of indebtedness or obligations of a corporation. Total assets consist of both current and long-term assets. Likewise, total liabilities consist of both current and long-term liabilities.

Current assets are quick assets such as cash, raw materials, inventory, accounts receivable, and other items that can be readily turned into cash as opposed to long-term assets such as plant, equipment, and other assets which cannot readily be turned into cash.

Current liabilities represent short-term indebtedness such as accounts payable, expenses, taxes payable, and other debts owed within a year as opposed to long-term debt, bonding issues, preferred stock, and common stock.

The total assets of a company indicate not only the total value of a corporation but also the size of a corporation. A corporation with over $1 billion in total assets is a large corporation. A corporation with total assets between $100 million and $1 billion is medium-sized. A corporation with under $100 million in total assets is considered small.

Current ratio

The current ratio is the mathematical ratio of current assets to current liabilities. It strikes the balance between what a corporation owns and owes on a short-term basis, and it determines the credit risk of a corporation. It is determined by dividing current assets by current liabilities. For example, if a corporation has $150 million in current assets and $100 million in current liabilities, it has a current ratio of 1.5. The higher the ratio, the stronger the corporation is financially. If a current ratio is below 1.00, the corporation has a negative net worth.

Common shares outstanding

Shares of common stock represent that portion of a corporation's capitalization which is not preferred, such as debt, bonding issues, and preferred stock. In either the payment of common stock dividends or the default of a corporation, the common stockholders receive payment only after the indebtedness of all senior or preferred obligations have been met.

Revenues

Revenues represent the income or cash receipts of a company.

Net income

Net income is synonymous with net earnings. It is that amount which may be applied to surplus and dividends after deducting the cost of goods sold, including all overhead, administrative, and selling expenses.

Earnings per share

The per share earnings are calculated by dividing net income by the total number of common shares outstanding.

Dividends per share

The common stock dividend is that amount of per share earnings paid to the stockholder. The remaining goes into the coffers of the corporation for further expansion and investment.

A stock dividend is payable in shares of stock to the common stockholder. For example, a 10% stock dividend means that a common shareholder will receive 10 additional shares of common stock for each 100 shares held. Since stock dividends merely subdivide the total pie, they are nontaxable. Stock dividends are paid usually by rapidly growing companies that are preserving capital for expansion.

Prices (HI and LO)

It is important to note that all per share earnings, dividends, and all yearly hi and lo prices have been adjusted to reflect stock dividends.

Abbott Laboratories

Abbott Park
North Chicago, Illinois 60064
Tel. (708) 937-6100
Listed NYSE
Investor contact: V.P. Investor Relations Ellen M. Walvoord
Ticker symbol: ABT
S&P rating: A+

From humble beginnings in the home laboratory of Dr. Wallace G. Abbott in 1888, Abbott Laboratories has grown into one of America's largest, consistently profitable, and most diversified health-care companies.

Its products can be divided roughly into (1) pharmaceutical and nutritional products and (2) hospital supplies and diagnostic laboratory equipment. In 1990, pharmaceutical and nutritional products represented 51% of sales and 60% of profits, while hospital supplies and diagnostic products represented 49% of sales and 40% of profits.

In the pharmaceutical and nutritional line, Abbott is the producer of such ethical (prescription) drugs as the antibiotic Erythromysin, the antianxiety product Traxene, and the anticonvulsant drug Depakote. Also, Abbott produces such over-the-counter sundries as Similac, the nation's leading infant feeding formula; Selsun Blue, an antidandruff shampoo; and Murine for eye care. The infant formula Similac and Isomil have a dominant 50% market share.

In the hospital supply and diagnostic product line Abbott was first (and is still the leader) in the development of an AIDS antibody test. Also, Abbott is a leading contender in the fields of intravenous fluids, cardiovascular products, and diagnostic tests and equipment.

A few years ago, Abbott shifted its research and development budget 80% toward more profitable pharmaceuticals and diagnostics. This has begun to pay off with such new products as Zileuton for ulcerative colitis, rheumatoid arthritis, asthma, and allergies; ProSom for insomnia; and Lupron for Endometriosis. Also, Abbott has developed the only injectable form of a drug that raises the calcium levels of patients who have no kidney function.

33

Promising drugs introduced in various overseas markets include Clarithromysin, an antibiotic; Tosufluxacin, an antiinfective; Forane, an inhalation anesthetic; and Abbott Matrix, a diagnostic test for allergies.

Abbott has paid consecutive cash dividends since 1926. It has increased earnings for 19 consecutive years. Institutions control over 50% of the outstanding shares. Abbott paid a 100% stock dividend in 1981, a 100% stock dividend in 1986, and another 100% stock dividend in 1990.

Total assets: $5.6 (Billion)
Current ratio: 1.2
Common shares outstanding: 429.1 million

		1981	1982	1983	1984	1985	1986	1987	1988	1989	1990
REVENUES (MIL.)		2,343	2,602	2,928	3,104	3,360	3,808	4,388	4,937	5,380	6,159
NET INCOME (MIL.)		247	289	348	403	465	540	633	752	860	966
EARNINGS PER SHARE		.51	.60	.72	.84	.97	1.16	1.39	1.67	1.93	2.22
DIVIDEND PER SHARE		.17	.20	.24	.29	.34	.40	.48	.58	.68	.81
PRICES	Hi	8.1	10.3	13.4	12.3	18.0	27.5	33.5	26.2	35.2	46.4
	Lo	5.9	6.4	9.1	9.3	9.9	15.9	20.0	21.4	23.1	31.3

Albertson's Inc.

250 Parkcenter Blvd.
Boise, Idaho 83726
Tel. (208) 385-6200
Listed NYSE
Investor contact: V.P.-Treas. David I. Connolly
Ticker symbol: ABS
S&P rating: A+

Albertson's is a supermarket, food, and drugstore chain operating approximately 530 stores in 17 Western and Southern states. It owns more than 135 supermarkets, more than 215 superstores, more than 145 combination food and drug units, and approximately 30 warehouse stores.

Albertson's opened 40 additional stores in 1991.

Supermarkets measure about 30,000 square feet, superstores about 42,000 square feet, combination food and drug stores about 58,000 square feet, and warehouse stores anywhere from 65,000 to 73,000 square feet.

Through aggressive merchandising, the opening of additional new stores, the remodeling of existing stores, and a consistent reduction of expenses, Albertson's has grown rapidly during the past ten years. Management, under the control of the original founder, Joe Albertson, has an ambitious five-year $2.1 billion expansion plan, which calls for the opening of 240 new stores and the remodeling of 175 existing stores. The plan also calls for the installation of computer scanning equipment in all stores and the opening of three new distribution centers.

While new store construction is the preferred expansion route for Albertson, it nevertheless purchased eight stores from the Cullem chain in Texas and four stores from Harvest Foods in Wichita, Kansas.

Albertson's is characterized by strong management, excellent operating skills, and a healthy balance sheet. The company's long- term liabilities account for only 20% of its total capital in contrast to a 40% average for other food retailers. Albertson's, with about 23.7% (128 stores) of its operations in California is now the nation's sixth-largest food and drug chain and the seventeenth-largest retailer.

Albertson's has paid consecutive cash dividends since 1960. It has experienced 21 years of consecutive earnings increases and 17 years of consecutive dividend increases. The shares paid a 100% stock dividend in 1980, a 100% stock dividend in 1983, a 100% stock dividend in 1987, and a 100% stock dividend in 1990.

Total assets: $2.0 billion
Current ratio: 1.2
Common shares outstanding: 133.8 million

		1982	1983	1984	1985	1986	1987	1988	1989	1990	1991
REVENUES (MIL.)		3,481	3,940	4,297	4,736	5,060	5,380	5,869	6,773	7,423	8,219
NET INCOME (MIL.)		49	58	70	80	85	100	125	163	197	234
EARNINGS PER SHARE		.40	.48	.54	.61	.65	.75	.94	1.22	1.47	1.75
DIVIDEND PER SHARE		.11	.13	.15	.17	.19	.21	.23	.27	.37	.46
PRICES	Hi	6.3	7.6	7.4	8.3	12.4	17.0	19.4	30.1	37.8	51.4
	Lo	3.1	4.9	5.7	6.6	7.7	10.1	12.0	18.3	24.4	32.6

ALLTEL Corporation

One Allied Drive
Little Rock, Arkansas 72202
Tel. (501) 661-8000
Listed: NYSE
Investor contact: V.P. Corporate Communications, Ronald D. Payne
Ticker symbol: AT
S&P rating: A

 ALLTEL operates one of the largest independent telephone companies in the United States. It provides local telephone service to about 1.2 million customers in 25 states. Most of its service areas are located in or near suburban markets.

Recognizing that growth in telephone service is more modest than in the past, ALLTEL has established a strong presence in a number of related growth businesses such as cellular telephone, product distribution, and information services.

As profiled in its 1990 Annual Report, "The company's cellular operations serve 6.4 million 'pops' in 21 states. By strategically positioning its metropolitan service areas (MSAs) in key Sun Belt markets and clustering its rural service areas around existing MSAs, ALLTEL has created excellent operating properties.

"ALLTEL distributes equipment nationwide through two subsidiaries: ALLTEL Supply, Inc., a leading supplier of telecommunications equipment, and HWC Distribution Corp., one of the nation's largest master distributors of specialty wire and cable products.

"Systematics, Inc., ALLTEL's entry in the high-growth information services market, handles data processing for more than 575 of the nation's banks, savings institutions, and mortgage companies either on-site or from one of Systematics' data centers. In addition, Systematics serves more than 300 software clients in the United States and 26 foreign countries. The company also performs data processing services and provides applications software for local and cellular telephone companies."

Likewise, ALLTEL publishes telephone directories, operates paging systems, and has a 26% interest in Advanced Telecommunications Corp., a Southern-based regional long-distance company.

In 1990, ALLTEL purchased a 19.8% interest in Chillicothe Telephone Co. and in 1991, for $85 million, acquired Missouri Telephone Company, with 20,000 telephone and 2,500 cable customers.

In 1990, revenues and profits were divided as follows: telephone operation, 52% of revenues and 80% of profits; information services, 16% of revenues and 9% of profits; product distribution, 21% of revenues and 6% of profits; cellular, 3% of revenues and 1% of profits; and other, 8% of revenues and 4% of profits.

ALLTEL has paid consecutive cash dividends since 1961. Institutions control about 35% of the common shares. It paid a 6% stock dividend in 1983, a 50% stock dividend in 1987, and a 50% stock dividend in 1989.

Total assets: $2.6 billion
Current ratio: 1.1
Common shares outstanding: 79.2 million

		1981	1982	1983	1984	1985	1986	1987	1988	1989	1990
REVENUES (MIL.)		646	735	812	933	1,035	1,074	1,152	1,265	1,451	1,574
NET INCOME (MIL.)		55	68	77	87	101	89	135	143	175	193
EARNINGS PER SHARE		.88	1.01	1.04	1.18	1.34	1.40	1.63	1.91	2.13	2.35
DIVIDEND PER SHARE		.73	.74	.77	.81	.83	.88	.93	1.05	1.18	1.31
PRICES	Hi	7.6	9.8	11.6	11.3	13.4	20.0	22.8	25.1	41.9	39.1
	Lo	6.4	6.9	9.0	8.9	10.6	12.9	15.4	17.1	23.4	24.8

American Business Products, Inc.

2100 River Edge Parkway, Suite 1200
Atlanta, Georgia 30328
Tel. (404) 953-8300
Listed: NYSE
Investor contact: Pres. Thomas R. Carmody
Ticker symbol: ABP
S&P rating: A-

American Business Products, Inc.

As profiled in its 1990 Annual Report, "American Business Products, Inc. is a leading manufacturer and supplier of business forms for computers and other uses, envelopes, business supplies, books and extrusion coating with 46 production facilities located throughout the continental United States and Hawaii. The Company's products are marketed and distributed in all 50 states through its operating companies, principally by a combined direct sales force of approximately 800 people. A joint venture company based in Germany produces and distributes envelope products in Europe.

American Business Products has five subsidiary companies which it acquired over the years, namely Curtis 1000 Inc., Vanier Graphics Corporation, BookCrafters USA Inc., American Fiber-Velope Mfg. Co., and Jen-Coat, Inc.

"Curtis 1000 Inc. is a world leader in the direct marketing of business envelopes and also boasts a full line of business forms, letterheads, multipart mailers and other supplies. Curtis serves over 70,000 customers coast-to-coast.

"Vanier Graphics Corporation ranks among the leading U.S. producers of business forms and mailers with a line of more than 2,000 products ranging from basic invoices and statements to complex multipart forms.

"BookCrafters USA, Inc. capitalizes on its speciality of short and medium run printing for publishers in the $4.5 billion book printing industry.

"American Fiber-Velope Mfg. Co. is one of the world's leading producers of Tyvek envelopes."

In 1990, American Business acquired Jen-Coat, Inc., a Massachusetts-based specialty extrusion coater of papers, films, and nonwoven fabrics used in packaging.

In 1990, sales and profits were apportioned as follows: business supplies and printing, 87% of sales and 83% of profits; book manufacturing, 11% of sales and 15% of profits; and extrusion coating and laminating, 2% of sales and 2% of profits.

1990 marked the 52nd consecutive year of increased sales and 33rd consecutive year of increased dividends. The Curtis family controls about 30% and institutions about 25% of the common shares. American Business paid a 50% stock dividend in 1983, a 25% stock dividend in 1989, and a 50% stock dividend in 1991.

Total assets: $207 million
Current ratio: 2.7
Common shares outstanding: 10.7 million

		1981	1982	1983	1984	1985	1986	1987	1988	1989	1990
REVENUES (MIL.)		210	223	236	280	300	314	326	358	387	399
NET INCOME (MIL.)		7	8	9	10	11	10	11	13	14	14
EARNINGS PER SHARE		.67	.71	.85	.92	1.07	.95	1.04	1.21	1.27	1.33
DIVIDEND PER SHARE		.17	.20	.24	.30	.34	.40	.43	.47	.52	.59
PRICES	Hi	5.9	6.8	12.2	12.6	18.2	19.6	16.8	14.2	18.0	15.9
	Lo	3.7	4.2	5.7	9.5	10.9	12.4	8.2	9.6	13.0	12.2

American Family Corporation

1932 Wynnton Road
Columbus, Georgia 31999
Tel. (404) 323-3431
Listed: NYSE
Investor contact: Senior V.P. R. Lee Anderson
Ticker symbol: AFL
S&P rating: A

As profiled in its 1990 Annual Report, "American Family Corporation, through its principal subsidiary, American Family Life Assurance of Columbus, is a market leader in the supplemental health insurance business. AFLAC's primary markets are the United States and Japan. American Family Broadcast Group, Inc., another American Family subsidiary, owns and operates seven  network-affiliated televisions stations in small to medium sized markets. The Company also owns a small printing and market communications company, Communicorp, Inc.

"Founded in Columbus, Georgia, in 1955, AFLAC entered the supplemental health insurance market in 1958 with the development of the world's first cancer expense insurance policy. The Company also pioneered a unique distribution system called cluster-selling, whereby sales associates use their time efficiently by meeting with groups of prospective customers at their workplace. Currently AFLAC markets a broad line of supplemental health insurance to over 84,000 payroll groups in the U.S.

"In 1974, AFLAC became the second American company in Japan's history to be licensed to sell insurance to Japanese citizens. AFLAC not only introduced supplemental cancer expense insurance in Japan, it also adapted cluster-selling to the Japanese marketplace. That new distribution system, comprised primarily of exclusive, corporate insurance agencies, enables employees to purchase AFLAC's insurance on a payroll deduction basis. Today AFLAC Japan has more than 41,000 payroll groups.

"The company has 3,144 full-time employees worldwide; 4,174 sales associates producing business monthly in the U.S.; and 3,150 agencies in Japan with 15,892 associates. Since 1970 the Company has paid approximately $4.7 billion in claims."

While broadly licensed to sell individual and group life and accident and health insurance, American Family's primary product is a supplemental medical and surgical expense cancer policy. In 1990, revenues were apportioned as follows: insurance 97%, broadcasting 2.3%, and other 0.7%.

Consecutive cash dividends have been paid since 1975. Institutions control about 35% of the outstanding common shares. American Family paid a 20% stock dividend in 1983, a 10% stock dividend in 1984, a 50% stock dividend in 1955, a 33⅓% stock dividend in 1986, and a 100% stock dividend in 1987.

Total assets: $8.0 billion
Common shares outstanding: 81.5 million

		1981	1982	1983	1984	1985	1986	1987	1988	1989	1990
REVENUES (MIL.)		514	578	699	824	954	1,431	1,893	2,328	2,438	2,678
NET INCOME (MIL.)		18	25	32	55	55	101	102	109	81	117
EARNINGS PER SHARE		.21	.30	.40	.55	.68	.98	1.27	1.35	1.00	1.44
DIVIDEND PER SHARE		.11	.11	.12	.14	.18	.21	.23	.25	.29	.33
PRICES	Hi	1.9	3.1	4.6	6.3	11.7	18.7	18.5	17.0	22.5	19.3
	Lo	1.3	1.4	2.8	3.4	5.7	10.4	9.9	11.5	13.4	12.1

American Home Products Corporation

685 Third Avenue
New York, New York 10017
Tel. (212) 878-5000
Listed: NYSE
Investor contact: Asst. Treasurer Claire A. Ball
Ticker symbol: AMP
S&P rating: A+

With revenues of $7 billion, 49,000 employees and 70,000 shareholders, American Home Products is one of the world's largest health-care and food-products companies. In 1990, health-care products accounted for 87% of sales and 91% of profits and food products accounted for 13% of sales and 9% of profits.

The most important category of its health-care items is prescription drugs, which account for about 63% of health-care sales. Prescription items include such well know pharmaceuticals as Premarin (estrogen replacement), Inderal (heart medication), and Triphasal (oral contraceptive). Recent drug approvals in the United States include Orudis (analgesic and antiarthritic) and Norplant (subdermal contraceptive implant); recent foreign approvals include Minulet and Tri-Minulet (both oral contraceptives). Lodine (analgesic and antiarthritic) received approval both in the United States and abroad. Consumer pharmaceuticals include Advil, Anacin, and Preparation H. Medical supplies include diagnostic kits, thermometers, catheters, and synthetic dressings.

Food products include Chef Boyardee, Guldens Mustard, Jiffy Popcorn and others.

American Home Products took over the bankrupt A. H. Robins firm for about $3.2 billion on December 15, 1989. Approximately $2.3 billion went into trust funds to settle claims against Robins arising from the Dalkon Shield. In addition to funding the trusts, American Home Products issued common stock valued at approximately $900 million, which was exchanged for all the outstanding stock of A. H. Robins. Robins is the maker of

Robitussin, America's largest-selling cough syrup.

American Home Products has paid consecutive cash dividends since 1919. 1990 represented American Home Products' 38th consecutive year of higher sales, earnings, and dividends. Institutions control about 60% of the outstanding shares. American Home Products split two-for-one effective April 19, 1990.

Total assets: $5.6 billion
Current ratio: 3.7
Common shares outstanding: 314.1 million

		1981	1982	1983	1984	1985	1986	1987	1988	1989	1990
REVENUES (MIL.)		3,895	4,428	4,807	5,089	5,358	5,684	5,805	6,401	6,747	6,775
NET INCOME (MIL.)		542	609	686	695	818	866	928	995	1,102	1,231
EARNINGS PER SHARE		1.64	1.85	2.08	2.14	2.54	2.73	2.98	3.22	3.54	3.92
DIVIDEND PER SHARE		.95	1.08	1.20	1.32	1.45	1.55	1.67	1.80	1.95	2.15
PRICES	Hi	18.6	24.0	27.1	27.9	33.4	47.4	48.4	42.1	54.6	54.9
	Lo	14.1	16.6	20.9	23.4	25.1	30.6	31.0	35.2	40.1	44.0

American International Group, Inc.

70 Pine Street
New York, New York 10270
Tel. (212) 770-7000
Listed: NYSE, London, Paris, Switzerland, and Tokyo
Investor contact: Asst. Director Investor Relations, Brian A. Jones
Ticker symbol: AIG
S&P rating: A

American
International
Group, Inc.

American International Group, Inc. is a premier international insurance holding company with over 45% of its policies written overseas. In addition to being the nation's largest writer of commercial and industrial coverage, AIG companies write property, casualty, marine, life, and financial-services insurance in approximately 130 countries and jurisdiction. Also, AIG provides risk management for self-insurers, agency management, and a range of financial services. The company is very strong in specialty insurance lines of business. Most of its life, health, and accident insurance is written abroad.

AIG is one of the nation's largest and financially soundest property and casualty companies. It is noted for its strong, disciplined and underwriting practices. Consistently its loss and expense ratios remain among the lowest for large American insurance companies. AIG has decreased its underwriting in less profitable workers' compensation, transportation insurance, and agency written personal lines. AIG is gradually returning to the underwriting of personal lines domestically through direct writing and in Europe, through a distribution agreement with Credit Lyonnais. Its life operations are rapidly expanding in the Pacific Rim and it plans to enter Eastern Europe.

Slowly, AIG has expanded its financial services, including interest-rate and currency swaps, cash management, and private banking. In 1990, it acquired International Lease Finance Corp. (ILFC). ILFC is a major lessor of commercial aircraft to domestic and foreign airlines. Over 95% of its aircraft, expected to be delivered in 1992, are leased, and it intends to increase its fleet of 115 aircraft to about 350 by 1995.

AIG's investment portfolio is very sound, with little real estate exposure and very few junk bonds. It has a rock solid balance sheet with a strong commitment to the insurance business.

In 1990, AIG's general insurance net premiums written were broken down as follows: commercial casualty, 58%; foreign, 24%; reinsurance, 9%; property, 5%; personal lines, 3%; and other, 1%.

Consecutive cash dividends have been paid since 1969. Institutions control over 50% of the common shares. AIG paid a 50% stock dividend in 1981, a 25% stock dividend in 1983, a 100% stock dividend in 1986, and a 25% stock dividend in 1990.

Total assets: $60.7 billion
Common shares outstanding: 212.2 million

		1981	1982	1983	1984	1985	1986	1987	1988	1989	1990
REVENUES (MIL.)		3.191	3.537	4.012	4,300	5,895	8,776	11,027	12,844	14,150	15,702
NET INCOME (MIL.)		363	384	412	302	420	791	1,033	1,209	1,367	1,442
EARNINGS PER SHARE		2.02	2.09	2.22	1.62	2.21	3.90	5.02	5.88	6.64	6.92
DIVIDEND PER SHARE		.12	.15	.18	.18	.18	.18	.21	.28	.35	.41
PRICES	Hi	22.2	26.9	31.1	29.2	44.0	57.4	67.0	55.0	89.6	84.8
	Lo	15.6	17.5	20.9	20.4	26.0	41.6	42.9	39.2	53.0	57.0

Anheuser-Busch Companies, Inc.

One Busch Place
St. Louis, Missouri 63118
Tel. (314) 577-3314
Listed: NYSE
Investor contact: V.P.-Treas. Gerald C. Thayer
Ticker symbol: BUD
S&P rating: A+

As profiled in its 1991-92 Fact Book, "Anheuser-Busch Companies, Inc. is a St. Louis-based diversified corporation with subsidiaries that include the world's largest brewing organization, the country's second-largest producer of fresh-baked goods and the second-largest theme park operation in the United States. It also has interests in container manufacturing and recycling, malt production, rice milling, international brewing and beer marketing, snack foods, international baking, refrigerated and frozen foods, real estate development, major league baseball, turf farming, stadium ownership, creative services, railcar repair, transportation services and metalized label printing."

The company's core product is Budweiser beer. It also brews and markets Bud Light, Bud Dry, Michelob Dry, and Michelob Classic Dark. With 43% market share and the consumption of beer holding steady at 175–178 million barrels a year, Anheuser-Busch is clearly growing at the expense of a large number of regional and foreign brands.

With 12 breweries, Anheuser-Busch has the capacity to produce over 90 million barrels of beer a year. National distribution gives Anheuser the ability to sponsor major sporting events on national TV. Shear size gives Anheuser the advantage of lower costs than competitors.

Subsidiary Campbell Taggart, with 67 plants operating in the United States, Spain, and France, is primarily involved in the production and distribution of baked goods, refrigerated dough products, frozen foods, refrigerated salad dressing, snack dips, and toppings to retail and food-service customers. It is the leading commercial baker in the Sunbelt and second-largest commercial baker in the United States.

Busch operates 9 U.S. theme parks: Busch Gardens—The Dark Continent, Busch Gardens—The Old Country, Sea World of California, Sea World of Ohio, Cypress Gardens, Adventure Island, and Sesame Place. Busch also owns the major league baseball team known as the St. Louis Cardinals.

In 1990, beer accounted for 76% of revenues and 91% of profits, food for 18% of revenues and 5% of profits, and entertainment for 6% of revenues and 4% of profits.

1990 marked Anheuser's 14th consecutive year of earnings and dividend increases. It has paid consecutive cash dividends since 1932. It paid a 200% stock dividend in 1985 and a 100% stock dividend in 1986.

Total assets: $9.6 billion
Current ratio: 1.0
Common shares outstanding: 283.9 million

	1981	1982	1983	1984	1985	1986	1987	1988	1989	1990
REVENUES (MIL.)	4,436	5,251	6,715	7,219	7,757	8,479	9,110	9,705	10,284	11,612
NET INCOME (MIL.)	217	287	348	392	444	518	615	716	767	842
EARNINGS PER SHARE	.80	1.00	1.08	1.23	1.42	1.69	2.04	2.45	2.68	2.96
DIVIDEND PER SHARE	.19	.23	.27	.31	.37	.44	.54	.66	.80	.94
PRICES Hi	7.5	11.9	12.9	12.5	22.9	29.1	40.1	34.4	46.0	45.3
Lo	4.6	6.5	9.9	9.0	11.9	19.8	25.8	29.0	30.6	34.0

Automatic Data Processing, Inc.

One ADP Boulevard
Roseland, New Jersey 07068
Tel. (201) 994-5000
Listed: NYSE
Investor contact: S.V.P. Administration and Finance, Arthur F. Weinbach
Ticker symbol: AUD
S&P rating: A+

As profiled in its 1991 Annual Report, "ADP is one of the largest independent companies in the United States dedicated to providing com-

puterized transaction processing, data communications, and information services.

"ADP's mission is to help clients improve their business performance by using our services.

"Our major services include: payroll and human resource information, market data and back-office services to the brokerage industry, industry-specific services to auto and truck dealerships, and computerized repair and replacement estimating for auto insurance companies and body repair shops. We serve more than 225,000 clients."

ADP's strategy for expansion is to concentrate on core businesses, which evidence clear market leadership and growth potential. Employer Services (payroll processing and tax filing), Brokerage Services, Dealer Services and Automotive Claims Services are its core units and all occupy leadership positions. Expansion of its core businesses requires little in the way of capital infusion and generates consistently higher profits. These four segments contributed 90% of 1991 revenues. Employer Services is ADP's largest segment, contributing over 55% of total revenues and growing at a double-digit rate. During fiscal 1991, ADP made ten relatively small acquisitions of which Robert F. White & Co., a Chicago payroll processor, was the largest.

While ADP has experienced some deterioration in brokerage revenues since the 1987 stock market crash, it has generated substantially increased payroll services to banks and claims services to insurance companies. ADP has been pruning services such as its electronic funds transfer business and real-estate services, which it feels do not fit well with its main operations.

ADP has been noted for its consistency in earnings and dividends. 1991 marked ADP's 42nd year of record revenues and earnings. It completed its 120th consecutive quarter of double-digit growth in earnings per share. ADP has paid consecutively increased cash dividends for the past 17 years, since their initiation in 1974. During 1991, ADP acquired 12 million (8%) of its outstanding common shares and the board of directors has authorized the purchase of an additional 7 million shares. ADP paid a 100% stock dividend in 1981, a 100% stock dividend in 1986, and a 100% stock dividend in 1991.

Total assets: $1.6 billion
Current ratio: 1.8
Common shares outstanding: 139.9 million

	1982	1983	1984	1985	1986	1987	1988	1989	1990	1991
REVENUES (MIL.)	669	753	889	1,030	1,204	1,384	1,549	1,678	1,714	1,772
NET INCOME (MIL.)	58	65	75	88	106	132	170	188	212	228
EARNINGS PER SHARE	.43	.47	.54	.62	.73	.88	1.10	1.27	1.44	1.63
DIVIDEND PER SHARE	.12	.13	.15	.16	.18	.20	.23	.27	.31	.36
PRICES Hi	9.5	11.2	10.1	15.0	19.5	27.3	23.7	25.4	30.2	46.4
Lo	5.2	8.3	7.4	9.7	14.0	13.9	17.3	17.9	22.7	25.0

Banc One Corporation

100 East Broad Street
Columbus, Ohio 43271
Tel. (614) 248-5944
Listed: NYSE
Investor contact: V.P.–Treas. George R.L. Meiling
Ticker symbol: ONE
S&P rating: A+

Banc One, based in Columbus, Ohio, is one of the most profitable and superbly managed banks in the United States. Both return on assets and return on equity are consistently above average. Banc One targets its activities to the middle market and consumer lending. Its strength is in retail banking and credit-card processing.

Banc One has expanded by acquisition. It has 51 affiliated banks with 747 branches in Ohio, Indiana, Kentucky, Michigan, Texas, and Wisconsin. It is the largest bank in Indiana, the second-largest in Ohio, and the third-largest in Wisconsin and Texas. It has 89 offices in Texas. In 1990, it had a high 1.53% return on assets.

In 1990, earnings of roughly $24.6 billion were divided as follows: commercial loans, 35%; real estate loans, 19%; consumer loans, 24%;

investments, 20%; and other, 2%.

Banc One processes nearly 9 million credit card accounts, of which over 4 million are its own.

In January 1990, Banc One purchased from the FDIC for $39 million an initial 7.5% interest in a bridge bank consisting of the 20 insolvent banks of M Corp in Dallas, Texas. The bank, now 23% owned by Banc One, is known as Banc One Texas and has approximately $13 billion in assets. Banc One is entitled to purchase the remaining 77% stake from the FDIC over four years at a total cost of $462 million. Meanwhile, the FDIC will assume the costs and risks associated with about $2.5 billion in nonperforming loans.

In 1991, Banc One acquired First Illinois Corp., a $1.6 billion bank holding company in suburban Chicago. Likewise, in late 1991, Banc One acquired the 1.6 billion asset First Security Corp. of Lexington, Kentucky, a bank holding company which consists of the flagship bank, First Security National Bank and Trust Co., and three smaller banks: First Security Bank and Trust Co. of Clark County, First Security Bank and Trust Co. of Danville, and First Security Bank and Trust Co. of Madison.

Banc One has paid consecutive cash dividends since 1933. It has increased earnings for the past 21 years. In 1987, when Banc One charged off 33¢ a share for loans to less-developed countries, it still yielded an annual increase in earnings. Banc One paid stock dividends of 10% in 1980; 10% in January 1982; 50% in December 1982; 50% in 1983; 10% in 1984; 50% in 1985; 10% in 1986; 10% in 1988; and 10% in 1990.

Total assets: $30.3 billion
Common shares outstanding: 158.9 million

		1981	1982	1983	1984	1985	1986	1987	1988	1989	1990
NET INCOME (MIL.)		39	58	83	108	130	200	209	340	348	423
EARNINGS PER SHARE		1.00	1.09	1.27	1.45	1.66	1.76	1.80	2.37	2.52	2.76
DIVIDEND PER SHARE		.33	.36	.43	.48	.58	.68	.74	.84	.95	1.04
PRICES	Hi	7.5	12.1	14.1	13.1	20.9	27.4	24.4	25.1	33.6	33.1
	Lo	5.9	7.0	10.9	10.5	12.5	17.8	19.6	19.1	20.3	19.0

Bandag, Inc.

Bandag Center
Muscatine, Iowa 52761
Tel (319) 262-1400
Listed NYSE
Investor contact: Senior V.P.–C.F.O. Thomas E. Dvorchak
Ticker symbol: BDG
S&P rating: A+

This Muscatine, Iowa, company is the world's leading manufacturer of retread rubber used primarily in the retreading of tires for buses and trucks. Its profitability rests upon two sound pillars of strength: a superb high-quality product and a distribution system of over 1,000 franchised dealers in over 100 countries.

Bandag's primary operation (88%) is the manufacture and sale of retread rubber material and equipment for the retreading of tires (primarily buses and trucks). In the process of cold bonding, the treads are cured prior to being bonded to the tire casing. The dealers bind the treads to the tire casing with bonding material using heat and pressure. The Bandag system is more costly than the conventional hot cap process, but tires recapped by the cold-process method run much longer, thereby reducing the end user's cost per mile driven. With the recent expansion of its Muscatine, Iowa, and Griffen, Georgia, plants, Bandag increased its tread rubber capacity by 25%. The remaining operations (12%) consist of a custom rubber compounding operation and the sale of new and retreaded tires.

The U.S. market is somewhat mature, Bandag each year gains an increasing share of the market. It now controls about 50–55% of the domestic market, which provides 73% of profits. Foreign markets contribute about 36% of revenues and 27% of profits. Bandag is particularly strong in Western Europe, where there is an increasing demand for retreads.

The founding Carver family owns about 34% of all outstanding shares and, through a Class B weighted common share issue, controls about 72% of the voting power. Bandag is in excellent financial condition with long-term debt about 3% of capital. Management has been using Bandag's very strong cash flow to repurchase its common stock.

Since 1982, the number of outstanding shares has decreased by 40%.

Bandag's dividends have increased each year since initiation in 1976. It paid a 50% stock dividend in 1982, a 100% stock dividend in 1986, and a 50% stock dividend in 1987.

Total assets: $347 million
Current ratio: 2.1
Common shares outstanding: 2.7 million

	1981	1982	1983	1984	1985	1986	1987	1988	1989	1990
REVENUES (MIL.)	313	286	303	319	330	370	423	491	525	586
NET INCOME (MIL.)	34	35	39	44	43	49	63	70	76	79
EARNINGS PER SHARE	1.38	1.54	1.94	2.42	2.51	2.85	3.90	4.68	5.22	5.50
DIVIDEND PER SHARE	.40	.45	.50	.55	.60	.66	.73	.83	.93	1.03
PRICES Hi	14.1	21.1	29.9	27.9	31.0	45.8	69.0	67.3	89.3	91.0
Lo	10.0	10.5	19.5	19.0	24.4	28.5	42.0	52.9	64.3	66.0

C.R. Bard, Inc.

730 Central Avenue
Murray Hill, New Jersey 07974
Tel. (908) 277-8000
Listed: NYSE
Investor contact: V.P.–Treas. William C. Bopp
Ticker symbol: BCR
S&P rating: A

C.R. Bard is both a manufacturer and a distributor of medical, diagnostic, and surgical equipment. Its emphasis is on cardiovascular, urological, surgical, and to a lesser degree patient-care products. Bard was a pioneer in the development of single-patient-use medical products for standard hospital procedures.

Management spends about $40 million a year on research and development and is currently involved in the development of a new PET balloon technology utilizing lasers as a device to clear arteries of debris. It is also working in conjunction with Collagen Corp. on the development of a product to treat urinary incontinence.

Bard's primary sales are to hospitals, physicians, and nursing homes. Cardiovascular products account for 42% of sales, surgical instruments for 26% of sales, urological products for 24% of sales, and miscellaneous medical products for 8% of sales. In 1990, international operations accounted for 27% of sales and 47% of profits.

Concerns regarding Bard's Probe angioplasty catheter have had a negative impact on 1989 earnings. There were reports that the tips of the Probe catheter were breaking off after insertion. Bard worked immediately to rectify the problem. The Food and Drug Administration (FDA) requested Bard to stop shipments and to resubmit the modified catheter for approval. The question revolves around whether Bard pursued the "proper regulatory path" in reintroducing this product. Bard, with FDA approval, reintroduced this product in early 1991.

Bard has been in business for 82 years. It has paid consecutive cash dividends since 1960. Institutions control approximately 65% of the outstanding shares. Bard paid a 50% stock dividend in 1982, a 100% stock dividend in 1986, and a 100% stock dividend in 1988.

Total assets: $613 million
Current ratio: 2.0
Common shares outstanding: 53.0 million

		1981	1982	1983	1984	1985	1986	1987	1988	1989	1990
REVENUES (MIL.)		330	343	397	417	465	548	641	758	778	785
NET INCOME (MIL.)		23	27	33	35	42	51	62	79	65	40
EARNINGS PER SHARE		.39	.46	.56	.59	.70	.86	1.07	1.38	1.18	.76
DIVIDEND PER SHARE		.08	.09	.10	.11	.13	.17	.22	.28	.36	.42
PRICES	Hi	5.5	8.9	11.8	9.5	11.0	20.3	25.1	24.6	26.5	22.5
	Lo	3.4	4.6	6.9	4.9	5.5	9.5	12.5	16.9	18.8	12.9

Barnett Banks, Inc.

50 Laura Street
Jacksonville, Florida 32202
Tel. (904) 791-7720
Listed: NYSE
Investor contact: V.P. Finance, Helen C. Rowan
Ticker symbol: BBI
S&P rating: A

Despite a decline in economic growth both nationally and in Florida, Barnett has expanded rapidly both internally and by the acquisition route. The migration of about a thousand people a day to Florida has swelled Barnett's deposit base. Barnett is the leading bank in 43 of Florida's 45 counties with over 550 offices across Florida and over 40 offices in Georgia.

Barnett has been steadily acquiring small banks around Atlanta, Georgia, and total assets in Georgia now total over $1.5 billion. Barnett's emphasis is on retail banking. It is focusing increased attention on commercial lending. In 1990, assets of $27.5 billion were apportioned as follows: real estate loans, 43%; consumer loans, 26%; commercial loans, 16%; investments, 14%; and other, 1%.

In 1990, sources of funds were time deposits, 46%; savings deposits, 31%; demand deposits, 11%; borrowings, 5%; equity, 5%; and other, 5%.

Nonbanking activities include trusts ($5.2 billion), credit cards, mortgage banking, bond sales, and reinsurance. These nonbanking assets are playing an increasing role in Barnett's earnings.

Because Barnett experienced a decline in earnings due to condominium loans during the 70's, management has been much more cautious and has diversified its real estate portfolio both as to types of loans and geographically.

Barnett has paid consecutive cash dividends since 1945. Its shares are over 50% owned by institutions. 1989 marks the 14th year of consecutive earnings increases. Barnett paid a 50% stock dividend in 1981, a 50% stock dividend in 1985, and a 50% stock dividend in 1986.

Total assets: $32.2 billion
Common shares outstanding: 63.7 million

		1981	1982	1983	1984	1985	1986	1987	1988	1989	1990
NET INCOME (MIL.)		41	57	82	103	128	162	196	226	257	101
EARNINGS PER SHARE		1.38	1.54	2.05	2.44	2.65	2.99	3.26	3.75	4.07	1.61
DIVIDEND PER SHARE		.41	.47	.52	.59	.67	.77	.89	1.01	1.16	1.29
PRICES	Hi	13.1	15.5	18.9	19.5	30.0	40.9	41.8	37.4	40.0	37.8
	Lo	8.3	8.4	11.5	14.5	18.8	25.6	27.1	29.0	32.3	14.1

Bausch & Lomb, Inc.

1 Lincoln First Square
Rochester, New York 14604
Tel. (716) 338-6000
Listed: NYSE
Investor contact: Mgr. Investor Relations, Ruth A. Sleeman
Ticker symbol: BOL
S&P rating: A

Bausch & Lomb is the world's leader in eye care, optical, and ophthalmological health-care products. It has a dominant share of the sunglasses market with its Ray-Ban line, controlling over 40% of the premium-priced segment of the market. With increased concern over the effects of the ultraviolet rays of the sun and the continual introduction of new styles and frames, Bausch & Lomb remains out front in the sunglasses market.

Its personal health-care products consist of contact lens solutions and over the counter products such as Sensitive Eyes and ReNu and prescription pharmaceuticals used in the treatment of eye irritation. Its acquisition of Interplak, a patented electronic toothbrush used in the home removal of plaque, has become an expanding source of revenues. With $110 million in sales in 1990, Interplak is expected to reach over $300 million in sales by 1994-95. Bausch & Lomb's entry into the manufacture of generic prescription ophthalmological pharmaceuticals, a relatively new field, holds long-term promise.

Medical products consist of soft and rigid gas-permeable contact lenses such as the SeeQuence disposable lens and the Medalist lens used in planned replacement programs. Medical products also include dental diagnostic equipment and hearing aids. Bausch & Lomb is in the process of developing a new soft-shell hearing aid with superior competitive qualities. It also offers an insurance service plan on optical products.

Biomedical products consist primarily of small animals such as rats, mice, and guinea pigs sold for research purposes by the Charles River Breeding Laboratories, acquired in 1984.

Optical products include everything from sunglasses to binoculars and telescopes. The manufacture of sophisticated ophthalmological equipment was discontinued in 1984.

Traditionally an optical company, Bausch & Lomb's strategy is to expand into the more profitable health-care and overseas market.

In 1990, health-care items represented 63% of sales and 56% of profits, optical products represented 37% of sales and 44% of profits. Overseas operations accounted for 42% of sales and 43% of profits.

Bausch & Lomb has paid consecutive cash dividends since 1952. Institutions control over 75% of the common shares. Bausch & Lomb paid a 100% stock dividend in 1983 and another 100% stock dividend in 1991.

Total assets: $1.7 billion
Current ratio: 1.6
Common shares outstanding: 29.4 million
Class B: 226.0 thousand

	1981	1982	1983	1984	1985	1986	1987	1988	1989	1990
REVENUES (MIL.)	533	510	568	534	596	699	840	978	1,220	1,369
NET INCOME (MIL.)	47	30	43	59	67	75	85	98	114	131
EARNINGS PER SHARE	.99	.62	.86	.99	1.11	1.24	1.41	1.64	1.89	2.19
DIVIDEND PER SHARE	.39	.39	.39	.39	.39	.39	.43	.50	.58	.66
PRICES Hi	15.4	13.1	15.2	13.9	17.8	22.0	24.8	24.0	32.9	36.5
Lo	10.3	8.4	9.7	8.8	12.4	15.9	15.4	17.2	20.4	26.4

Betz Laboratories, Inc.

4636 Somerton Road
Trevose, Pennsylvania 19058
Tel. (215) 355-3300
Listed: NASDAQ
Investor contact: V.P.–Treas. R. Dale Voncanon
Ticker symbol: BETZ
S&P rating: A

Although committed to cyclical end markets, Betz Laboratories, since going public in 1965, has compiled an excellent long-term growth record. Essentially, Betz manufactures specialty chemicals used to treat water in industrial processes. Its chemicals prevent corrosion, scaling, and other water-related problems in industrial equipment. They are used primarily in the chemical, petrochemical, refining, paper, steel, mining, and manufacturing industries and utility companies.

Betz Laboratories, Inc.

The future growth of Betz is assured by its "added value" approach, the efficiency-enhancing nature of its water treatment chemicals, and tougher environmental requirements.

Betz consistently outpaces its competitors. Its return on equity has averaged over 20% during the past decade. A key to Betz's success is the valued advice of its highly trained sales engineers on the prevention of equipment deterioration, plant efficiency and wastewater output. Also important is Betz's tight focus on a highly technical niche market. Its marketing and servicing policies enhance its ability to acquire and retain customers. More recently it has computerized its systems so as to automatically dispense, monitor, and control its treatment programs. Betz's automation of the water treatment industry and the customized tailoring of programs to specific industries will both reduce account turnover and increase the productivity of the sales force.

Over 40% of Betz' products are manufactured from petrochemicals. Its technical sales force numbers over 1,300. It has 15 manufacturing plants in the United States and seven abroad. Also, Betz markets pumps and equipment for applying its chemicals. Its Clam-Trol CT-1 has been exceptionally effective in controlling zebra mussels, which cause extensive damage to water cooling systems in the Great Lakes area.

In 1990, revenues were apportioned as follows: sales to basic industries, 48%; paper chemicals, 15%; commercial and industrial markets, 9%; process and energy chemicals, 8%; foreign operations, 15%; and Canadian markets, 5%.

Consecutive cash dividends have been paid since 1958. Institutions control over 75% of the outstanding common shares. Betz paid a 100% stock dividend in 1981 and a 100% stock dividend in 1990.

Total assets: $427 million
Current ratio: 2.3
Common shares outstanding: 28.4 million

	1981	1982	1983	1984	1985	1986	1987	1988	1989	1990
REVENUES (MIL.)	253	255	267	304	319	344	386	448	517	597
NET INCOME (MIL.)	29	31	33	37	37	36	41	48	56	66
EARNINGS PER SHARE	.92	.97	1.04	1.16	1.17	1.12	1.29	1.57	1.76	2.12
DIVIDEND PER SHARE	.34	.41	.47	.55	.63	.68	.73	.80	.89	1.01
PRICES Hi	16.6	21.1	22.4	19.5	19.1	22.4	29.1	26.3	31.3	43.3
Lo	10.9	12.4	16.1	13.6	15.1	17.5	17.5	20.6	23.6	27.8

H & R Block, Inc.

4410 Main Street
Kansas City, Missouri 64111
Tel. (816) 753-6900
Listed: NYSE
Investor contact: V.P. & Treas. D.W. Ayers
Ticker symbol: HRB
S&P rating: A

H & R Block is the largest U.S. and Canadian preparer of individual income tax returns. It completes over 12% of both U.S. federal and Canadian individual income tax returns. Block has over 8,900 owned and franchised tax preparation offices in the United States, Canada, Europe, Australia, and New Zealand.

The 1986 Tax Reform Act, which was billed as "tax simplification," actually has sent more clients to Block. Although the tax preparation business is somewhat mature, Block registers an increase in volume each year.

Block has sought to expand and diversify its operations so that its services now consist not only of tax preparation but also of personnel and computer services.

Its Personnel Pool of America, with over 505 owned and franchised offices in the United States (including Puerto Rico) and Canada, provides industry with supplemental personnel in medical, industrial, food, and clerical employment.

Another subsidiary, Compu-Serv, processes information and provides specialized computer programs to a number of customers, both individual and corporate. Yet another subsidiary, Path Management Industries, was sold in late 1990.

In 1991, tax return preparation provided 53% of revenues and 73% of profits, computer services provided 21% of revenues and 21% of profits, temporary help services provided 22% of revenues and 6% of profits, and other operations provided 4% of revenues and 0% of profits.

The H.R. Block family controls about 6% and institutions about 70% of the outstanding common shares. H & R Block has paid consecutive cash dividends since 1962. Block paid a 100% stock dividend in 1985, a 100% stock dividend on 1987, and a 100% stock dividend in 1991.

Total assets: $1.0 billion
Current ratio: 1.5
Common shares outstanding: 106.5 million

		1982	1983	1984	1985	1986	1987	1988	1989	1990	1991
REVENUES (MIL.)		319	343	419	497	615	722	812	900	1,053	1,191
NET INCOME (MIL.)		38	41	48	55	62	75	90	100	124	140
EARNINGS PER SHARE		.39	.41	.47	.54	.60	.71	.86	.95	1.15	1.31
DIVIDEND PER SHARE		.24	.24	.26	.29	.33	.36	.42	.50	.61	.75
PRICES	Hi	5.5	6.2	6.3	10.0	13.3	16.7	17.2	18.7	22.8	38.3
	Lo	3.2	4.5	4.8	5.5	9.0	10.0	11.4	13.1	15.0	19.9

America's GROWTH STOCKS

Bob Evans Farms, Inc.

3776 South High Street
Box 07863, Station G
Columbus, Ohio 43207-0863
Tel. (614) 491-2225
Listed: NASDAQ
Investor contact: Exec. V.P. & Treas. Keith P. Bradbury
Ticker symbol: BOBE
S&P rating: A

Bob Evans Farms is a combination of a sausage manufacturer and a high-quality restaurant chain. Bob Evans features more than 257 family style restaurants operating in 16 states. Bob Evans has expanded both by acquisitions and new installations. The restaurants feature Bob Evans sausage, but recently the menu has expanded to include charbroiled dinners and lighter items such as fruit and chicken salad.

Bob Evans manufactures sausage at five Midwestern and two Texas plants. Truck diver–salesmen distribute the sausage to supermarkets and retail grocery stores in 23 states.

The 1987 acquisition of the Owens Family Restaurant chain and Owens Country sausage of Longview, Texas, brought Bob Evans into the Southwest. Owens sausage is widely distributed throughout Texas. In Texas Bob Evans uses the Owens name both in its restaurant operation and in the distribution of its sausage.

In 1991, Bob Evans Farms, Inc. acquired Mrs. Giles Country Kitchens, a division of Campbell's Fresh Inc. Mrs. Giles Country Kitchens, Lynchburg, Virginia, is a producer and distributor of salads in the Southeastern U.S. Products such as potato salad, chicken salad, and cole slaw are sold by the company in bulk and smaller deli-style containers.

With the consumption of red meat declining and the cost of labor rising, Bob Evans has consistently increased earnings by expansion.

Bob Evans's strategy, when entering a new area, is to first introduce its sausage product by saturation advertising. With the quality image of its sausage established, Bob Evans then proceeds to open restaurants in the area. Bob Evans has a long-term record of superior growth, an almost debt-free balance sheet, and a strong brand franchise.

Bob Evans has paid a consecutive cash dividend since 1964. Bob Evans paid a 100% stock dividend in 1978; a 50% stock dividend in 1981; a 10% stock dividend in 1982; a 33⅓% stock dividend in January 1983; a 25% stock dividend in September 1983; a 25% stock dividend in 1986; a 25% stock dividend in 1987; and a 10% stock dividend in 1989.

Total assets: $287 million
Current ratio: 1.2
Common shares outstanding: 32.2 million

		1982	1983	1984	1985	1986	1987	1988	1989	1990	1991
REVENUES (MIL.)		173	188	202	228	263	327	395	420	454	501
NET INCOME (MIL.)		14	14	16	18	21	21	29	31	28	34
EARNINGS PER SHARE		.45	.47	.52	.59	.67	.69	.91	.95	.87	1.07
DIVIDEND PER SHARE		.12	.13	.13	.16	.16	.20	.22	.23	.25	.26
PRICES	Hi	12.4	14.4	12.6	13.5	16.9	20.0	16.4	16.1	15.1	26.6
	Lo	6.3	10.3	7.8	9.3	11.9	12.0	13.1	12.9	11.3	13.8

America's GROWTH STOCKS

Borden, Inc.

277 Park Avenue
New York, New York 10172
Tel. (212) 573-4000
Listed: NYSE
Investor contact: H.A. Clemente
Ticker symbol: BN
S&P rating: A

Borden, founded in 1857, is one of the nation's preeminent food companies. It is the largest dairy and pasta company in the United States. Despite its huge size, Borden has only one national brand, Creamette pasta. Borden is an amalgamation of a large number of regional brands. Since 1986, Borden has made 65 small to medium-size acquisitions.

Regional brands have a number of pluses. If a problem develops with a product, it can effect only limited damage. Also, advertising can be pitched to local tastes.

Another characteristic of Borden is product diversification. In addition to regional food brands such as Eagle condensed milk and Kava instant coffee, Borden makes a market in such nonfood items as Krylon spray paint and Wall-Tex covering. In early 1990, Borden acquired the flexible packaging businesses of both Printpac-U.E.B. of New Zealand and The Abbot/Polyaustro Group of Australia.

Borden's sales can be divided into dairy products, 23%; snacks, 19%; pasta, 10%; grocery items, 19%; nonfood consumer products, 8%; films and adhesives, 18%; and discontinued items, 3%. Most rapid growth is taking place in grocery products and snack foods. In snack foods Borden ranks second to Pepsi-owned Frito Lay.

In 1990, packaging and industrial products represented 24% of sales and 21% of income, dairy products 23% of sales and 10% of income, snack foods and consumer items 26% of sales and 24% of income, and grocery products 27% of sales and 45% of income. International operations accounted for 28% of sales and 28% of income.

Earnings declined in 1989 due to a $2.73 per share charge for plant closings and upgrading. About 30% of dairy operations were involved in this restructuring. Earnings rebounded sharply to $2.46 per share in 1990.

Borden has paid consecutive cash dividends since 1899. Institutions control some 50% of the common shares. Borden paid a 100% stock dividend in 1985, a 50% stock dividend in 1986, and a 100% stock dividend in 1989.

Total assets: $5.3 billion
Current ratio: 1.1
Common shares outstanding: 147.3 million

		1981	1982	1983	1984	1985	1986	1987	1988	1989	1990
REVENUES (MIL.)		4,415	4,111	4,265	4,568	4,716	5,002	6,154	7,244	7,653	7,633
NET INCOME (MIL)		160	166	189	191	194	223	267	312	(61)	364
EARNINGS PER SHARE		.91	.97	1.10	1.19	1.25	1.50	1.81	2.11	(.41)	2.46
DIVIDEND PER SHARE		.34	.36	.40	.44	.49	.55	.62	.75	.90	1.04
PRICES	Hi	5.0	8.8	10.3	10.9	17.9	26.3	32.0	30.6	38.6	37.9
	Lo	4.3	4.5	7.6	8.3	10.6	15.9	15.0	23.6	27.8	27.0

Bristol-Myers Squibb Company

345 Park Avenue
New York, New York 10022
Tel. (212) 546-4000
Listed: NYSE
Investor contact: Asst. Treasurer, Jonathan B. Morris
Ticker symbol: BMY
S&P rating: A+

In October, 1989, Bristol-Myers merged with Squibb Corp. to form the world's second-largest pharmaceutical company. In a tax-free exchange, Bristol-Myers issued 240 million Bristol-Myers common shares for 97 million Squibb common shares. The merger created a giant in ethical pharmaceuticals, drug sundries, and medical and consumer products. Bristol-Myers Squibb realizes revenues in excess of $10 billion and has a research budget in excess of $900 million and prospects for earnings growth between 15% and 20% per share for the next five years.

Squibb's strength in blood pressure (Capoten and Congard) and cholesterol-control (Pravachol) pharmaceuticals blends well with Bristol-Myers' anti-depressant (Burspar), anti-cancer, anti-AIDS, antibiotic, and anti-viral drugs.

Its medical products include orthopedic implants and surgical supplies. Non-prescription drugs and sundries include Bufferin, Excedrin, Nuprin, Comtrex, Keri Lotion, No Doz, and Ammens Medicated Powder. Bristol-Myers, through its subsidiary Mead Johnson, is a major distributor of the infant feeding formula Enfamil. Toiletries and beauty aids include Clairol, Vitalis, Ultress, and Clairesse. Household products include such items as Vanish, Endust, Draino, Windex, and Renuzit.

Bristol-Myers now has 22 products each producing in excess of $100 million a year in sales. New products include such items as Videx, an anti-AIDS product, Pravachol, and Monopril, an antihypertensive drug. Pharmaceutical sales are now about 51% of the company's revenue and expanding at an 18% rate.

In 1990, sales and earnings were divided as follows: pharmaceutical and medical products, 65% of sales and 72% of profits; nonprescription drugs and sundries, 17% of sales and 15% of profits; and toiletries and household products, 18% of sales and 13% of profits. Foreign operations represent 39% of sales and 34% of profits.

Consecutive cash dividends have been paid since 1933. Institutions control approximately 60% of the outstanding shares. Bristol-Myers Squibb authorized a two-for-one stock split in 1983 and a two-for-one split in 1987.

Total assets: $9.2 billion
Current ratio: 2.0
Common shares outstanding: 522.4 million

		1981	1982	1983	1984	1985	1986	1987	1988	1989	1990
REVENUES (MIL.)		3,497	3,600	3,917	4,189	4,444	4,836	5,401	5,972	9,189	10,300
NET INCOME (MIL.)		306	349	408	472	531	590	710	829	747	1,748
EARNINGS PER SHARE		1.15	1.30	1.50	1.73	1.93	2.07	2.47	2.88	1.43	3.33
DIVIDEND PER SHARE		.45	.51	.60	.80	.94	1.18	1.47	1.76	2.03	2.19
PRICES	Hi	14.8	18.5	23.9	26.4	34.4	44.4	55.9	46.5	58.0	68.0
	Lo	11.5	12.8	15.6	20.5	24.5	30.1	28.3	38.1	44.0	50.5

Browning-Ferris Industries, Inc.

Browning-Ferris Building
757 N. Eldrige, P.O. Box 1351
Houston, Texas 77253
Tel. (713) 870-8100
Listed: NYSE
Investor contact: V.P. Fletcher Thorne-Thomsen, Jr.
Ticker symbol: BFI
S&P rating: A

Browning-Ferris is the second-largest company dealing in solid and liquid waste disposal with over 402 waste locations. It is engaged in the collection, processing, and disposal of waste for commercial, industrial, and residential customers. It is especially significant in rubbish and waste collection for municipalities.

Increasingly, the company is engaged in the recovery and recycling of waste material, particularly plastics. In May 1989, Browning-Ferris signed an agreement with Wellman Inc. to reprocess collected plastic material. It is seeking a waste-to-fuel development in a joint venture with

American Re-Fuel. Also, it has a rapidly growing medical waste collection business.

Its hazardous waste disposal business is somewhat impeded by the company's difficulty in obtaining hazardous waste permits in New York and Ohio. However, it does have a new landfill hazardous waste site in Colorado.

Much of Browning-Ferris's growth can be attributed to the rather steady acquisition of a large number of small independent trash haulers. An international operation, CECOS International, has had difficulty in obtaining waste sites and is not very profitable. Browning-Ferris is engaged in a number of related business such as portable toilets and asbestos abatement.

Commercial and industrial waste collection produces 58%, residential collection 16%, processing 16%, special services 8%, and chemical waste 2% of revenues.

Browning-Ferris has paid consecutive cash dividends since 1950. It paid a 50% stock dividend in 1983, a 100% stock dividend in 1985, and a 100% stock dividend in 1987.

Total assets: $3.5 billion
Current ratio: 1.0
Common shares outstanding: 153.2 million

		1982	1983	1984	1985	1986	1987	1988	1989	1990	1991
REVENUES (MIL.)		715	776	909	1,068	1,243	1,580	1,990	2,491	2,967	3,183
NET INCOME (MIL.)		63	77	87	113	131	166	225	278	257	65
EARNINGS PER SHARE		.48	.58	.64	.81	.91	1.11	1.50	1.84	1.68	.42
DIVIDEND PER SHARE		.17	.20	.24	.27	.32	.40	.48	.56	.64	.68
PRICES	Hi	9.3	11.9	11.3	16.0	23.6	35.8	29.3	42.8	49.3	30.8
	Lo	4.1	8.3	6.8	9.3	15.1	17.5	20.9	26.9	20.5	16.9

Bruno's, Inc.

300 Research Parkway
Birmingham, Alabama 35201
Tel. (205) 940-9400
Listed: NASDAQ
Investor contact: Exec. V.P.–Secy. G. J. Griffin
Ticker symbol: BRNO
S&P rating: A+

Bruno's, INC   Bruno's, an independent investor-owned supermarket chain, is based in Alabama but also has stores in Georgia, Florida, Mississippi, Tennessee, and South Carolina. Its more than 230 stores operate under a variety of names: Food World, Consumer Warehouse Food Stores, Bruno's Food and Pharmacy, Food Max, Food Fair, and Piggly Wiggly. The 76 Piggly Wiggly stores, located in Georgia, were acquired in 1988. The Food World stores are large supermarkets, the Consumer Warehouse Stores are small warehouse units, the Bruno's Food and Pharmacy units are large food and drug stores, and Food Max stores are large warehouse units. Aggressive pricing and a strong cap on expenses have turned around the Piggly Wiggly stores.

Bruno's entered into partnership with Kmart and has a 49% interest in an American Fare 240,000-square-foot hypermarket. The first one is located in Atlanta, Georgia. It offers food, general merchandize, and apparel. A second American Fare store opened in Charlotte, North Carolina, in early 1990, a third opened in Jackson, Mississippi in mid-1990, and additional ones are planned.

Part of Bruno's success is a variety of store formats designed for local market conditions and a cost structure that is extremely competitive. Although Bruno's is the largest supermarket chain in Alabama, there is additional opportunity for further market penetration in that state as well as in other states in the Southeast.

The Bruno family controls about 25% of the common stock; institutions control another 35%. Bruno's has paid consecutive cash dividends since 1974. Bruno's paid a 100% stock dividend in 1980, a 100% stock dividend in 1983, a 100% stock dividend in 1985, and a 100% stock dividend in 1987.

Total assets: $773 million
Current ratio: 1.8
Common shares outstanding: 81.9 million

		1982	1983	1984	1985	1986	1987	1988	1989	1990	1991
REVENUES (MIL.)		549	605	716	887	1,018	1,143	1,982	2,134	2,395	2,618
NET INCOME (MIL.)		12	15	19	25	30	31	43	48	60	67
EARNINGS PER SHARE		.19	.23	.27	.35	.38	.40	.53	.59	.74	.82
DIVIDEND PER SHARE		.04	.05	.06	.07	.08	.09	.10	.12	.14	.18
PRICES	Hi	3.8	5.4	5.3	9.0	11.8	12.6	12.9	15.1	16.8	21.6
	Lo	1.5	3.5	3.3	5.1	7.5	7.6	9.6	10.1	12.9	12.1

CCB Financial Corporation

Main and Corcoran Streets (P.O. Box 931)
Durham, North Carolina 27702
Tel. (919) 683-7777
Listed: NASDAQ
Investor contact: Controller, W. Harold Parker, Jr.
Ticker symbol: CCBF
S&P rating: A

As profiled in its 1990 Annual Report, "CCB Financial Corporation is a bank holding company whose principal subsidiaries are Central Carolina Bank and Trust Company and Republic Bank & Trust Co. Through its subsidiary banks, CCB Financial Corporation offers a wide variety of retail, commercial and trust banking services through its 98 offices located primarily in the Piedmont section of North Carolina."

Central Carolina Bank serves 33 communities with 82 branch of-

CCB Financial Corporation

fices in Guilford, Forsyth, and five neighboring counties. This is North Carolina's second-largest metropolitan area, with a 10.6% growth rate. Republic Bank has 16 branch offices in the Mecklenburg area, which includes the city of Charlotte and seven other counties. It is North Carolina's largest metropolitan area, with an 18.0% growth rate.

Southland Associates, a subsidiary of Central Carolina Bank and Trust Company, is engaged in real estate sales, insurance sales, and real estate development. Southland serves six communities with offices in Durham, Chapel Hill, Greensboro, Raleigh, Roxboro, and Wilmington.

CCB is a minor but dynamic player in a market dominated by three major regional financial institutions. Its strategic plan calls for increasing market share by mergers, acquisitions, the development of new branches in selected growth areas, and technology conversion. CCB remains consistently profitable in a geographic area experiencing some real-estate softness.

In 1990, loans of $1.4 billion were divided as follows: commercial, financial, and agricultural, 20.2%; real-estate construction, 12.5%; real-estate mortgage, 43.8%; installment, 13.7%; credit card, 7.3%; and lease financing, 2.5%.

In 1990, deposits of $1.75 billion were divided as follows: savings, 5.1%; money market, 37.3%; time, 42.4%; and demand, 15.2%.

In 1990, income of $225.9 million was apportioned as follows: interest on fees and loans, 67.0%; investment securities, 15.1%; federal funds, 3.2%; service charges, 5.5%; trust, 2.4%; and other, 6.8%.

CCB has paid consecutive cash dividends since 1934 and has increased its cash dividends for 27 consecutive years. Institutions control about 35% and officers and directors about 20% of the outstanding common shares. CCB paid a 100% stock dividend in 1984.

Total assets: $2.1 billion
Common shares outstanding: 5.1 million

		1981	1982	1983	1984	1985	1986	1987	1988	1989	1990
NET INCOME (MIL.)		5.2	6.2	8.6	11.3	14.4	18.0	17.0	19.7	21.0	20.5
EARNINGS PER SHARE		1.26	1.48	2.07	2.70	3.43	3.60	3.40	3.94	4.17	4.05
DIVIDEND PER SHARE		.46	.52	.61	.73	.94	1.12	1.21	1.30	1.40	1.48
PRICES	Hi	8.1	12.5	17.0	24.5	34.3	45.0	45.3	36.0	43.8	40.3
	Lo	6.6	6.9	9.9	16.6	24.5	32.8	29.5	32.0	33.3	24.3

Capital Cities/ABC, Inc.

77 West 66th Street
New York, New York 10023
Tel. (212) 456-7777
Listed: NYSE
Investor contact: V.P. J.M. Fitzgerald
Ticker symbol: CCB
S&P rating: A+

Capital Cities/ABC is the product of the 1986 acquisition of the American Broadcasting Companies by Capital Cities Communications. The company has three basic divisions, broadcasting, publishing, and cable TV.

> **Capital Cities/ ABC, Inc.**

The broadcast division owns and operates both the ABC Television Network and the ABC Radio Network. It has 227 primary television affiliates and six radio networks with 3,050 affiliates. It owns and operates eight TV stations in Philadelphia, Houston, Durham, Fresno, New York, Los Angeles, Chicago, and San Francisco. It owns 21 radio stations (11 AM and 10 FM) in such markets as New York, Chicago, Los Angeles, and San Francisco. The Federal Communications Commission has granted Capital Cities a permanent waiver in markets where it has both a TV and a radio outlet. In the future, Capital Cities hopes to profit from the syndication of TV programs developed by its own in-house TV production studios in New York.

Capital Cities publishes nine daily newspapers in eight markets, 77 weekly newspapers and shopping guides, and 39 specialty and trade publications. Its Fairchild Publications publishes numerous trade periodicals such as *Women's Wear Daily* and *Electronic News*. ABC Publishing markets such periodicals as *COMPUTEL*, *McCall's*, *Needlework & Crafts*, *Los Angeles Magazine*, *Institutional Investor*, and *Practical Homeowner's*.

Capital Cities Broadcasting has an equity interest in three cable television channels: ESPN (80%), Arts & Entertainment (38%), and Lifetime (33.3%).

Capital Cities/ABC has paid consecutive cash dividends since 1976. It has increased earnings for 18 consecutive years. Warren Buffett (via Berkshire Hathaway) controls 17.2% of the common stock, and directors control 21.6%.

Total assets: $6.7 billion
Current ratio: 3.1
Common shares outstanding: 16.7 million

		1981	1982	1983	1984	1985	1986	1987	1988	1989	1990
REVENUES (MIL.)		574	664	762	940	1,021	4,124	4,440	4,773	4,957	5,386
NET INCOME (MIL.)		81	96	115	135	142	182	279	387	486	478
EARNINGS PER SHARE		6.12	7.25	8.53	10.40	10.87	11.20	16.46	22.31	27.25	27.71
DIVIDENDS PER SHARE		.20	.20	.20	.20	.20	.20	.20	.20	.20	.20
PRICES	Hi	80.5	136.8	157.5	174.5	229.0	279.8	450.0	369.8	568.0	633.0
	Lo	56.5	64.4	114.8	123.5	152.3	208.3	268.0	297.0	353.0	380.0

Capital Holding Corporation

Commonwealth Building
Louisville, Kentucky 40202
Tel. (502) 560-2000
Listed: NYSE
Investor contact: V.P. E. W. Baucom
Ticker symbol: CPM
S&P rating: A

CapitalHolding

This Louisville, Kentucky-based life insurance holding company is an amalgamation of several life and health companies offering an array of products through varied distribution channels. Its marketing efforts are targeted to the middle-income population. Subsidiary companies sell insurance through agents, direct mail, and door to door (industrial policies). Industrial policies account for about 50% of Capital's total revenues.

68

Capital is one of the largest and most profitable stock life companies in the United States. It underwrites life, annuity, accident and health, and a small amount of property and casualty insurance. The agency segment primarily sells individual life and health policies. The direct response segment utilizes television, newspaper, and direct mailing. The accumulation and investment group sells through stockbrokers, banks, and financial planners.

Capital is experiencing explosive growth in its asset accumulation and investment spread contracts. These consist of fixed and variable annuities, single premium annuities, IRA products, and GICs (guaranteed investment contracts) sold to pension funds. The sales of a Medicare supplement is expanding as the policy is being approved by an increasing number of states.

Acquisitions play a major role in Capital's growth. During 1991, it acquired Durham Corp., a North Carolina industrial life insurance company, operating in 12 Southeastern, Mid-Atlantic, and Midwestern States. In 1989, it acquired Montgomery Ward's personal insurance lines and Southlife Holding.

Also, Capital owns First Deposit Corp., a holding company for a commercial bank, a savings and loan, and a life insurance company.

Capital Holding has increased dividends for the past 21 years. Institutions control about 65% of the common shares. Capital has paid consecutive cash dividends since 1941. It paid a 100% stock dividend in 1985.

Total assets: $16.7 billion
Common shares outstanding: 44.6 million

		1981	1982	1983	1984	1985	1986	1987	1988	1989	1990
REVENUES (MIL.)		1,003	1,286	1,581	1,746	2,163	2,292	3,351	2,046	2,500	2,577
NET INCOME (MIL.)		95	102	122	122	143	273	172	190	276	166
EARNINGS PER SHARE		1.70	1.89	2.17	2.19	2.63	5.25	3.35	4.00	5.85	3.39
DIVIDEND PER SHARE		.60	.66	.70	.74	.77	.82	.88	.94	1.00	1.08
PRICES	Hi	12.5	18.9	19.9	22.0	29.4	38.8	36.9	34.0	52.3	54.1
	Lo	8.9	10.5	15.4	15.1	20.1	25.8	24.3	26.8	31.3	26.3

America's GROWTH STOCKS

Carter-Wallace, Inc.

1345 Avenue of the Americas
New York, New York 10105
Tel. (212) 339-5000
Listed: NYSE
Investor contact: V.P.–Secy. R. Levine
Ticker symbol: CAR
S&P rating: A+

 Carter-Wallace manufactures and markets a combination of ethical pharmaceuticals and a large number of personal-care and over-the-counter drugs and sundries. Some of its better known personal care items are the Answer-2 home pregnancy test, Carters Little Liver Pills, and Sea and Ski sun care lotion. Health-care products represent 45% of sales and include such items as tranquilizers, muscle relaxants, and antibiotics.

Consumer products account for 55% of annual revenues. Its Arrid deodorant accounts for about 21% of annual sales. Trojan condoms represent over 50% of all condoms sold in the United States. Also, Carter is involved in the pet care market with such products as Chirp vitamins for birds, Boundary Mosquito Repellant, and Femalt Hair Ball Remover.

Carter-Wallace continues to expand by both the development of new products and acquisitions. In 1990, it acquired Lady's Choice deodorant from American Cyanamid; Hygeia, a first-response home pregnancy kit from Tambrands; and an exclusive license from Ivax to sell, Doral, a prescription sedative, in the United States.

Health-care products represent 45% of sales and 60% of profits, deodorants 21% of sales and 1% of profits, and other consumer items 34% of sales and 39% of profits.

The United States represents 75% of sales and 85% of profits. Foreign operations account for 25% of sales and 15% of profits. The international value of the dollar is obviously a factor in earnings. Carter-Wallace is controlled by the Hoyt family, which owns 37% of the Class A common stock and 86% of the Class B shares.

Carter-Wallace has increased earnings for the past 13 consecutive years. It has paid consecutive cash dividends since 1883. It paid a 100% stock dividend on the Class B common shares in 1987.

Total assets: $562 million
Current ratio: 2.1
Common shares outstanding: Class A 10.9 million
Class B 4.3 million

		1982	1983	1984	1985	1986	1987	1988	1989	1990	1991
REVENUES (MIL.)		261	290	323	349	400	451	483	515	555	635
NET INCOME (MIL.)		12	17	18	21	28	32	38	45	50	52
EARNINGS PER SHARE		.78	1.06	1.19	1.33	1.81	2.14	2.50	2.97	3.30	3.37
DIVIDEND PER SHARE		.20	.22	.23	.25	.29	.38	.51	.65	.79	.90
PRICES	Hi	11.0	14.5	13.9	25.8	43.1	75.5	43.3	60.5	58.6	125.6
	Lo	4.5	8.9	9.8	12.5	24.0	24.0	31.9	39.1	44.9	52.6

Central Fidelity Banks, Inc.

1021 East Cary Street
Richmond, Virginia 23261
Tel. (804) 742-4000
Listed: NASDAQ
Investor contact: Mgr. Public Relations, Peggy Cummings
Ticker symbol: CFBS
S&P rating: A+

As described in its 1990 Form 10K, "Central Fidelity is a bank holding company headquartered in Richmond, Virginia, created December 31st, 1978, upon the con- solidation of two bank holding companies, Central National Corporation and Fidelity American Bankshares, Inc.

"At year-end 1990, the company operated 196 banking offices, including 25 super-market full service locations, and 157 automated teller machines throughout the Commonwealth of Virginia. Virtually all of its revenue is earned by providing a wide range of commercial banking services to a broad customer base consisting of individuals, corporations, institutions and governments, primarily located in Virginia."

Fidelity has three bank-related subsidiaries, namely Central Fidelity Services, Inc., Central Fidelity Properties, Inc., and Central Fidelity Insurance Agency, Inc., none of which contribute substantially to earnings.

Fidelity targets certain markets for deposits such as a No Penalty Certificate of Deposit, and Individual Retirement Account guaranteeing a minimum rate, a Best Rate Money Market Account guaranteeing a rate tied to the Treasury bill rate of return, a Focus 55 Certificate of Deposit, and an Investment Services Group, which brings together estate planning and personal financial management.

At year-end 1990, the loan portfolio of $3.58 billion was divided as follows: commercial, 44.2%; construction, 14.6%; real estate, 4.8%; installment, 20.7%; and bank card, 15.7%. Income of $605.2 million was apportioned as follows: interest, 71.1%; investment securities, 17.2%; fees and charges, 4.0%; and other income, 7.7%.

Central Fidelity has paid consecutive cash dividends since 1911. Earnings have increased for 16 consecutive years. Institutions control about 36% of the outstanding common shares. Central Fidelity paid a 5% stock dividend in February 1979, a 5% stock dividend in December 1979, a 50% stock dividend in 1983, a 50% stock dividend in 1985, and a 50% stock dividend in 1991.

Total assets: $6.2 billion
Common shares outstanding: 21.5 million

		1981	1982	1983	1984	1985	1986	1987	1988	1989	1990
NET INCOME (MIL.)		16	18	25	29	33	42	47	50	54	56
EARNINGS PER SHARE		.89	1.05	1.39	1.52	1.63	1.84	2.01	2.13	2.35	2.47
DIVIDEND PER SHARE		.34	.38	.42	.48	.54	.62	.70	.76	.81	.93
PRICES	Hi	5.2	6.7	10.7	12.9	20.7	24.3	20.0	19.7	23.0	21.6
	Lo	3.7	4.9	5.9	8.4	12.7	16.5	15.3	16.6	17.7	12.0

Circuit City Stores, Inc.

2040 Thalbro Street
Richmond, Virginia 23230
Tel. (804) 257-4292
Listed: NYSE
Investor contact: Mgr. Financial Relations, Ann M. Collier
Ticker symbol: CC
S&P rating: A

Circuit City Stores, Inc. is one of the nation's largest retailers of brand-name electronic products and appliances. Its products include audio and video equipment, televisions, personal computers, word processors, compact disks, microwave ovens, washers, dryers, refrigerators, and ranges. Formerly Wards Co., Circuit City has more than 185 stores including 14 Circuit City stores, 157 Circuit City Superstores, and 14 Impulse stores. Stores are located in 11 Mid-Atlantic and Southeastern states, Nevada, and California. Circuit City plans about 20 more Circuit City Superstores and entrance into the Phoenix and Philadelphia markets.

Circuit City stores are typically between 4,000 and 15,000 square feet and sell primarily audio and electronic items. Circuit City Superstores are between 15,000 and 47,000 square feet and carry both consumer electronic items and major appliances. Impulse stores, located in shopping malls, are relatively small, between 2,000 and 4,000 square feet, and carry a limited supply of fast-moving smaller electronic items.

While same store profits are somewhat level due to decreased consumer spending, earnings continue to expand because of a steady stream of new store openings.

Revenue sources for 1991 were broken down as follows: television, 24%; VCR, 22%; audio, 22%; other electronic, 14%; and appliances, 18%.

Consecutive cash dividends have been paid since 1979. Institutions control about 80% of the outstanding common shares. Circuit City Stores paid a 100% stock dividend in 1981; a 50% stock dividend in March 1983; a 200% stock dividend in November 1983; a 100% stock dividend in 1986; and a 100% stock dividend in 1989.

73

Total assets: $874 million
Current ratio: 1.7
Common shares outstanding: 46.3 million

	1982	1983	1984	1985	1986	1987	1988	1989	1990	1991
REVENUES (MIL.)	176	246	357	519	705	1,011	1,350	1,721	2,097	2,367
NET INCOME (MIL.)	1.9	4.3	12	20	22	35	50	70	78	57
EARNINGS PER SHARE	.06	.12	.31	.49	.50	.80	1.13	1.53	1.70	1.22
DIVIDEND PER SHARE	.008	.008	.010	.020	.024	.029	.038	.055	.075	.095
PRICES Hi	1.1	4.5	7.5	7.8	17.1	20.9	22.6	27.0	29.0	26.0
Lo	0.5	0.9	3.0	4.8	5.9	8.5	9.4	17.8	9.0	11.3

Citizens Utilities Company

High Ridge Park, P.O. Box 3801
Stamford, Connecticut 06905
Tel. (203) 329-8800
Listed: NASDAQ
Investor contact: Investor Relations, Arthur D. Dague
Ticker symbol: CITUB
S&P rating: A+

1990 was the 46th consecutive year Citizens Utilities has reported higher net income, higher revenues, higher earnings, and higher dividends per share. 1991 is likely to extend that record to 47.

Citizens provides telecommunications, electric, gas, water, and waste-water services to more than 760,000 customers in 13 states. Operations are widely scattered in mostly underdeveloped but rapidly growing areas including parts of Arizona (27% of 1990 revenues), California (26% of 1990 revenues), and the island of Kauai in Hawaii (10% of 1990 revenues). Other states in which Citizens has operations are Colorado, Idaho, Illinois, Indiana, Louisiana, Nevada, Ohio, Pennsylvania, Utah, and Vermont.

Both service and geographic diversification help insulate Citizens from any catastrophic problems affecting any one service or area. In 1990, telecommunications accounted for 33% of revenues, electricity for 26%, gas for 30%, and water and wastewater for 11%.

In addition to utility services, Citizens has expanded into radio paging in Arizona, California, and Utah. In 1991 Citizens' cellular telephone interests (limited partner in six partnerships in Arizona, California, Nevada, and Pennsylvania) were merged into Century Cellular Corp., a division of Century Communications. In 1989, Century Investors, a subsidiary of Century Communications, acquired slightly more than a 2% interest in Citizens.

Citizens Utilities has both Class A and Class B common shares. From 1956 through 1989 Class B shares paid a cash dividend (taxable) and Class A shares paid an equivalent dividend in stock (nontaxable on receipt). Under this arrangement cash dividends accounted for less than 20% of net income, and thus Citizens could internally generate cash for its construction projects. Class A shares are convertible into Class B shares on a one-for-one basis. However, Class B shares are not convertible into Class A shares.

The IRS exemption that allowed the dual payment of stock on Class A shares and cash on Class B shares expired in 1990 and this privilege was not renewed. As a result, since 1990, Citizens has been paying quarterly stock dividends (nontaxable on receipt) on both its Class A and Class B shares. In addition, a new plan beginning in 1992 will enable Class B shareholders to have their quarterly stock dividends sold for their accounts and the cash distributed quarterly. Class A is still convertible into Class B.

Higher dividends have been paid for 47 consecutive years (including 1991). Citizens had a two-for-one stock split in 1982 and another one in 1986. In 1990, Citizens paid a 1.33% stock dividend on both Class A and B in March, June, and September, and a 2.4% stock dividend in December, equalling a stock dividend cash equivalent of $1.76. The company paid a 2.0% stock dividend in March and a 1.9% stock dividend in June, September, and December 1991 on the Class A and B shares.

Total assets: $1.5 billion
Current ratio: 0.6
Common shares outstanding: Class A 42.2 million
Class B 12.9 million

		1981	1982	1983	1984	1985	1986	1987	1988	1989	1990
REVENUES (MIL.)		180	202	222	251	267	268	282	302	339	528
NET INCOME (MIL.)		29	34	38	44	51	58	67	77	89	106
EARNINGS PER SHARE		.77	.83	.90	.97	1.09	1.18	1.34	1.55	1.75	1.94
DIVIDEND PER SHARE		.63	.67	.71	.79	.85	.94	1.04	1.17	1.34	—
PRICES	Hi	7.3	9.5	11.7	13.1	18.6	26.6	28.0	29.1	37.2	34.5
	Lo	6.0	6.6	9.5	9.1	11.8	16.6	18.6	21.1	25.1	19.0

City National Corporation

400 North Roxbury Drive
Beverly Hills, California 90210
Tel. (213) 550-5400
Listed: NYSE
Investor contact: V.P.–Treas. J. F. Schulte
Ticker symbol: CYN
S&P rating: A

City National, based in Beverly Hills, is one of Southern California's most successful banks. Most of its 24 offices are in Los Angeles County, but it does have some presence in other parts of Southern California. Its success lies in its ability to adapt its products to its customers' needs. Many of its customers are both professional and entertainment people for whom City National provides personal service banking. City National strongly controls this niche and avoids much of the rough and tumble of retail banking.

In 1990, its loans of $3.1 billion were apportioned as follows: commercial, 57%; real estate mortgage, 26%; real estate construction, 15%; and installment, 2%. In 1990, sources of funds were as follows: time deposits, 52%; demand deposits, 21%; borrowings, 11%; additional deposits, 8%; shareholders equity, 7%; and other, 1%.

Each year City National attains the highest return on assets of California banks. It also has the lowest charge-off rate of California banks with assets over $1 billion and the lowest ratio of nonperforming assets to loans.

City National also derives substantial earnings from City National Information Systems, which supplies data processing to over 200 Western banking institutions. It also markets the Instant Teller, the largest teller machine operation in the West.

Consecutive cash dividends have been paid since 1963. Insiders control about 23% of the common shares, and institutions hold about 21%. City National paid a 10% stock dividend in 1982, a 10% stock dividend in 1984, a 10% stock dividend in 1982, a 100% stock dividend in 1986, a 10% stock dividend in 1987, a 20% stock dividend in 1988, and a 25% stock dividend in 1989.

Total assets: $4.95 billion
Common shares outstanding: 32.1 million

	1981	1982	1983	1984	1985	1986	1987	1988	1989	1990
NET INCOME (MIL.)	20	15	17	20	24	30	41	49	59	44
EARNINGS PER SHARE	.65	.48	.58	.66	.80	.98	1.34	1.62	1.86	1.35
DIVIDEND PER SHARE	.16	.20	.22	.22	.23	.30	.40	.47	.58	.64
PRICES Hi	8.8	8.4	8.8	7.4	10.3	14.1	20.3	21.6	28.0	24.8
Lo	5.1	4.1	5.5	5.6	6.3	9.4	12.4	13.5	18.0	11.0

The Clorox Company

1221 Broadway
Oakland, California 94612
Tel. (415) 271-7000
Listed: NYSE
Investor contact: W. Osterland
Ticker symbol: CLX
S&P rating: A+

Clorox was originally a one-product liquid bleach company. In 1957, it was acquired by Procter & Gamble, but the U.S. Supreme Court upheld a Federal Trade Commission ruling that Procter & Gamble must divest itself of Clorox. In 1969, the divestiture was completed and Clorox once again became a single-product company.

From 1969 on, Clorox acquired numerous relatively small, regionally strong consumer products companies. Clorox attempted to market these products heavily on a national scale. With most of them it succeeded, in others it didn't.

Clorox produces such grocery items as Clorox liquid bleach, Clorox 2 (a bleach for colored fabrics), Soft Scrub, Fresh Step cat litter green, Kingsford Charcoal, Deer Park bottled water, Kitchen Bouquet (a gravy browner and seasoner), and Liquid Plumr. In 1990, Clorox acquired the Shulton home products division of American Cyanamid; brands include Pine-Sol disinfectant and Combat insecticide. Also, Clorox markets food, cleaning products and restaurant equipment to restaurants, hotels, and schools. In 1991, Clorox left the highly competitive detergent business. In 1989, Clorox divested itself of its architectural coatings (Lucite and Olympic paints and stains) business because of low margins.

Future growth is expected to come both from new products and from increased market share of existing products. Clorox and the Henkel Company of Germany have agreed to joint research and a sharing of marketing and research information.

Henkel now owns about 27.3% of Clorox's common stock. Institutions hold about 45%. Clorox has paid consecutive cash dividends since 1968. It paid a 100% stock dividend in 1987.

Total assets: $1.6 billion
Current ratio: 1.3
Common shares outstanding: 55.4 million

		1982	1983	1984	1985	1986	1987	1988	1989	1990	1991
REVENUES (MIL.)		867	914	975	1,055	1,089	1,126	1,260	1,356	1,484	1,646
NET INCOME (MIL.)		45	66	80	86	96	105	133	146	154	53
EARNINGS PER SHARE		.94	1.34	1.52	1.61	1.77	1.93	2.42	2.24	2.80	.98
DIVIDEND PER SHARE		.43	.48	.54	.62	.70	.79	.92	1.09	1.29	1.47
PRICES	Hi	14.0	18.4	15.5	25.4	30.3	36.0	33.8	44.5	45.4	42.4
	Lo	5.4	10.4	11.4	13.9	22.0	23.5	26.1	30.1	32.1	35.0

The Coca-Cola Company

1 Coca-Cola Plaza
Atlanta, Georgia 30313
Tel. (404) 676-2121
Listed: NYSE
Investor contact: Juan D. Johnson
Ticker symbol: KO
S&P rating: A+

Coca-Cola is the world's leading purveyor of soft drinks. In recent years it has expanded from tonic to the fruit juice market with the purchase of Minute Maid and Hi-C. Coca-Cola makes soft drink syrups and concentrates, which it sells to licensed independent bottlers and wholesalers around the world. Its major brands include Coca-Cola, Diet Coke, Tab, Sprite, Diet Sprite, Fresca, Fanta, Cherry Coke, and Minute Maid soda.

Coca-Cola also markets fruit juice, juice concentrates, other beverages, mixers and snacks. These products are sold under the Minute Maid, Hi-C, and Bacardi labels.

Soft drinks provide 84% of revenues and 96% of profits. Food products provide 18% of revenues and 4% of profits. Coke has an annual cash flow of over $1 billion.

Coca-Cola owns a 49% interest in Coca-Cola Enterprises, its largest bottler, which is also based in Atlanta. Also, it has acquired its French bottler and is seeking greater control of its far flung operations. Through consolidation and centralization, Coke can reduce costs and become even more competitive.

Coke controls about 40% of the United States soft drink market. Foreign operations are playing an increasing role in Coke's bottom line and now account for 61% of sales and 80% of profits.

In early 1991, Coca Cola purchased a soft drink and bottling operation in eastern Germany. Also, it entered into an agreement with Nestle to form a joint venture, the Coca-Cola Refreshments Company. It will manufacture and distribute coffee, tea, and chocolate concentrate under the Nestle brand name.

In 1989, Coke sold its 49% interest in Columbia Pictures & Entertainment to Sony Corp. for $1.55 billion in cash.

Berkshire Hathaway—that is, Warren Buffet—controls about 7% and has federal approval to purchase up to 15% of the common shares. Institutions control about 54% of the common shares. Coke has paid consecutive cash dividends since 1893. It paid a 200% stock dividend in 1986 and a 100% stock dividend in 1990.

Total assets: $9.3 billion
Current ratio: 1.0
Common shares outstanding: 667.5 million

		1981	1982	1983	1984	1985	1986	1987	1988	1989	1990
REVENUES (MIL.)		5,889	6,250	6,829	7,364	7,904	8,669	9,658	8,338	8,966	10,236
NET INCOME (MIL.)		447	512	558	629	678	934	916	1,045	1,193	1,382
EARNINGS PER SHARE		.61	.66	.69	.80	.86	1.21	1.22	1.43	1.70	2.04
DIVIDEND PER SHARE		.39	.41	.45	.46	.49	.52	.56	.60	.68	.80
PRICES	Hi	6.8	8.9	9.6	11.0	14.8	22.4	26.6	22.6	40.5	49.0
	Lo	5.1	4.9	7.6	8.2	9.9	12.8	14.0	17.5	21.6	32.6

Colgate Palmolive Company

300 Park Avenue
New York, New York 10022
Tel. (212) 310-2000
Listed: NYSE
Investor contact: V.P. Investor Relations, Katharine Tarbox
Ticker symbol: CL
S&P rating: B

Colgate is a major consumer products company, whose personal care and oral-hygiene products and household items are sold throughout the world. It has operations in 65 countries and exports to about 100 more. It manufactures and markets such items as Colgate toothpaste, Palmolive soap, Ajax cleansers, and Fab detergents. Its revenues continue to climb as consumers remain loyal to brand names except in times of severe recession and unemployment.

Household cleaners and detergents account for 45% of sales and 30% of operating profits. However, Colgate is expanding its product mix. New products are playing an increasing role in Colgate's revenues and earnings. Among these new products are concentrated detergents, personal care items, and in particular oral care and dental products.

Oral care products now account for over 20% of Colgate's total revenues and profits. Important in these sales is Colgate's acquisition of Vipoint Pharmaceutical in early 1990. Vipoint's products are marketed under the Viadent name. Viadent products, both toothpaste and mouthwash, are far superior to those of competitors in that they contain an extract of the bloodroot plant which has been found to be exceptionally effective in fighting plaque. Colgate's long-term strategy is to deemphasize detergents and to concentrate on more profitable personal care and oral products.

Colgate is also engaged in specialty marketing of products such as Hills pet foods, Princess House crystal, and Sterno canned heat. The Kendall Company, which manufactures bandages, tissues, and other products used by the health care industry, is a major subsidiary.

Colgate continues to expand internationally. Already in over 160 countries, it more recently has expanded into Pakistan, Turkey, Saudi Arabia, eastern Europe, and the republics of the former Soviet Union. With more than 60% of its revenues and earnings abroad, dollar translation is a major factor in earnings.

Colgate has paid consecutive cash dividends since 1895. Institutions control over 50% of the outstanding common shares. It paid a 100% stock dividend in 1991.

Total assets: $4.2 billion
Current ratio: 1.4
Common shares outstanding: 133.6 million

		1981	1982	1983	1984	1985	1986	1987	1988	1989	1990
REVENUES (MIL.)		5,261	4,888	4,865	4,910	4,524	4,985	5,647	4,734	5,039	5,691
NET INCOME (MIL.)		208	197	198	54	168	177	1	153	280	321
EARNINGS PER SHARE		1.28	1.21	1.21	.32	1.07	1.26	.39	1.11	1.99	2.28
DIVIDEND PER SHARE		.57	.60	.63	.64	.65	.68	.70	.74	.78	.90
PRICES	Hi	9.2	11.3	12.7	13.3	16.7	23.5	26.3	24.8	32.4	37.8
	Lo	6.9	8.0	9.5	10.3	11.3	15.2	14.0	19.3	22.1	26.4

Comerica Incorporated

211 West Fort Street
Detroit, Michigan 48275
Tel. (313) 222-3300
Listed: NYSE
Investor contact: Sr. V.P. Paul D. Tobias
Ticker symbol: CMA
S&P rating: A-

Founded in 1849, Comerica (formerly Detroitbank) is a $13 billion bank holding company with over 220 banking offices throughout eight of Michigan's largest cities. Its 350-unit automated teller network is one of Michigan's largest. Comerica has nine full-service ComeriMart branches located within Kroger supermarkets in southeast Michigan. Comerica has a bank in Toledo, Ohio, and banking offices in Dayton, Indianapolis, and Chicago. Comerica's banking strategy is directed toward consumer borrowers and depositors, small-business owners, middle market companies, and affluent individuals.

Comerica has expanded operations from the Midwest to California, Texas, and Florida. From a one-man office in San Jose, California, in 1983, Comerica has expanded banking operations to five offices in key California markets, with over $1.5 billion in assets. In the early 1980's Comerica entered Texas, and it now has 25 banking locations with over $1.2 billion in assets. Because a large number of Michigan customers were retiring to Florida, Comerica, in 1982, established Comerica Trust Company of Florida N.A. In 1990, Comerica purchased $400 million in trust assets from Lakeworth based First American Bank & Trust and $35 million in deposits from Enterprise Federal Savings of Clearwater, Florida, which led to the creation of Comerica Bank-Florida F.S.B. Eventually Comerica intends to merge these two Florida entities.

In 1990, Comerica acquired $1.0 billion in deposits and 18 branch offices of the failed Michigan bank, Empire Federal Savings Bank of America. During 1989 and 1990, Comerica acquired, with federal assistance, $600 million in deposits from 12 financially troubled Texas financial institutions. In early 1991, Comerica merged into its California entity, the financially sound, well-managed, $500 million-asset, San Jose-based Plaza Commerce Bancorp. Later in 1991, Comerica purchased for $35 million InBancshares of Los Angeles, and Comerica Bank-Texas acquired $102 million of deposits from the Metropolitan National Bank of Dallas.

In 1990, loans of $8.4 billion were divided as follows: commercial loans, 41.5%; commercial mortgages, 13.7%; construction, 2.5%; residential mortgages, 13.1%; and consumer loans, 29.2%. In 1990, income of $1.3 billion was divided as follows: interest, 69.7%; securities, 18.3%; trust, 3.3%; service charges, 3.6%; bank card, 1.3%; and other, 3.8%.

Comerica has paid consecutive cash dividends since 1936. Institutions control over 50% of the outstanding common shares. Comerica paid a 5% stock dividend in 1982, a 5% stock dividend in 1983, a 50% stock dividend in 1988, and a 50% stock dividend in 1991.

Total assets: $13.3 billion
Common shares outstanding: 28.1 million

		1981	1982	1983	1984	1985	1986	1987	1988	1989	1990
NET INCOME (MIL.)		30	36	49	57	53	62	71	112	78	128
EARNINGS PER SHARE		1.70	1.86	2.20	2.41	2.24	2.73	3.10	5.09	3.49	5.66
DIVIDEND PER SHARE		.91	.92	.97	1.01	1.06	1.10	1.15	1.43	1.73	1.95
PRICES	Hi	11.9	12.7	15.2	17.5	22.5	30.4	36.3	38.6	44.1	36.8
	Lo	8.9	8.9	11.2	13.1	17.1	19.4	23.7	29.3	34.0	24.2

Commerce Bancshares, Inc.

1000 Walnut (P.O. Box 13686)
Kansas City, Missouri 64199-3686
Tel. (816) 234-2000
Listed: NASDAQ
Investor contact: Treas. Charles E. Templer
Ticker symbol: CBSH
S&P rating: A

 Commerce

As profiled in its 1990 Annual Report, "Commerce Bancshares, Inc. is a registered, multi-bank holding company organized as a Missouri corporation in 1966. With $6.7 billion in total assets at December 31, 1990, the Company is the third largest bank holding company in Missouri. The Company, through its 14 subsidiary banks, conducts a general banking business in over 100 locations throughout Missouri, including credit card issuance by a subsidiary bank in Nebraska. These banks provide a comprehensive range of financial services including trust, retail, commercial and correspondent banking services. All of the Company's banking subsidiaries are members of the Federal Deposit Insurance Corporation and are regulated and examined by various governmental authorities. The Company also has non-banking subsidiaries involved in small business investment, credit and related insurance, mortgage banking, discount brokerage services and real estate activities for the Company."

Commerce's strategy is to expand in existing markets with concentration in the five largest markets in Missouri, namely St. Louis, Kansas City, Springfield, St. Joseph, and Columbia. Ninety-two percent of its total assets and 99 of its 114 branches are in these key areas. It plans a new regional headquarters building in fast-growing Springfield. Its commercial banking niche is the Midwestern middle market. In 1990, it acquired $190 million in deposits from a failed savings and loan in Kansas City and St. Joseph.

In a 1990 study, conducted by Olsen Research Associates for the magazine *United States Banker*, Commerce Bancshares was rated as the best overall performing and safest bank holding company of the top 100 banking organizations in the country: "Commerce Bank's Total Return Bond Fund and Employees Benefits Equity Fund were ranked second and third respectively in the nation for their outstanding performance."

In 1990, loans of $3.3 billion were apportioned as follows: business, 32.3%; real estate construction, 3.4%; real estate mortgage, 29.4%; consumer, 26.7%; and credit card, 8.3%.

Commerce has paid consecutive cash dividends since 1936. Institutions control about 15% of the outstanding shares. It paid a 100% stock dividend in 1986 and another 100% stock dividend in 1989.

Total assets: $6.7 billion
Common shares outstanding: 18.6 million

		1981	1982	1983	1984	1985	1986	1987	1988	1989	1990
NET INCOME (MIL.)		11	32	35	31	38	39	40	49	59	58
EARNINGS PER SHARE		.55	1.60	1.65	1.48	1.81	1.88	1.95	2.46	3.12	3.02
DIVIDEND PER SHARE		.42	.46	.48	.50	.52	.54	.56	.59	.63	.70
PRICES	Hi	7.3	8.0	11.4	11.8	16.1	21.1	19.4	21.1	29.5	27.4
	Lo	5.5	6.5	7.8	10.0	11.3	15.5	13.4	14.3	19.6	18.5

Community Psychiatric Centers

24502 Pacific Park Drive
Laguna Hills, California 92656
Tel. (714) 831-1166
Listed: NYSE
Investor contact: Pres. C.F.O., Richard L. Conte
Ticker symbol: CMY
S&P rating: A

Since August 1989, Community Psychiatric Centers has once again limited its operations to acute-care psychiatric hospitals. At that time shareholders voted a spinoff of the dialysis and home health-care units on the basis of one share of Vivra, a new corporation, for every 10 shares of Community. Specifically, Vivra took over Community's 85 dialysis centers and 15 health-care offices.

Community Psychiatric Centers

Community operates 50 short-term acute-care psychiatric centers in 18 states, Puerto Rico, and the United Kingdom. In 1991, Community opened a 120-bed psychiatric center in Streamwood, Illinois, and another center in Little Rock, Arkansas. In 1990, Community opened new centers in California, Wisconsin, and Oklahoma City. Also, in 1990 Community acquired from Comprehensive Care the newly rebuilt 152-

bed Brea Neuropsychiatric Hospital in California and purchased from Humana the 174-bed psychiatric Brentwood Hospital in Shreveport, Louisiana. Likewise, it acquired the Harvard Medical Services, a mental health referral agency for psychiatric patients from Western Europe.

In 1990, the average length of stay by patients was 21.5 days, and the average occupancy rate was 90%. Approximately 60% of revenues are derived from private and direct payment sources and 40% from governmental or contractual reimbursement.

Despite rapid expansion in recent years, Community is in excellent financial condition. Community charges less and earns more than its competitors. It owns all the land and buildings on which its hospitals are located. The demand for facilities to treat mental health disorders, including drug and alcohol abuse, shows no sign of abatement.

In 1991, Community acquired for about $77 million the financially ailing Austin, Texas-based, Healthcare International, Inc., and Health-Vest, Inc. Healthvest is a real-estate investment trust that owns many of the hospitals that Healthcare manages. This acquisition adds 1,400 psychiatric beds and 16 hospitals in Virginia, Texas, Colorado, and Hawaii and takes Community into seven new markets.

Since its founding in 1969, Community has experienced rapid and consistent growth. It has increased earnings in each of the past 21 years. Institutions control about 65% of the common shares. It has paid consecutive cash dividends since 1974. Community Psychiatric paid a 100% stock dividend in 1980, a 50% stock dividend in 1982, a 50% stock dividend in 1983, a 50% stock dividend in 1984, and a 50% stock dividend in 1987.

Total assets: $571.8 million
Current ratio: 5.1
Common shares outstanding: 46.4 million

		1981	1982	1983	1984	1985	1986	1987	1988	1989	1990
REVENUES (MIL.)		90	117	138	174	205	231	285	347	320	374
NET INCOME (MIL.)		13	18	27	36	45	51	60	71	72	83
EARNINGS PER SHARE		.35	.47	.63	.81	1.01	1.14	1.32	1.54	1.56	1.80
DIVIDEND PER SHARE		.08	.10	.12	.14	.17	.20	.29	.34	.36	.36
PRICES	Hi	7.1	11.8	20.3	20.0	23.9	26.5	32.3	26.1	35.0	30.6
	Lo	4.4	5.4	10.4	11.3	15.9	14.8	18.0	19.0	22.3	19.8

ConAgra, Inc.

One ConAgra Drive
Omaha, Nebraska 68102
Tel. (402) 595-4000
Listed: NYSE
Investor contact: V.P. Walter H. Casey
Ticker symbol: CAG
S&P rating: A+

This Omaha-based company is an agricultural conglomerate which combines a diversified array of farm and food companies under one roof. It produces frozen foods, red meats, processed meats, poultry, cheese, peanut butter, jelly, pet foods, seafoods, and other grocery products.

It also is engaged in corn, wheat, and oat milling; slaughtering cattle and poultry; operating about 120 commodities brokerage offices; and selling fertilizers, pesticides and grain for livestock feed. Some of its brand names are Banquet, Armour, Country Pride, Real peanut butter, and Chun King Frozen foods. It is the No. 2 producer of poultry in the United States. Prepared foods is ConAgra's largest and fastest-growing segment.

ConAgra owns about 189 retail stores in rural America. These include Country General Stores, Wheelers, S & S, Sandvigs, Peavey Ranch and Home Stores, and Northwest Fabric and Craft stores.

ConAgra has purchased for $52 million the remaining (50%) interest in Swift Independent Packing Co. and is prepared to consolidate this beef, pork, and lamb processor into its own operations. To satisfy the increased demand for oat bran and to a lesser extent corn and barley, ConAgra has quadrupled its milling capacity. Having lost Holly Farms to Tyson Foods, ConAgra is gearing up for increased penetration of the poultry market.

In 1991, ConAgra acquired Golden Valley Microwave Foods, Inc. for 18.8 million shares of ConAgra common stock. In mid-1990, ConAgra acquired Beatrice Co., of Chicago (a major U.S. food products company) from Kohlberg, Kravis, Roberts & Co. for $1.34 billion in cash and stock.

In 1991, prepared foods accounted for 77.1% of sales and 76.2% of profits, agricultural products for 12.5% of sales and 10.8% of profits, trading and processing for 9.5% of sales and 11.5% of profits, and finance for 0.9% of sales and 1.5% of profits.

ConAgra has paid consecutive cash dividends since 1976. It paid a 100% stock dividend in 1980, a 50% stock dividend in 1984, a 100% stock dividend in 1986, a 50% stock dividend in 1989, and a 50% stock dividend in 1991.

Total assets: $9.4 billion
Current ratio: 1.1
Common shares outstanding: 209.5 million

	1982	1983	1984	1985	1986	1987	1988	1989	1990	1991
REVENUES (MIL.)	1,710	2,309	3,302	5,498	5,991	9,002	9,475	11,340	15,501	19,505
NET INCOME (MIL.)	33	48	63	92	105	149	155	198	232	311
EARNINGS PER SHARE	.37	.39	.46	.59	.68	.82	.86	1.09	1.25	1.42
DIVIDEND PER SHARE	.12	.14	.16	.19	.22	.25	.29	.33	.39	.45
PRICES Hi	4.4	5.3	6.2	10.5	14.3	16.9	15.1	20.2	25.5	36.3
Lo	2.5	3.9	4.4	5.7	8.6	9.3	10.6	12.9	15.2	22.3

Crawford & Company

5620 Glenridge Drive NE
Atlanta, Georgia 30342
Tel. (404) 256-0830
Listed: NYSE
Investor contact:E.V.P. D. R. Chapman
Ticker symbol: CRD.B
S&P rating: A+

Crawford & Co. is the world's largest independent insurance adjustment firm. In addition, Crawford is engaged in operating employers' self-insurance plans and in loss-control services, health-care management, and rehabilitation services. Crawford derives most of its business from insurance companies, a substantial portion (16–20%) from the American International Group. Its major competitor is the General Adjustment Bureau.

Crawford & Company

Property and casualty claims adjustment (particularly automobile) is by far the largest segment of Crawford's business. An insurance company may hire an independent adjuster for a variety of reasons. It may not have a claims office in a given region, or may have an excessive number of claims in a given area, or may not have an experienced adjustor in a specific line of insurance.

Likewise, insurance companies hire an independent to inspect potential risks for about the same reasons they hire an independent adjustor. The independent inspector often performs loss control services.

Many employers hire an independent to manage a self-insurance plan. The idea of a self-insurance plan is to save money. The independent manages and coordinates the health insurance program and the workers compensation plan.

Separate health maintenance programs are often administered by the independent adjuster. The independent handles everything from the underwriting to medical case management and final claims payment.

Crawford expands to a large degree through the acquisition of smaller independent adjusters. In 1991, Crawford acquired Rosemurgy & Co., which adjusts aviation hull and marine claims. In 1990, it acquired the F.E.P. Group (loss control and fire protection) from Sedgewick James; it also acquired the Graham Miller Group, an international London-based, adjustment firm.

In 1990, revenues were divided as follows: claims, 78%; health and rehabilitation, 19%; and other, 3%.

Crawford has both Class A and Class B shares of common stock. The Crawford family controls about 60% of both the Class A and Class B shares. Consecutive cash dividends have been paid since 1968. Crawford paid a 50% stock dividend in 1986, a 50% stock dividend in 1989, and a 100% stock dividend in 1990.

Total assets: $271 million
Current ratio: 1.6
Common shares outstanding: Class A 17.8 million
Class B 17.8 million

		1981	1982	1983	1984	1985	1986	1987	1988	1989	1990
REVENUES (MIL.)		142	157	167	186	214	244	265	294	374	449
NET INCOME (MIL.)		10	11	11	12	13	15	16	19	28	32
EARNINGS PER SHARE		.29	.30	.32	.35	.39	.44	.47	.54	.79	.91
DIVIDEND PER SHARE		.12	.12	.13	.15	.16	.17	.19	.21	.26	.32
PRICES	Hi	4.4	4.3	5.5	4.3	6.4	8.8	9.5	7.8	18.1	18.3
	Lo	3.3	2.7	2.8	2.9	4.0	6.0	4.9	5.6	7.4	10.1

Crown Cork & Seal Company, Inc.

9300 Ashton Road
Philadelphia, Pennsylvania 19136
Tel. (215) 698-5100
Listed: NYSE
Investor contact: V.P. Henry E. Butwel
Ticker symbol: CCK
S&P rating: B+

As described in its 1990 Annual Report, "The Company's business is the manufacture and sale of metal cans, crowns and closures and the building of filling, packaging and handling machinery. These products are manufactured in sixty-three (63) plants within the United States and seventy-one (71) plants outside the United States and are sold through our own sales organization to the food, citrus, brewing, soft drink, oil, paint, toiletry, drug, antifreeze, chemical and pet food industries."

Fabricated products represent 90% and machinery 10% of Crown Cork & Seal's operations. Fabricated products include aerosol cans, beer and beverage cans, food cans, crowns, closures, and cone-top cans; machinery products include bottle washers, bottle fillers, can fillers, process equipment, and rotary printers.

In 1990, Crown Cork acquired for $336 million the metals packaging operation of Continental Holdings, Inc. This doubled the size of domestic operations and to reflect this size, Crown Cork has restructured into two operating divisions. The North American Division encompassing the United States, Canada, Mexico, and Central America and the International Division handles worldwide operations.

Crown Cork has expanded its human resources department, has incorporated into its operations the Oakbrook Technical Center, formerly a product research and quality control unit of Continental Can, and has established a corporate environmental department.

In March 1991, Crown Cork acquired the Ball General Packaging can business and in May 1991, purchased the non-European international operations of Continental Can, from Kiewit & Sons for $125 million.

Rescued by the late John F. Connelly from near financial collapse in 1957, Crown Cork & Seal has grown consistently over the years both through increased volume of business and acquisitions. It has not paid a cash dividend for more than 30 years. Institutions control over 35% of the outstanding shares. It paid a 200% stock dividend in 1988.

Total assets: $2.6 billion
Current ratio: 1.3
Common shares outstanding: 28.9 million

		1981	1982	1983	1984	1985	1986	1987	1988	1989	1990
REVENUES (MIL.)		1,374	1,352	1,298	1,370	1,487	1,619	1,718	1,834	1,910	3,072
NET INCOME (MIL.)		65	45	52	60	72	79	88	93	94	107
EARNINGS PER SHARE		1.48	1.05	1.28	1.59	2.17	2.49	2.86	3.37	3.58	3.71
DIVIDEND PER SHARE		—	—	—	—	—	—	—	—	—	—
PRICES	Hi	12.4	10.8	13.0	15.3	29.9	38.1	46.6	47.3	57.0	67.0
	Lo	8.4	7.6	9.6	11.6	14.8	25.8	28.5	30.1	43.9	49.5

Dauphin Deposit Corporation

South Market Square
213 Market Street
Harrisburg, Pennsylvania 17105
Tel. (717) 255-2121
Listed: NASDAQ
Investor contact: Corp. Secy. Claire D. Flemming
Ticker symbol: DAPN
S&P rating: A

As profiled in its 1990 Annual Report, "Dauphin Deposit Corporation is a multi-bank holding company headquartered in Harrisburg, Pennsylvania.

"The Corporation's banks are Dauphin Deposit Bank and Trust Company, headquartered in Harrisburg, Pennsylvania, which operates 59 branches in Dauphin, Cumberland, Lancaster, Lebanon and York counties, and Bank of Pennsylvania, which serves Berks and Lehigh counties

Dauphin Deposit Corporation

with 25 branches.

"Other subsidiaries of the Corporation include Dauphin Life Insurance Company, Dauphin Investment Company and Financial Realty, Inc.

"Dauphin Deposit Corporation's business philosophy is to maintain strong profit growth and increased rate of return to stockholders while continuing to reinvest in and serve the communities in its marketplace. This philosophy is supported by financial soundness, a competitive spirit and a keen sense of social responsibility."

In 1990, Dauphin Corp. completed the consolidation of the operations departments of Dauphin Deposit Bank and Bank of Pennsylvania, resulting in cost savings and improvement in efficiency. Also in 1990, Dauphin purchased Hopper Soliday & Co., Inc. a securities broker/dealer headquartered in Lancaster, Pennsylvania. Hopper Soliday is one of Pennsylvania's leading underwriters of municipal bonds, provides institutional and retail securities sales and offers financial advisory services to privately owned businesses.

In 1990, Dauphin Deposit Bank's return on assets was a high 1.35% and its return on equity a high 15.81%. Likewise, Bank of Pennsylvania's return on assets was a high 1.66% and its return on equity a high 18.25%.

In 1990, loans of $1.8 billion were apportioned as follows: commercial, financial, and agricultural, 48.1%; real estate construction, 5.9%; real estate residential, 29.3%; consumer, 15.6%; and lease financing, 1.1%.

Dauphin has experienced 156 years of prudent banking. It has increased earnings for the past 19 consecutive years. It has paid consecutive cash dividends since 1910. Institutions control about 20% of the common shares. It paid a 10% stock dividend in 1981, a 100% stock dividend in 1983, a 100% stock dividend in 1985, and a 5% stock dividend in 1989.

Total assets: $3.5 billion
Common shares outstanding: 12.4 million

	1981	1982	1983	1984	1985	1986	1987	1988	1989	1990
NET INCOME (MIL.)	10	13	17	21	24	29	35	41	44	45
EARNINGS PER SHARE	1.81	1.68	1.96	2.12	2.43	2.76	2.97	3.14	3.42	3.56
DIVIDEND PER SHARE	.64	.73	.80	.88	.96	1.06	1.16	1.24	1.38	1.44
PRICES Hi	11.6	14.6	17.1	15.8	27.1	37.4	34.0	32.6	37.5	35.3
Lo	6.1	10.0	11.4	12.0	15.8	26.9	24.5	27.1	28.0	24.0

Deluxe Corporation

1080 West County Road
St. Paul, Minnesota 55126-8201
Tel. (612) 483-7111
Listed: NYSE
Investor contact: V.P. Corporate Public Relations, Stuart Alexander
Ticker symbol: DLX
S&P rating: A+

Deluxe has been the leading provider of checks and related forms to banking institutions and their customers for almost 75 years. Deluxe does business with most of the nation's banking institutions and controls over 50% of the market.

In recent years, via acquisitions, operations have expanded beyond check printing. Some of Deluxe's more important acquisitions have been Chex Systems (1984), A.O. Smith Data Systems (1986), and Current, Inc. (1987). In 1990, it acquired A.C.H. Systems, Inc. of Phoenix, which gave Deluxe entry into the automated clearing house market. Likewise, it acquired Seattle-based, Electronic Transaction Corp., a large check authorization service. The synergy created by Electronic Transaction Corp. (check authorization), Chex Systems (account verification), and Deluxe Data systems (electronic transaction processing) should bode well for future earnings.

Deluxe Data Systems provides softwear and processing services to

93

the electronic-payment transfer market. Business System is a supplier of computer forms and record-keeping systems. Current Inc. is a large mail-order retailer of stationary and greeting cards.

Also, Deluxe is engaged in plant modernization and the installation of new, modern check-printing equipment.

The check printing aspect of Deluxe is somewhat mature, but it is the electronic transfer of funds and newly acquired businesses that are driving Deluxe upward and onward. Deluxe Data Systems is the largest electronic funds interchange in the United States.

Deluxe is now aiming to become a major factor in the point of sale market. In 1988, Deluxe installed point of sale equipment in a 12-store St. Louis supermarket chain. It subsequently signed distributor contracts with marketing firms in France and the United Kingdom. Also, it was selected to provide software for Canada's national point of sale network. Information Sciences Pte., Ltd. of Singapore is marketing Deluxe's software on the Pacific Rim.

By 1990, Deluxe had increased its sales for 52 consecutive years and its dividends for 30 consecutive years. It has paid consecutive cash dividends since 1921. Among Fortune 500 companies, Deluxe has recorded above-average profitability for more than five decades. It paid a 100% stock dividend in 1981, a 100% stock dividend in 1985, and a 100% stock dividend in 1986.

Total assets: $924 million
Current ratio: 1.7
Common shares outstanding: 84.1 million

		1981	1982	1983	1984	1985	1986	1987	1988	1989	1990
REVENUES (MIL.)		504	550	620	683	764	867	948	1,196	1,316	1,414
NET INCOME (MIL)		53	65	77	88	104	121	149	143	153	172
EARNINGS PER SHARE		.59	.71	.85	1.01	1.22	1.42	1.74	1.68	1.79	2.03
DIVIDEND PER SHARE		.22	.27	.31	.39	.49	.58	.76	.86	.98	1.10
PRICES	Hi	7.9	10.3	12.0	14.5	24.9	38.0	42.3	28.4	35.8	35.9
	Lo	3.0	4.8	8.8	8.9	13.6	21.5	20.0	21.0	24.0	26.6

Diagnostic Products Corporation

5700 West 96th Street
Los Angeles, California 90045
Tel. (213) 776-0180
Listed: NYSE
Investor contact: V.P. Julian R. Bockserman
Ticker symbol: DP
S&P rating: B+

As profiled in its 1990 Annual Report, "Diagnostic Products Corporation is the world's leading independent manufacturer of immunodiagnostic kits. Representing state-of-the-art technology derived from immunology and molecular biology, these kits can measure hormones, drugs, and other medically important substances present in body fluids and tissues at infinitesimal concentrations. They provide information vital to the diagnosis and management of thyroid disorders, diabetes, infertility, infections, diseases, allergy, drugs of abuse, and certain forms of cancer.

Diagnostic Products Corporation

"The Company—with its affiliated R&D and manufacturing facilities in England and Japan—distributes its products through a national sales force, and through a world-wide distributor network covering over 90 countries. DPC products are used in hospitals, clinical and veterinary laboratories, and doctors' offices.

"With increased commitment to molecular biology research in regard to the development of monoclonal antibodies and practical applications of recombinant DNA and genetic engineering, plus the recent development of new automated instrumentation, DPC enters the new decade as a complete source of diagnostic and therapeutic advances benefitting mankind."

Diagnostic Products worldwide operations and affiliates span 94 countries.

In 1990, Diagnostic Products acquired its French and Benelux distributor, purchased the remaining 26% of its German affiliate, and turned over the management of its Spanish affiliate to its superbly managed Italian affiliate.

During 1990, revenues were apportioned geographically as follows: United States, 29%; Western Europe, 54%; and other, 17%.

Diagnostic Products has no long-term debt. Cash dividends were initiated in 1988. Institutions control more than 25%, and Chairman Ziering and Vice President Mailyn Ziering control more than 20%, of the outstanding common shares. Diagnostic Products paid a 900% stock dividend in 1982, a 50% stock dividend in 1983, and a 100% stock dividend in 1989.

Total assets: $102 million
Current ratio: 4.2
Common shares outstanding: 12.1 million

	1981	1982	1983	1984	1985	1986	1987	1988	1989	1990
REVENUES (MIL.)	9.4	12.3	14.8	17.7	22.7	29.0	36.9	47.0	60.3	75.9
NET INCOME (MIL.)	1.4	2.8	2.8	2.9	3.9	6.3	9.3	12	15	17
EARNINGS PER SHARE	.15	.28	.26	.27	.37	.54	.75	1.00	1.20	1.35
DIVIDEND PER SHARE	—	—	—	—	—	—	—	.12	.20	.24
PRICES Hi	—	6.9	10.5	6.9	7.9	13.6	20.3	22.8	38.0	44.0
Lo	—	3.1	5.0	3.5	4.4	7.4	10.3	14.0	19.3	22.3

Dillard Department Stores, Inc.

900 West Capitol Avenue
P.O. Box 486
Little Rock, Arkansas 72203
Tel. (501) 376-5200
Listed: NYSE
Investor contact: V.P.–C.F.O. James I. Freeman
Ticker symbol: DDS
S&P rating: A+

DILLARD DEPARTMENT STORES, INC.

Dillard operates about 185 department stores in the Midwest and Southwest. It has expanded aggressively through store remodeling and acquisitions. The stores carry mostly branded merchandise directed toward the middle-income market. Sales are divided roughly as follows: apparel, 65%; home furnishings, 14%; shoes, jewelry, etc., 21%. Credit sales accounted for 50.2% of revenues.

The company's strategy is to acquire small regional department store chains that are either marginally profitable or in the red. Dillard takes control in a merger and through economies of scale, lean overhead, buying acumen, computerized inventory, and financial controls, quickly turns them around. Stores are approximately 40,000 to 380,000 square feet. In 1984, Dillard acquired Stix, Baer & Fuller, and Brown and Diamond Department Stores; in 1987, it acquired Joske's and the Cain Sloan's divisions of Allied Stores. In 1989 Dillard entered the Southeast with the purchase of D.H. Holmes Co. Ltd., an 18-store chain, for 870,902 Dillard Class A Shares. Dillard has a 50% interest in Higbee's 12 stores in Ohio, acquired in 1988 for $30 million in a joint venture with the Edward J. Bartolo Corp. In 1990, Dillard acquired, for $110 million, the 23 stores of J. B. Ivey. In late 1990 Dillard opened three new stores one in Tennessee, one in North Carolina, and one in Arizona.

Dillard's earnings have improved dramatically in the recent past because of an economic turnaround in the previously depressed energy states of Texas, Oklahoma, and Louisiana.

There are both Class A and Class B shares. The Class A common shares are 25% owned by a Dutch company, but the Class B controlling shares, which elect two-thirds of the directors, are owned by the Dillard family, which is active both in the control and the day-to-day operation of the business.

Dillard has paid consecutive cash dividends since 1969. It paid a 100% stock dividend in 1983, a 100% stock dividend in 1984, and a 100% stock dividend in 1985.

Total assets: $3.0 billion
Current ratio: 2.8
Common shares outstanding: Class A 365.7 million
Class B 1.3 million

		1982	1983	1984	1985	1986	1987	1988	1989	1990	1991
REVENUES (MIL.)		593	711	847	1,277	1,601	1,851	2,206	2,655	3,160	3,734
NET INCOME (MIL.)		16	22	34	50	67	74	91	114	148	183
EARNINGS PER SHARE		.70	.94	1.39	1.82	2.29	2.35	2.83	3.53	4.36	5.01
DIVIDEND PER SHARE		.05	.05	.075	.088	.11	.12	.14	.16	.18	.20
PRICES	Hi	6.9	15.8	20.9	38.5	45.8	57.5	46.5	74.3	96.0	136.8
	Lo	2.8	5.6	10.8	18.1	32.0	24.0	25.1	41.0	61.8	82.5

The Walt Disney Company

500 South Buena Vista Street
Burbank, California 91521
Tel. (818) 560-1000
Listed: NYSE
Investor contact: Wendy Webb
Ticker symbol: DIS
S&P rating: A-

The Walt Disney Co. (formerly Walt Disney Productions) is one of America's foremost entertainment companies. The able chairman and CEO, Michael Eisner, has combined excellent creative talent with strong financial controls. Essentially, Disney has three operations, theme parks with attendant resorts and hotels, film entertainment, and consumer products.

Theme parks and resorts are Disney's primary operations. These began with the opening of Disneyland Park in Anaheim, California in 1955 and expanded with the opening of Disney World (Magic Kingdom, Disney Village, and resort hotels) in Orlando, Florida. In 1989, it added a new major attraction, Disney-MGM Studio Theme Park, to its Florida complex. Also, Disney receives substantial royalties from an independently owned Disneyland which opened in Tokyo in 1983. A partially owned "Euro Disney" 30 miles outside Paris is scheduled to open in 1992.

Filmmaking for theater, television, and the home video market, is Disney's second most important operation. Also, it owns a cable TV service known as the Disney Channel and a Hollywood TV station, KCAL. Disney developed a number of big box office hits such as "Good Morning Vietnam," "Three Men and a Baby," and "The Color of Money." Jeffrey Katzenberg, Chairman of Walt Disney Studios, intends to refocus Disney's filmmaking away from big-star, high-budget productions toward low-cost films with good stories.

Disney's consumer products divisions has a chain of retail stores, a licensing division, and a publishing arm. The retail stores sell Disney-related merchandise such as Mickey Mouse dolls, T-shirts, and coffee mugs. The licensing division collects fees from distributors who sell Disney merchandise, and the publishing division is responsible for the creation of Disney books, magazines, and comic books.

In 1990, revenues and profits were divided as follows: theme parks, 52% of revenues and 62% of profits; filmmaking, 38% of revenues and 22% of profits; and consumer products, 10% of revenues and 16% of profits.

Disney has paid consecutive cash dividends since 1957. Institutions control over 40% of the common shares. Disney paid a 300% stock dividend in 1986.

Total assets: $8.0 billion
Current ratio: 1.1
Common shares outstanding: 130.2 million

		1982	1983	1984	1985	1986	1987	1988	1989	1990	1991
REVENUES (MIL.)		1,030	1,307	1,656	2,015	2,166	2,877	3,438	4,594	5,844	6,182
NET INCOME (MIL.)		100	92	22	173	247	445	522	703	824	637
EARNINGS PER SHARE		.75	.68	.15	1.29	1.82	3.23	3.80	5.10	6.00	4.78
DIVIDEND PER SHARE		.30	.30	.30	.30	.32	.32	.38	.46	.56	.64
PRICES	Hi	17.9	21.3	17.1	29.5	54.9	82.5	68.4	136.3	136.5	129.8
	Lo	11.9	11.9	11.3	14.9	28.1	41.3	54.0	64.9	86.0	93.6

R.R. Donnelley & Sons Company

2223 Martin Luther King Blvd.
Chicago, Illinois 60616
Tel. (312) 326-8000
Listed: NYSE
Investor contact: S.V.P. and Treas., Ronald G. Eidell
Ticker symbol: DNY
S&P rating: A+

Chicago-based R.R. Donnelley & Sons Company, founded in 1912, is the largest printer in the world. Also, Donnelley known as Lakeside Press, prints phone directories, magazines, catalogs, tabloids, and books

and is engaged in the computer documentation business, which is growing at more than 20% a year. Lakeside prints over 200 magazines, including *Time*, *Newsweek*, *Sports Illustrated*, *Family Circle*, and *Modern Maturity*. It prints Sunday insert magazines for such newspapers as the *New York Times* and the *Chicago Tribune*. It has contracts with over 900 book publishers and prints all types of books, including textbooks, subscription and mail order books, encyclopedias, and Bibles. Donnelley prints catalogs for Sears and J. C. Penney. Also, it prints newspaper inserts for such retailers as K-Mart, Wal-Mart, and Macy's. Donnelley is the nation's leading printer for the financial industry.

In 1991, Donnelley entered into a joint venture with Groupe Presse Hachette to form a new company called Print Holdings, B.V., which holds an 80% interest in Heliocolor, S.A., a state-of-the-art gravure printing facility near Madrid, Spain. Also in 1991, Donnelley purchased an interest in Dataware Technologies, a software firm in Massachusetts. In 1990, it acquired the Meredith/Burda commercial printing business for $570 million. With the 1987 acquisition of Metromail, Donnelley has become a major factor in direct mail listing. In the past 12 years Donnelley has spent over $2 billion in capital improvement and development.

Donnelley operates an international communications system between New York, London, and Tokyo. Also, it has acquired a Tokyo printing firm. Foreign operations are not yet a major factor in Donnelley's revenues.

Catalogs and tabloids account for 37% , magazines 18%, books 11%, directories 17%, and other items 17% of revenues.

The Donnelley family controls 18% and institutions about 85% of the outstanding common shares. 1990 marked the 16th year of consecutive earnings increases. Donnelley has paid consecutive cash dividends since 1911. A 100% stock dividend was paid in 1983, and another 100% stock dividend was paid in 1987.

Total assets: $3.3 billion
Current ratio: 1.8
Common shares outstanding: 78.0 million

	1981	1982	1983	1984	1985	1986	1987	1988	1989	1990
REVENUES (MIL.)	1,244	1,404	1,546	1,814	2,038	2,234	2,483	2,878	3,122	3,498
NET INCOME (MIL.)	79	91	114	134	148	158	218	205	222	226
EARNINGS PER SHARE	1.05	1.20	1.50	1.75	1.94	2.03	2.80	2.64	2.85	2.91
DIVIDEND PER SHARE	.32	.36	.41	.50	.58	.64	.70	.78	.88	.96
PRICES Hi	10.9	16.9	24.0	24.6	32.3	40.0	45.4	38.8	51.3	52.6
Lo	7.6	9.0	14.6	16.0	23.0	29.5	25.5	29.9	34.3	34.1

Dow Jones & Company, Inc.

200 Liberty Street
New York, New York 10281
Tel. (212) 416-2000
Listed: NYSE
Investor contact: Investor Relations, Jan Wilson
Ticker symbol: DJ
S&P rating: A+

Dow Jones is the publisher of the *Wall Street Journal*, with about 2 million daily circulation, and *Barron's National Business and Financial Weekly*, a tabloid magazine with a circulation of 241,321. A subsidiary, Ottaway Newspapers, publishes 83 daily newspapers. Dow Jones also operates news wire and data retrieval services. It has a 100% interest in Telerate, which provides computerized data to banks, insurance companies, and brokerage firms. Also, Dow Jones owns a 40% equity interest in a Quebec newsprint manufacturer and a 33% equity interest in one in Virginia.

DOW JONES & COMPANY

The *Wall Street Journal* is America's largest-circulation daily newspaper. It is edited in New York and beamed by satellite to 18 printing plants across the nation. There is also a European and an Asian edition.

Telerate began in partnership with AT&T, but Dow Jones purchased AT&T's remaining interest in late 1989 and now owns 100%. Telerate and Intex Holdings, Ltd. entered into a partnership to provide fully automated trading for the London International Financial Futures Exchange under the title of Trading Service, but because of a disagreement on the terms of the contract, it is now in arbitration.

In 1990-91, the *Journal* suffered a plunge in ad linage due to a combination of the recession and problems in the financial industry, from which the *Journal* obtains most of its advertising. The information group is now Dow Jones's chief moneymaker, and during 1991 Telerate evidenced some recovery in earnings momentum.

In 1990, business publications provided 43% of revenues and 34% of operating income, information services provided 43% of revenues and 53% of operating income, and daily newspapers provided 14% of revenues and 13% of operating income.

Dow Jones has both a common stock issue and a Class B common stock issue. Each share of Class B stock has 10 votes per share. The Bancroft family controls 67% of both the Class A and Class B shares.

Consecutive cash dividends have been paid since 1906. Cash dividends have been increased in each of the past 15 years. Dow Jones paid a 100% stock dividend in 1981, a 100% stock dividend in 1983, and a 50% stock dividend on the Class B shares in 1986.

Total assets: $2.6 billion
Current ratio: 0.6
Common shares outstanding: 77.8 million
Class B 23.1 million

		1981	1982	1983	1984	1985	1986	1987	1988	1989	1990
REVENUES (MIL.)		641	731	866	966	1,040	1,135	1,314	1,603	1,688	1,720
NET INCOME (MIL.)		71	88	114	129	139	183	203	228	317	107
EARNINGS PER SHARE		.76	.93	1.19	1.34	1.43	1.89	2.10	2.35	3.15	1.06
DIVIDEND PER SHARE		.31	.36	.40	.48	.52	.55	.64	.68	.72	.76
PRICES	Hi	18.5	23.5	38.0	34.3	33.4	42.1	56.3	36.5	42.5	33.8
	Lo	9.9	11.9	21.4	23.5	24.5	28.1	28.0	26.8	29.3	18.1

Dun & Bradstreet Corporation
299 Park Avenue
New York, New York 10171

Tel. (212) 593-6800
Listed: NYSE
Investor contact: V.P. Investor Services, Frank L. Alexander
Ticker symbol: DNB
S&P rating: A+

Dun & Bradstreet is the world's largest marketer of business information and related services. Dun & Bradstreet provides business and credit information through Dun & Bradstreet Information Services; computer software services through Dun & Bradstreet Software; marketing information services through Nielsen Marketing Re-  search, Nielsen Media Research, and IMS International. Dun & Bradstreet publishes yellow classified telephone directories through its Reuben H. Donnelley division. Dun & Bradstreet provides financial information through Moody's Investors Service and provides credit insurance through its wholly-owned subsidiary American Credit Indemnity.

Dun & Bradstreet has a solid grasp on its markets and strong financial resources, making it extremely difficult for a competitor to gain a foothold.

In 1991, Dun & Bradstreet sold Donnelley Marketing for $200 million. However, it retained Donnelley Marketing Information Services. Also, in 1991, plans sold the communications medical publishing unit of IMS International.

In 1990, Dun & Bradstreet sold Zytron, Neodata Services, and Petroleum Information.

Dun & Bradstreet has rapidly expanded due to a combination of aggressive marketing and acquisitions. Due to problems in its Credit Services unit, Nielsen Clearing House, and Nielsen Marketing Research, net operating earnings declined for the first time in 26 years in 1990. Dun & Bradstreet expects some growth in its 1991 earnings, but worldwide economic conditions, as well as adverse effects of industry conditions on Dun & Bradstreet Software, continue to add elements of uncertainty to this outlook. 1991 growth is not expected to be up to the company's long-term expectations.

Dun & Bradstreet is exceptionally strong financially and has no long-term debt. It has paid consecutive cash dividends since 1934. It paid a 100% stock dividend in 1983 and another 100% stock dividend in 1987.

Total assets: $4.8 billion
Current ratio: 1.1
Common shares outstanding: 181.6 million

	1981	1982	1983	1984	1985	1986	1987	1988	1989	1990
REVENUES (MIL.)	1,818	2,041	2,267	2,625	3,022	3,463	3,789	4,267	4,322	4,818
NET INCOME (MIL.)	171	199	235	281	325	379	439	499	586	508
EARNINGS PER SHARE	.93	1.08	1.27	1.51	1.75	2.04	2.36	2.67	3.14	2.80
DIVIDEND PER SHARE	.57	.67	.77	.91	1.06	1.24	1.45	1.68	1.94	2.09
PRICES Hi	17.6	26.0	35.0	33.9	43.9	60.3	71.8	57.5	60.3	48.6
Lo	13.4	14.8	24.5	25.6	31.5	40.5	44.5	45.9	41.3	36.1

Durr-Fillauer Medical, Inc.

218 Commerce Street
Montgomery, Alabama 36124
Tel. (205) 241-8800
Listed: NYSE
Investor contact: Treas. Charles T. Gross
Ticker symbol: DUFM
S&P rating: A+

Durr-Fillauer is basically a wholesale drug and medical supply distributor in the Southeast. It also has an orthopedic manufacturing division based in Chattanooga, Tennessee.

The wholesale drug division distributes some 28,000 items to about 4,200 customers. Approximately 54% of sales are to hospital pharmacies, 39% to independently operated pharmacies, and 7% to drugstore chains. Durr-Fillauer's "Priceguard" program does much to cement its strong relations with independent pharmacists. This program gives independent druggists discounts, electronic ordering, and other benefits usually available only to large drug chains. Durr-Fillauer has an agreement with Voluntary Hospitals of America whereby Durr-Fillauer is exclusive distributor of pharmaceuticals to some 130 V.H.A. hospitals in the Southeast.

The medical-surgical division supplies medical, surgical, and veterinary products to hospitals, physicians' offices, outpatient clinics, emergency centers, nursing homes, medical laboratories, and veterinary sites. In 1990, sales to hospitals represented 43% of revenues and sales to others, 57%. Due to the steady erosion of hospital admissions, Durr-Fillauer is emphasizing sales to alternative medical treatment facilities.

The orthopedic division manufactures artificial limbs and braces for more than 2,000 wholesale customers.

In 1988, Durr-Fillauer acquired Spokane Surgical Supply, Co., expanding operations into the Pacific Northwest. In 1989, Durr-Fillauer acquired both the medical and surgical segments of J. M. Keckler Medical Co. in northern California and Nevada and opened a distribution center in Seattle, Washington.

In 1990, wholesale drug sales represented 72% of revenues and 61% of profits; medical and surgical sales, 27% of revenues and 33% of profits; and orthopedic sales, 1% of revenues and 6% of profits. The medical surgical operations are clearly the most profitable.

Durr-Fillauer has increased sales and earnings for the 31st consecutive year. It has paid consecutive cash dividends since 1937. It paid a 25% stock dividend in 1980, a 50% stock dividend in 1981, a 100% stock dividend in 1982, a 25% stock dividend in 1985, a 25% stock dividend in 1990, and a 25% stock dividend in 1991.

Total assets: $244 million
Current ratio: 2.0
Common shares outstanding: 12.6 million

	1981	1982	1983	1984	1985	1986	1987	1988	1989	1990
REVENUES (MIL.)	154	205	263	342	427	489	534	588	706	815
NET INCOME (MIL.)	3.2	4.0	5.0	5.8	6.1	6.5	6.8	11	15	17
EARNINGS PER SHARE	.40	.47	.51	.59	.62	.66	.70	1.22	1.22	1.35
DIVIDEND PER SHARE	.067	.078	.088	.10	.11	.13	.13	.14	.18	.23
PRICES Hi	6.3	10.6	14.4	10.4	12.3	13.7	11.2	14.8	19.5	22.6
Lo	3.3	4.2	8.5	6.6	7.4	8.6	5.7	6.8	14.4	15.6

Eaton Vance Corp.

24 Federal Street
Boston, Massachusetts 02110
Tel (617) 482-8260
Listed: NASDAQ
Investor contact: Treas. Curtis H. Jones
Ticker symbol: EAVN
S&P rating: A-

Eaton Vance Corporation

As profiled in its 1990 Annual Report, "Eaton Vance is a holding company deriving its revenues primarily from investment management activities. Eaton Vance Management, a wholly owned subsidiary, acts as advisor to 30 mutual funds, various institutional accounts (including corporations, hospitals, retirement plans, universities, foundations and trusts) and individuals.

"The Company's five main lines of business are: (1) management of investment companies, distribution of investment company shares and investment counseling for individuals and institutions; (2) trust and banking services and mutual fund custody, accounting and pricing services through a 77.3 percent interest in Investors Bank & Trust Company; (3) real estate investment and consulting through wholly owned Northeast Properties, Inc.; (4) the development of precious metal properties through wholly owned Fulcrum Management, Inc., and Min Ven, Inc. and (5) oil and gas activities through wholly owned Energex Corporation and 56.5 percent owned Serio Exploration Company."

Under the able leadership of Chairman Landon T. Clay, one of Harvard's most distinguished alumni, Eaton Vance manages some $7.5 billion in portfolios with objectives ranging from high current income to maximum capital gains. In 1990, Eaton introduced the Eaton Vance Short-Term Global Income Fund, the Eaton Vance Florida Tax Free Fund, and the Eaton Vance New York Tax Free Fund. Also in 1990, Eaton Vance Prime Rate Reserves established a $300 commercial paper program, a first for the mutual fund industry. In early 1991, Eaton introduced two additional single-state municipal bond funds, one for New Jersey and the other for Pennsylvania.

In 1990, Investors Bank & Trust, specializing in mutual fund custody and accounting services, acquired the entire fund-custody business of the Bank of New England. This acquisition tripled assets under custody from $9 billion to over $27 billion and raised annual revenues from $10 million to $30 million.

In 1990, income was derived as follows: investment advisory fees, 54%; distribution plan payments, 18%; other investment management income, 1%; banking, 20%; real estate, 3%; and mining oil, and gas, 4%.

Eaton has paid consecutive cash dividends since 1976. It paid a 100% stock dividend in 1983 and another 100% stock dividend in 1986.

Total assets: $224 million
Current ratio: 0.7
Common shares outstanding: Nonvoting 3.6 million
Voting 9.7 thousand

		1982	1983	1984	1985	1986	1987	1988	1989	1990	1991
REVENUES (MIL.)		11	19	19	23	32	52	47	64	94	NA
NET INCOME (MIL.)		1.2	4.0	4.1	4.8	6.4	12	11	7.3	7.7	13
EARNINGS PER SHARE		.33	1.05	1.09	1.27	1.62	2.70	2.74	1.97	2.05	3.49
DIVIDEND PER SHARE		.15	.18	.20	.22	.25	.30	.37	.41	.47	.64
PRICES	Hi	6.9	13.0	12.0	23.0	30.1	32.8	23.5	28.3	28.0	33.0
	Lo	3.0	6.9	7.9	8.5	16.0	12.9	15.0	22.0	14.6	15.8

Emerson Electric Co.

8000 W. Florissant Avenue
St. Louis, Missouri 63136
Tel. (314) 553-2000
Listed: NYSE
Investor contact: Asst. Treas., Earle L. Weaver
Ticker symbol: EMR
S&P rating: A+

Emerson Electric is one of America's largest and most consistently profitably manufacturing concerns, with 34 years of uninterrupted earnings and dividend growth. Emerson combines outstanding management with a consistent process of investment, new product development, aggressive marketing, and acquisitions.

Emerson is a diversified manufacturer of electrical and electronic products for the commercial, industrial, and consumer markets.

The commercial and industrial segment manufactures and markets products for industrial automation and power regulation and transmission. Its products include electric motors, drives, switches, distribution equipment, and components for refrigeration.

The consumer segment manufactures and distributes power tools, electrical products for both residential and nonresidential lighting, welding equipment, and other products.

In 1990, Emerson spun off to shareholders its defense segment, consisting of Hazeltine and five other subsidiaries.

Emerson's strategy is one of constantly acquiring new companies that show promise and at the same time divesting itself of operations that don't live up to promise.

With foreign operations accounting for over 40% of revenues, Emerson has a strong stake in the international value of the dollar.

Commercial and industrial products account for 55% of revenues and 51% of earnings, appliance and construction-related products 45% of revenues and 45% of earnings, and corporate items 0% of revenues and 4% of earnings.

Emerson has had 34 years of uninterrupted earnings increases. It has paid consecutive cash dividends since 1947. Emerson split its common stock 3 for 1 in 1987.

Total assets: $6.4 billion
Current ratio: 1.4
Common shares outstanding: 238.3 million

		1982	1983	1984	1985	1986	1987	1988	1989	1990	1991
REVENUES (MIL.)		3,807	3,810	4,587	4,921	5,242	6,170	6,652	7,071	7,573	7,427
NET INCOME (MIL.)		325	330	383	416	427	467	529	588	613	632
EARNINGS PER SHARE		1.38	1.40	1.62	1.76	1.83	2.00	2.31	2.63	2.75	2.83
DIVIDEND PER SHARE		.67	.70	.77	.87	.92	.97	1.00	1.12	1.26	1.32
PRICES	Hi	21.4	22.9	23.9	27.5	30.9	42.4	36.0	39.9	44.4	55.0
	Lo	12.0	13.4	18.4	19.5	22.3	26.8	27.3	29.5	30.8	36.9

Ennis Business Forms, Inc.

107 North Sherman Street
Ennis, Texas 75119
Tel. (214) 875-6581
Listed: NYSE
Investor contact: Chairman Kenneth A. McCrady
Ticker symbol: EBF
S&P rating: A

Founded in 1909, Ennis markets a large and diverse supply of business forms. Ennis targets small companies away from large urban areas. Over 80% of forms are either custom or semicustom produced. They come in a wide variety of sizes and colors. They include continuous forms, data processing cards, sales books, tags, etc.

Ennis Business Forms, Inc.

Ennis operates 13 manufacturing plants and two warehouses across the United States. Products are distributed through 30,000 dealers, most of whom are independents, stationary supply firms, and printers.

Also, Ennis owns and operates Connolly Tool & Machine Company of Dallas, Texas. Acquired by Ennis in 1990, Connolly designs and manufactures tools, dies, and machinery, primarily for customers in the southwest.

In early 1991, Ennis Business Forms, Inc., acquired the assets and operations of Admore, Inc., a privately owned Michigan based specialty printing company with annual sales of $16 million.

In 1983, Ennis acquired American Business Equipment, Inc., which sells and services photocopier equipment. It also sells paper and other supplies needed to keep photocopiers in operation.

Business form sales account for 88% of total revenues. Ennis has authorized the expenditure of $10 million for the repurchase of its common stock.

Ennis has paid consecutive cash dividends since 1973. It paid a 100% stock dividend in 1983, a 100% stock dividend in 1985, a 50% stock dividend in 1987, a 50% stock dividend in 1989, and a 50% stock dividend in 1991.

Total assets: $73.2 million
Current ratio: 5.0
Common shares outstanding: 18.3 million

		1982	1983	1984	1985	1986	1987	1988	1989	1990	1991
REVENUES (MIL)		88	91	96	108	111	112	118	128	130	126
NET INCOME (MIL.)		6.5	7.2	7.9	9.4	11	13	16	19	21	21
EARNINGS PER SHARE		.25	.27	.33	.41	.49	.55	.74	.93	1.05	1.12
DIVIDEND PER SHARE		.053	.057	.064	.079	.10	.15	.22	.32	.41	.47
PRICES	Hi	2.2	4.2	4.3	7.1	8.2	13.7	12.3	18.3	17.1	21.4
	Lo	1.2	1.9	2.7	4.2	6.2	7.9	9.6	11.9	10.7	10.9

Equifax, Inc.

1600 Peachtree Street N.W.
Atlanta, Georgia 30302
Tel. (404) 885-8000
Listed: NYSE
Investor contact: Tom Maloy
Ticker symbol: EFX
S&P rating: A+

EQUIFAX®

Equifax (formerly Retail Credit Corporation) supplies business and industry with credit information. Other operations provide personnel information on prospective insureds, employees, and claimants. Also, it is engaged in marketing services, information services, and energy audits for utilities.

Equifax supplies most life insurance and property and casualty insurance companies in the United States with information on prospective insurance and employment applicants. In the case of life insurance applicants, it supplements, through its vast data bases, information furnished by the Medical Information Bureau. It provides information regarding the applicant's habits (smoking, substance abuse) and creditworthiness. In the case of property and casualty insurance companies, it provides previous accident history, age and physical condition of the property to be insured, and other information. Also, it provides insurance companies with personal and credit information on claimants.

Also, Equifax provides to business, government, and industry consumer and commercial credit reports, debt collection information, credit application processing, and marketing services. Likewise, Equifax conducts energy audits (both commercial and residential), provides energy consumption software and customer debt information to utilities.

In 1990, Equifax merged with Telecredit, which augments Equifax's operations. With the Telecredit acquisition, Equifax becomes one of the three largest providers of retail and credit information. Telecredit provides Equifax with a dominant share of the credit-card processing and check authorization business. Equifax is consolidating its marketing divisions and will cross-market its services through the Telecredit data base. Also, Telecredit provides Equifax with substantial cash reserves with which it can pay off debt. Equifax is planning to offer credit card solicitation and collection services.

In 1990, revenues and profits were broken down as follows: insurance accounts, 43% of revenues and 18% of profits; credit and marketing services, 50% of revenues and 69% of profits; and Canadian operations, 7% of revenues and 13% of profits.

Equifax has paid consecutive cash dividends since 1913. Institutions control over 50% of the outstanding common shares. Equifax paid a 100% stock dividend in 1982, a 50% stock dividend in 1985, a 100% stock dividend in 1985, a 100% stock dividend in 1986, and a 100% stock dividend in 1989.

Total assets: $754 million
Current ratio: 2.1
Common shares outstanding: 81.8 million

		1981	1982	1983	1984	1985	1986	1987	1988	1989	1990
REVENUES (MIL.)		402	435	471	507	564	635	670	743	840	1,079
NET INCOME (MIL.)		16	12	18	19	22	26	31	34	36	64
EARNINGS PER SHARE		.40	.30	.42	.44	.53	.60	.72	.73	.73	.79
DIVIDEND PER SHARE		.20	.22	.24	.27	.29	.32	.35	.39	.43	.48
PRICES	Hi	2.3	4.8	6.4	5.9	10.3	14.3	15.8	16.5	20.0	22.4
	Lo	1.8	2.0	4.4	4.0	5.4	9.5	8.8	12.3	13.0	13.5

Ethyl Corporation

330 South Fourth Street
Richmond, Virginia 23217
Tel. (804) 788-5000
Listed: NYSE
Investor contact: Director Investor Relations, John S. Patton
Ticker symbol: EY
S&P rating: A+

 Ethyl Corporation has undergone a metamorphosis from primarily a supplier of lead compounds as antiknock gasoline additives to a manufacturer of diverse specialty chemical products, including petroleum additives, industrial chemicals, bromine chemicals, and electronic materials. Ethyl remains one of the world's leading suppliers of lead antiknock compounds, largely for foreign markets. As the sale of antiknock lead compounds has steadily declined over the years, Ethyl has acquired new, largely chemical businesses.

A subsidiary, Whitby, Inc., manufactures and distributes ethical and over-the-counter drugs.

In 1990, Ethyl sold off its Hardwicke Chemical segment for $112 million. Hardwick, a synthetic pyrethoid intermediates producer, represented about $50 million in sales.

In 1989, Ehtyl spun off Tredegar Industries, Inc., to stockholders on the basis of one tax-free share of Tredegar for every ten shares of Ethyl. Tredegar Industries consists of Ethyl's former aluminum, plastics, and energy holdings. This left Ethyl primarily in the chemicals and life insurance businesses.

First Colony Life, acquired in 1982, underwrites life, individual annuity and employee benefit insurance. First Colony is experiencing strong growth in both immediate and deferred annuity policies. First Colony has been a very profitable addition to Ethyl's activities and now has nearly $1 billion in annual sales.

In 1990, chemicals represented 63% of sales and 69% of profits, while insurance supplied 37% of sales and 31% of profits. With the elimination of plastics, aluminum, and energy operations, specialty chemicals will play an increasing role in revenues and profits.

Since approximately 50% of chemicals sales are from U.S. exports, transfers, and foreign manufacturing, the international value of the dollar can play an important role in Ethyl's earnings.

Ethyl has paid consecutive cash dividends since 1957. Ethyl paid a 100% stock dividend in 1983, a 100% stock dividend in 1985, and a 100% stock dividend in 1986.

Total assets: $6.7 billion
Current ratio: 2.2
Common shares outstanding: 118.3 million

		1981	1982	1983	1984	1985	1986	1987	1988	1989	1990
REVENUES (MIL.)		1,082	1,220	1,388	1,465	1,461	1,516	1,713	2,093	2,432	2,514
NET INCOME (MIL.)		91	94	106	132	117	178	193	231	231	232
EARNINGS PER SHARE		.57	.59	.65	.86	.91	1.40	1.57	1.91	1.93	1.95
DIVIDEND PER SHARE		.19	.19	.21	.21	.29	.34	.40	.45	2.01	.60
PRICES	Hi	4.5	4.4	7.5	8.4	15.4	23.4	32.3	24.1	29.0	23.0
	Lo	2.9	2.4	3.8	5.0	7.9	13.5	15.0	17.3	21.0	20.5

Fifth Third Bancorp

38 Fountain Square
Cincinnati, Ohio 45263
Tel. (513) 579-5300
Listed: NASDAQ
Investor contact: C.F.O. P.M. Brumm
Ticker symbol: FITB
S&P rating: A+

Fifth Third Bank is one of America's fastest growing and highest quality banks. It derived its name from a merger of the Fifth National Bank and the Third National Bank of Ohio. Fifth Third has expanded rapidly through both the acquisition of small banks and the establishment of new branch offices. It has made acquisitions in Ohio, northern Kentucky, and southeastern Indiana.

Fifth Third is engaged in the commercial banking and trust business. It is now experimenting with so-called bank marts. These are small, full-service operations situated in retail outlets, primarily supermarkets.

While Fifth Third has banking offices in only three states, it operates in some 27 states through automatic teller machines. It opens about 20 to 25 new offices a year and now operates about 225 banking offices. It intends to focus on the more profitable areas of trust and data processing.

In 1989, Fifth Third made its first large acquisition, Toledo-based First Ohio Bancshares. In 1991, it purchased Pinnacle Bancorp Inc., a holding company for the $275 million Midfed Savings Bank of Middletown, Ohio and acquired the $149 million-asset Montgomery Bancorporation, which owns the Montgomery Traders Bank & Trust Co., and the Farmers Exchange Bank of Millersburg, Kentucky. Also, in 1991, Fifth Third purchased nine branches (five in Columbus and four in Cincinnati) from Chase Bank of Ohio, a subsidiary of Chase Manhattan Corp.

At the end of 1990, outstanding loans and leases of $5.6 billion were divided as follows: commercial, industrial, and agricultural, 41%; consumer, 25%; mortgage, 22%; lease, 8%; and construction, 4%. Also, in 1990, deposits of $6 billion were apportioned as follows: demand, 14%; checking, 11%; savings, 6%; money market, 19%; and time, 50%.

Cincinnati Financial, a strong regional property and casualty insurance company, owns 22% and Western-Southern Life Insurance Company owns 9% of the outstanding common shares of Fifth Third.

Fifth Third has increased earnings for the 16th consecutive year. It has paid cash dividends since 1952. It paid a 100% stock dividend in 1983, a 50% stock dividend in 1985, a 50% stock dividend in 1986, a 50% stock dividend in 1987, and a 50% stock dividend in 1990.

Total assets: $7.1 billion
Common shares outstanding: 39.2 million

		1981	1982	1983	1984	1985	1986	1987	1988	1989	1990
NET INCOME (MIL.)		23	27	30	35	44	55	60	84	108	120
EARNINGS PER SHARE		.99	1.13	1.26	1.44	1.71	2.01	2.03	2.62	2.79	3.07
DIVIDEND PER SHARE		.29	.33	.37	.42	.49	.56	.68	.78	.90	1.02
PRICES	Hi	5.0	6.5	11.1	11.5	19.4	28.9	28.0	30.4	39.9	37.0
	Lo	4.3	4.9	6.1	9.5	11.4	18.9	20.3	21.1	29.6	23.3

First Alabama Bancshares, Inc.

P.O. Box 1448
Montgomery, Alabama 36102
Tel. (205) 832-8486
Listed: NASDAQ
Investor contact: E.V.P. Robert P. Houston
Ticker symbol: FABC
S&P rating: A+

First Alabama Bancshares, based in Montgomery, Alabama, is a $6 billion plus bank and a leader in commercial middle-market and consumer loans. The bank has expanded both internally and by acquisitions. Its lead bank, First Alabama Bank, has over 143 full service office throughout Alabama.

First Alabama Bancshares

In 1987, it acquired Golden Summit Corp. of Florida and its one-bank subsidiary Santa Rosa State Bank. In 1988, it acquired Sunshine Bankshares of Florida and merged all its Florida operations into Sunshine Banks. In 1990, it acquired from Altus one bank and five supermarket locations in Birmingham, Alabama. Also during 1990, it acquired some assets and $600 million in deposits from the Baldwin County Federal Savings Bank and City Federal Savings and Loan Association, strengthening its base in Birmingham, Montgomery, and Baldwin Counties. Early in 1991, it acquired the St. Clair Federal Savings Bank with deposits of $83 million, and its Sunshine Bank Division acquired five offices and $160 million in deposits from the Great Western Bank of Pensacola, Florida.

First Alabama's capital ratio is consistently one of the best in the nation and the company's earnings have been on a consistently steady upward thrust. Conservative management aims for very high asset quality and retains more mortgages in its portfolio than the average bank. Unlike a number of other southern states, Alabama has a very diverse economy, which favors banks in an economic downturn.

In 1990, the loan portfolio of $4.2 billion was divided as follows: commercial, 33%; installment, 30%; real estate, 33%; and real estate construction, 4%.

In 1990, deposits of $4.83 billion were divided as follows: demand, 16%; large certificates of deposit, 13%; NOW accounts, 10%; money market, 11%; savings, 7%; and additional interest deposits, 43%.

First Alabama has paid consecutive cash dividends since 1968. It paid a 10% stock dividend in 1979, a 100% stock dividend in 1984, and a 100% stock dividend in 1986.

Total assets: $6.3 billion
Common shares outstanding: 34.1 million

		1981	1982	1983	1984	1985	1986	1987	1988	1989	1990
NET INCOME (MIL.)		30	33	40	44	51	54	56	58	63	69
EARNINGS PER SHARE		1.25	1.08	1.29	1.42	1.66	1.67	1.71	1.77	1.90	2.10
DIVIDEND PER SHARE		.38	.42	.45	.50	.56	.64	.76	.80	.84	.92
PRICES	Hi	7.4	7.3	9.8	12.3	18.6	26.5	24.1	16.8	19.4	18.5
	Lo	6.3	5.3	6.5	8.5	10.8	16.4	13.3	13.4	15.1	14.6

First Empire State Corporation
One M & T Plaza
Buffalo, New York 14240
Tel. (716) 842-4200
Listed: AMEX
Investor contact: S.V.P. Gary S. Paul
Ticker symbol: FES
S&P rating: A

First Empire State Corporation

As profiled in its 1990 Annual Report, "First Empire State Corporation is a regional bank holding company headquartered in Buffalo, New York. Its banking subsidiaries are Manufacturers and Traders Trust Company, The East New York Savings Bank and The First National Bank of Highland.

116

"M & T Bank, with $5.5 billion in assets as of December 31st, 1990, is a New York-chartered commercial bank with 80 offices throughout Western New York, plus offices in New York City, Albany, Syracuse and Nassau the Bahamas. East New York is a New York-chartered savings bank with 16 branches in metropolitan New York City and assets of $2.0 billion as of December 31, 1990. Highland, a national bank located in the Hudson Valley, operates 14 offices and had $449 million in assets at the recent year end.

"M & T Bank's subsidiaries include M & T Capital Corporation, a venture capital company, M & T Financial Corporation, an equipment leasing company, and M & T Discount Brokerage Services, Inc., a discount securities broker.

"On January 26, 1990 M & T Bank expanded its branch network into the Rochester, New York area by acquiring nearly $439 million of assets and assuming approximately $554 million of liabilities, including $470 million of deposits in 11 branches of the former Monroe Savings Bank, FSB.

"On September 28, 1990, M & T Bank acquired approximately $450 million of loans, predominantly secured by 1–4 family residential properties, and assumed approximately $1.2 billion of deposits of the former Empire Federal Savings Bank of America."

In 1990, income of $713 million was divided as follows: interest income, 77.6%; investment securities, 14.6%; service charges, 2.4%; trust income, 1.4%; credit charges, 0.8%; and other, 3.2%.

In 1990, loans and leases of $5.5 billion were divided as follows: commercial, financial, and agricultural, 19.0%; real estate construction, 0.6%; real estate mortgage, 61.9%; consumer loans, 16.8%; and leases, 1.7%.

First Empire State has paid consecutive cash dividends since 1979. Institutions control about 50% of the shares. First Empire State paid a 100% stock dividend in 1987.

Total assets: $7.7 billion
Common shares outstanding: 8.1 million

		1981	1982	1983	1984	1985	1986	1987	1988	1989	1990
NET INCOME (MIL.)		10	12	5	17	22	26	40	44	51	54.0
EARNINGS PER SHARE		1.80	2.06	.93	3.04	4.13	4.80	4.78	6.02	7.04	7.91
DIVIDEND PER SHARE		.19	.43	.50	.53	.63	.70	.80	.95	1.10	1.25
PRICES	Hi	10.0	13.0	18.9	23.3	35.8	49.5	59.0	56.3	72.5	67.5
	Lo	7.0	7.8	11.8	15.6	22.1	34.6	35.0	39.0	51.4	47.0

First Financial Management Corporation

3 Corporate Square
Atlanta, Georgia 30329
Tel. (404) 321-0120
Listed: NYSE
Investor contact: C.F.O. E. D. M. Schachner
Ticker symbol: FFM
S&P rating: B+

First Financial Management Corporation

As profiled in its 1990 Annual Report, "First Financial Management corporation is a national leader in information services, offering a vertically integrated set of data processing, storage and management products for the capture, manipulation and distribution of data. Services include merchant credit card authorization, processing and settlement; debt collection and accounts receivable management; data imaging, micrographics and electronic data base management; financial institutions processing; health and pharmaceutical claims processing; and the development and marketing of data communication and information systems. In addition, the Company owns the largest savings institution in Georgia and a major regional consumer finance company.

"Merchant Services consists of NaBANCO, the largest merchant credit card processor in the U.S.; Nationwide Credit, a leading provider of debt collection and accounts receivable management services; and MicroBilt, a major provider of data communications and information processing systems. Data Imaging Services include computer output micrographics, electronic laser printing, microfilm, micropublishing, high and low speed data capture, direct mail marketing services, and data base management systems. With 3,500 employees and 80 branch locations, First Image Management Company and Appalachian Computer Services provide over 10,000 customers these multiple services. Basic Information Technologies provides a wide range of processing services to over 1,100 financial institutions in 42 states through 7 host and 9 remote data centers with 800 employees. The Computer Company processes over 110 million health care claims annually representing close to $9 billion. Medicaid claims processing is provided in eight states and Washington D.C. and the company is also a leader in pharmaceutical claims processing. Consumer Services includes Georgia Federal Bank, the largest savings institution in Georgia and First Family Financial Services, a major regional consumer finance company. Georgia Federal has $4.7 billion in assets and 56 branches. First Family operates 191 consumer finance offices in eight southeastern states."

In 1990, First Financial Management acquired Electro Data Corporation, OnLine Financial Communications systems, Nationwide Credit, Zytron Corporation, the operating assets of Finance South and Post-Tron Systems Corporation, and certain assets of Chilton Data Services. Also, it acquired the merchant credit card portfolios of Bank of Boston, Bank of New York, and Southeast Bank of Florida.

First Financial Management initiated cash dividends in 1987. Institutions control over 60% of the common shares. It paid a 50% stock dividend in 1985, a 50% stock dividend in 1987, and a 5% stock dividend in 1989.

Total assets: $5.5 billion
Current ratio: 1.3
Common shares outstanding: 27.5 million

		1981	1982	1983	1984	1985	1986	1987	1988	1989	1990
REVENUES (MIL.)		—	18	24	36	52	70	175	424	667	925
NET INCOME (MIL.)		—	1.3	1.8	2.6	3.4	7.3	14	34	57	73
EARNINGS PER SHARE		—	.20	.26	.37	.48	.66	1.10	1.69	2.15	2.50
DIVIDEND PER SHARE		—	—	—	—	—	—	—	—	.10	.10
PRICES	Hi	—	—	10.5	7.6	15.4	17.6	30.3	31.9	39.0	33.8
	Lo	—	—	6.3	5.6	7.4	11.0	15.0	23.1	23.4	14.1

First Hawaiian, Inc.

165 South King Street
Honolulu, Hawaii 96813
Listed: NASDAQ
Investor contact: Asst. V.P. Lisa Halvorson
Ticker symbol: FHWN
S&P rating: A+

As described in its 1990 Annual Report, "First Hawaiian, Inc. is a bank holding company whose principal subsidiary is First Hawaiian Bank. First Hawaiian was founded in 1858 and is the state's oldest financial institution. The bank presently has 48 branches throughout Hawaii, two on Guam, an offshore branch in Grand Cayman, British West Indies and a representative office in Tokyo, Japan.

"Other major subsidiaries include First Interstate of Hawaii, Inc. and its wholly-owned subsidiary, First Interstate Bank of Hawaii, the state's fourth largest commercial bank; First Hawaiian Creditcorp. Inc., the state's largest locally-owned financial services loan company and First Hawaiian Leasing, Inc., which is primarily engaged in commercial equipment and vehicle leasing."

In May 1991, First Hawaiian completed the acquisition of First Interstate of Hawaii, holding company for Hawaii's fourth-largest bank, with 20 branch offices and approximately $900 million in assets. As a result of the acquisition of First Interstate of Hawaii, First Hawaiian's assets now exceed $6.4 billion.

In 1990, return on equity was 20.29% and return on assets was a strong 1.35%. In 1990, *Business Week* magazine named First Hawaiian, "The Most Solid" bank in the nation.

In 1990, loans and leases of $3.3 billion were divided as follows: commercial, financial and agricultural, 27.1%; real estate construction, 8.7%; real estate mortgage, 38.4%; consumer, 14.3%; lease financing, 4.6%; and foreign, 6.9%.

Also, in 1990, deposits of $4.8 billion were divided as follows: non-interest bearing demand, 16.4%; interest-bearing demand, 21.3%; savings, 13.3%; time, 42.9%; and foreign, 6.1%.

The provision for loan and lease losses rose to $39,847,000, or 1.22% of total outstanding loans and leases, at the end of December, 1990.

First Hawaiian has paid consecutive cash dividends since 1929. It has had 26 years of consecutive earnings growth. It paid a 10% stock dividend in 1981, a 100% stock dividend in 1984, a 100% stock dividend in 1986, a 100% stock dividend in 1989, and a 100% stock dividend in 1990.

Total assets: $6.4 billion
Common shares outstanding: 32.1 million

		1981	1982	1983	1984	1985	1986	1987	1988	1989	1990
NET INCOME (MIL)		18	19	21	24	27	31	36	43	57	72
EARNINGS PER SHARE		.68	.72	.79	.91	1.02	1.15	1.33	1.62	2.14	2.45
DIVIDEND PER SHARE		.29	.30	.32	.33	.36	.43	.48	.58	.70	.83
PRICES	Hi	4.0	4.1	5.3	6.3	8.9	13.8	15.4	16.5	26.8	25.8
	Lo	3.1	2.9	3.6	5.1	6.3	8.3	8.9	11.3	14.9	14.5

First Virginia Banks, Inc.
6400 Arlington Blvd.
Falls Church, Virginia 22042-2336
Tel. (703) 241-4000
Listed: NYSE
Investor contact: V.P. Ronald Locke
Ticker symbol: FVB
S&P rating: A

As profiled in its 1990 Annual Report, "First Virginia Banks, Inc., with assets of approximately $5.38 billion, is the oldest bank holding company headquartered in Virginia. At year-end 1990, its statewide network

 of 16 Virginia member banks with 257 offices served cities, towns, and counties accounting for over 85% of Virginia's population including the state's fastest growing and most affluent areas. The Corporation has three banks in Maryland which operate 34 offices in Hartford, Baltimore, Prince George's, Montgomery, Anne Arundel, St. Mary's, and Charles counties. Two thirds of the Corporation's banking offices are located in the urban corridor stretching from the metropolitan areas of Baltimore and Washington through Richmond and down into Tidewater. The Corporation also has two banks in Tennessee which operate 16 offices in the cities of Bristol, Kingsport, and Johnson City and the counties of Hawkins, Monroe, Sullivan and Washington in East Tennessee.

"At mid-year 1990, the Corporation's member banks accounted for 12.3% of the banking offices in Virginia and 7.5% of the total domestic bank deposits in Virginia. In addition, the Corporation and its member banks own several companies which are engaged in financially related activities such as mortgage banking and insurance in nine states."

First Virginia is highly liquid, with over 75% of loans consisting of consumer installments and one- to four-family mortgages, which amortize on a monthly basis. Its ratio of tangible equity capital to assets is a high 8.9%. In 1990, the bank's return on assets, the amount of money it earns on loans and investments, was a high 1.25% and return on equity a high 13.59%.

In 1990, loans of $3.8 billion were apportioned as follows: commercial, financial and agricultural, 11.3%; real estate construction, 3.5%; real estate mortgage, 15.3%; installment, 63.5%; and consumer, 6.4%.

In 1990, First Virginia acquired the $67 million-asset Clifton Trust Bank of Baltimore, Maryland.

First Virginia has paid consecutive cash dividends since 1960 and has increased cash dividends in each of the past nine years. Institutions control about 25% of the common shares.

Total assets: $5.4 billion
Common shares outstanding: 21.3 million

	1981	1982	1983	1984	1985	1986	1987	1988	1989	1990
NET INCOME (MIL.)	15	18	25	29	35	40	48	56	61	67
EARNINGS PER SHARE	1.60	2.00	2.30	2.44	2.59	2.78	2.75	2.90	3.20	3.05
DIVIDEND PER SHARE	.56	.64	.72	.80	.88	.96	1.04	1.12	1.20	1.28
PRICES Hi	10.0	12.5	20.0	20.0	28.8	37.5	35.0	28.0	35.6	30.6
Lo	6.3	6.8	11.3	14.8	19.0	25.4	21.3	22.6	23.8	16.8

America's GROWTH STOCKS

Fleet/Norstar Financial Group, Inc.

50 Kennedy Plaza
Providence, Rhode Island 02903
Listed: NYSE
Tel. (401) 278-5800
Investor contact: Director Corporation Communications, Robert W. Lougee, Jr.
Ticker symbol: FNG
S&P rating: A-

As described in its 1990 Annual Report, "Fleet/Norstar, founded in 1791, is a $33-billion diversified financial services company with 1,000 offices nationwide." Its approximately 18,000 employees work at nine banks throughout New England and New York State and at more than a dozen financial service companies located throughout the country, including Atlanta; Columbia, S.C.; Long Beach, California; Milwaukee; and New York City.

> Fleet/Norstar
> Financial
> Group, Inc.

Fleet/Norstar's nonperforming assets are not on the same scale as those of other New England banks for a number of reasons. First, Fleet/Norstar is more geographically spread out than most New England banks, with over half of its commercial loans originating in upper New York State. Second, in late 1987, Fleet/Norstar discounted underwriting New England condominium loans. Third, nonbank services count for about a quarter of revenues. It ranks second to Citicorp in servicing $35 billion in nationwide mortgages. It is third in the nation in student loan processing. It derives substantial revenues from investment banking, trust services, and consumer finance.

Fleet is still realizing a decline in overhead as the operations arising from the 1988 merger of Fleet and Norstar are consolidated. In April 1991, Fleet/Norstar in partnership with Kolberg, Kravis & Roberts, Inc., acquired the failed Bank of New England from the F.D.I.C. for $683 million. In addition, the F.D.I.C. will receive $25 million in cash and $100 million in preferred stock as a premium in the deal. With the acquisition of the Bank of New England banking franchise, Fleet transactions in New England will rise from about one-third of the bank's business to between 40% and 50%. The $23 billion-asset Bank of New England is now Fleet Bank of Massachusetts, Fleet Bank, N.A. (Connecticut), and Fleet Bank of Maine.

In 1990, loans (excluding leases net of unearned) of $18.8 billion were apportioned as follows: commercial, 42.9%; residential real estate, 7.7%; construction, 9.2%; permanent, 11.0%; consumer, 29.0%; and international, 0.2%. 1990 income of $4.0 billion is divided as follows: interest, 81.3%; mortgage, 6.0%;, student loans, 2.0%; trust, 1.9%; and other, 8.8%.

Consecutive cash dividends have been paid by the predecessor bank since 1791. Dividend payments have increased in each of the past 14 years. A 100% stock dividend was paid in 1985, and another 100% stock dividend was paid in 1987.

Total assets: $32.5 billion
Common shares outstanding: 110.2 million

		1981	1982	1983	1984	1985	1986	1987	1988	1989	1990
NET INCOME (MIL.)		47	100	136	173	209	253	200	336	371	(74)
EARNINGS PER SHARE		1.15	1.51	1.56	1.74	1.97	2.37	1.82	3.01	3.34	(.75)
DIVIDEND PER SHARE		.46	.52	.57	.62	.68	.74	.88	1.20	1.31	1.25
PRICES	Hi	6.9	9.9	12.7	14.5	21.5	28.1	30.6	27.9	30.9	27.6
	Lo	4.9	5.1	8.5	10.1	14.3	18.6	17.0	22.4	23.8	10.5

America's GROWTH STOCKS

FlightSafety International, Inc.

Marine Air Terminal
La Guardia Airport
Flushing, New York 11371
Tel. (718) 565-4100
Listed: NYSE
Investor contact: B. McDonald
Ticker symbol: FSI
S&P rating: A

FlightSafety International is the world's largest provider of training for private, commercial, and government aircraft pilots. Likewise, it trains pilots of large marine vessels and operators of industrial steam and power generating plants. It is involved in the manufacture of training equipment and audio-visual training materials. Flight-

Safety International has a virtual monopoly, its only competition being in-house airline training programs and the armed forces.

FlightSafety entered the training of commercial pilots in the early 80s, the training of Air Force personnel with the 1988 acquisition of FlightSafety Services Corp, which trains both U.S. Air Force C-5 cargo transport crews and controllers of the U.S. Air Force Space Command. In 1990 it entered the field of maintenance training.

FlightSafety trains over 30,000 pilots a year by means of simulators that reproduce the performance characteristics of aircraft made by 21 manufacturers. FlightSafety plans to add over 30 additional simulators in the next few years. The new simulators will include ones to train pilots and crew in the operation of Boeing aircraft. FlightSafety has over 35 training centers located in the United States, most of them near aircraft manufacturing plants.

MarineSafety International trains pilots and crews of large marine vessels. Training includes the piloting, cargo handling, and engine room procedures of large vessels, both the U.S. Navy and the Coast Guard are clients.

PowerSafety International, which is jointly owned by Babcock & Wilcox, trains personnel in the operating of power and steam generating plants.

FlightSafety International has paid consecutive cash dividends since

1976. Institutions control over 50% and Chairman Albert L. Ueltschi about 30% of the outstanding common shares. FlightSafety International paid a 50% stock dividend in 1981, a 50% stock dividend in 1985, and a 50% stock dividend in 1988.

Total assets: $621 million
Current ratio: 2.6
Common shares outstanding: 34.0 million

	1981	1982	1983	1984	1985	1986	1987	1988	1989	1990
REVENUES (MIL.)	63	71	75	94	104	101	130	175	222	273
NET INCOME (MIL.)	19	21	22	27	31	30	42	50	66	76
EARNINGS PER SHARE	.58	.65	.67	.81	.93	.88	1.25	1.48	1.93	2.22
DIVIDEND PER SHARE	.05	.07	.08	.09	.10	.11	.13	.15	.17	.21
PRICES Hi	15.9	14.6	17.5	15.5	19.8	20.1	28.9	29.3	51.0	65.3
Lo	9.5	7.1	9.9	8.8	13.4	13.1	14.1	21.0	24.1	35.5

Food Lion, Inc.

P.O. Box 1330
Salisbury, North Carolina 28145-1330
Tel. (704) 633-8250
Listed: NASDAQ
Investor contact: Corp. Communications Mgr., Mike Mozingo
Ticker symbol: FDLNB
S&P rating: A

Food Lion is one of the most rapidly growing supermarket chains in the Southeastern United States. Based in North Carolina, its more than 850 stores are located in North Carolina, South Carolina, Virginia, Tennessee, Georgia, Florida, Maryland, Delaware, West Virginia, Kentucky, Texas, and Pennsylvania. However, over half the stores are in North Carolina.

Stores range in size from 13,200 to 35,330 square feet. All are self-service and cash and carry. Food Lion carries a full line of groceries and health and beauty aids under both national brands and its private-label Food Lion Brand. In 1990, Food Lion opened over 100 new stores. In 1991, it opened new distribution centers in Plant City, Florida and Greencastle, Pennsylvania. Also in 1991, Food Lion opened more than 40 stores and a distribution center in the Dallas-Fort Worth region of Texas.

Food Lion combines strong management, effective marketing, and superior operating skills. Its selling and administrative expenses are 13% in contrast to an industry average of 21%. Its strategy is low cost. It does not use trading stamps or promotional gimmicks but concentrates on the reduction of cost through volume. When Food Lion expands into an area, it keeps opening stores in adjacent locales and then opens a distribution warehouse nearby, thus cutting down on warehouse and transportation costs. Food Lion currently has warehouse distribution centers in North Carolina, South Carolina, Virginia, Tennessee, Florida, and Pennsylvania.

Food Lion has both Class A and Class B common shares outstanding. Class A is nonvoting and Class B is voting. In general Class B shares trade slightly higher than Class A shares. A Belgian company, Establissements Delhaize Fere et Cie "Le Lion" S.A. owns almost 40% of the Class A shares and about 50% of the Class B voting shares. Stockholders have authorized the repurchase of 16.2 million Class A shares and 16 million of the Class B shares.

Food Lion has increased earnings for 19 consecutive years. Class B shares have paid consecutive cash dividends since 1971. It paid a 200% stock dividend in 1979, a 200% stock dividend in 1982, a 200% stock dividend in 1986, and a 100% stock dividend in 1987.

Total assets: $1.5 billion
Current ratio: 1.3
Common shares outstanding: Class A 162.6 million
Class B 159.7 million

		1981	1982	1983	1984	1985	1986	1987	1988	1989	1990
REVENUES (MIL.)		667	947	1,172	1,470	1,866	2,407	2,954	3,815	4,717	5,584
NET INCOME (MIL.)		19	22	28	37	48	62	86	113	140	173
EARNINGS PER SHARE		.06	.07	.09	.12	.15	.19	.27	.35	.43	.54
DIVIDEND PER SHARE		.005	.006	.007	.007	.012	.018	.046	.070	.10	.14
PRICES	Hi	1.1	2.4	2.5	2.5	3.8	9.4	14.5	13.5	13.6	16.6
	Lo	0.6	0.9	1.8	1.5	2.3	3.4	6.0	9.8	9.6	10.4

Franklin Resources, Inc.

777 Mariners Island Blvd.
San Mateo, California 94404
Tel. (415) 570-3000
Listed: NYSE
Investor contact: Treas. Kenneth Domingues
Ticker symbol: BEN
S&P rating: A-

Franklin Resources, Inc.

Franklin Resources is the holding company for the 56-member, California-based, Ben Franklin Group of Mutual Funds. It acts as investment manager, transfer agent, and distributor of the funds. With fund assets of $45.9 billion as of December 31st, 1990, Franklin is the largest fund group in the nation.

Franklin Funds represent a broad spectrum of objectives such as growth, balanced, tax-exempt, fixed income, bond, and capital appreciation funds. Despite its size, Franklin has a reputation for excellent service and consistent performance. Franklin has a high customer retention rate. Franklin has formulated tax-exempt unit trusts and tax exempt money funds for most of the high-income-tax states, such as New York and California.

In addition to investment management, Franklin provides custodial services for Individual Retirement Accounts and Keough plans. Also, it provides investment management to clients other than fund customers. It markets insurance products, in particular tax-sheltered annuities, and has recently acquired an insurance company. It is engaged in trust operations, real estate syndication, and property management. It sponsors oil and gas products and is currently engaged in the opening of three closed-end funds and one open-end fund.

At the close of 1990, fund assets of $45.9 billion were divided as follows: Tax-free Income Funds, 52%; U.S. Government (Ginnie Maes), 28%; Money Funds, 8%; and Equity/Income Funds, 12%.

Cash dividends were initiated in 1981. Officers and directors control 54% of the common shares (including 37% by the Johnson family), and institutions control 26%. A 25% stock dividend was paid in 1982; a 100% stock dividend was paid in 1983; a 25% stock dividend was paid in 1984; a 100% stock dividend was paid in 1985; a 100% stock dividend was paid in January, 1986; a 50% stock dividend was paid in October, 1986; a 25% stock dividend was paid in 1987; and a 50% stock dividend was paid in 1990.

Total assets: $479 million
Common shares outstanding: 39.0 million

		1981	1982	1983	1984	1985	1986	1987	1988	1989	1990
REVENUES (MIL.)		6	12	24	37	63	143	207	203	253	288
NET INCOME (MIL.)		0.6	1.8	3.1	6.1	14	32	59	66	79	89
EARNINGS PER SHARE		0.1	0.5	0.8	.15	.34	.81	1.47	1.67	2.00	2.28
DIVIDEND PER SHARE		.001	.004	.006	.019	.033	.064	.14	.28	.29	.40
PRICES	Hi	0.1	0.4	1.3	2.3	11.5	19.8	28.5	15.9	30.1	35.8
	Lo	0.1	0.1	0.1	1.1	2.3	10.6	8.0	11.4	15.0	22.5

Gannett Co., Inc.
1100 Wilson Blvd.
Arlington, Virginia 22234
Tel. (703) 284-6000
Listed: NYSE
Investor contact: V.P. Investor Relations, Susan V. Watson
Ticker symbol: GCI
S&P rating: A+

Gannett is one of the nation's largest newspaper publishers, with 82 dailies in 35 states and territories and 66 nondailies in 15 states and Washington, D.C. Its newspapers include such giants as the *Detroit News*, the *Des Moines Register*, the *Cincinnati Enquirer*, the *Louisville Courier Journal*, and the nationally distributed *USA Today*. With

approximately 1.8 million average daily circulation, *USA Today* is the second-largest national newspaper, the *Wall Street Journal* being first.

Also, Gannett owns and operates 15 radio stations and 10 T.V. stations, of which nine have network affiliations. It owns and operates Louis Harris & Associates (public opinion polls). Likewise, it owns Gannett Outdoor, the largest billboard firm in North America. Operating in 20 major markets in the U.S. and most major markets in Canada, Gannett Outdoor expanded operations through the 1988 acquisition of the New York Subways Advertising Co.

Throughout its 24 years of public ownership, Gannett has been a consistently profitable operation. However, there has been an earnings problem with *USA Today* which has operated at a loss since its founding in 1982. It has attained 6.3 million daily readers but has failed to attract sufficient advertising.

In 1991, Gannett's newspaper division introduced NEWS 2000, a program designed to improve the content of its newspapers. As its newspapers become more necessary to its readers, they become more attractive to its advertising customers. NEWS 2000 will focus the attention of reporters and editors on elements of quality, style, and community service in an effort to build circulation penetration in every Gannett newspaper market.

In 1990, newspaper publishing provided 81% of revenues and 83% of profits, broadcasting 11% of revenues and 12% of profits, and outdoor advertising 8% of revenues and 5% of profits.

Gannett has paid consecutive cash dividends since 1929. Institutions control about 66% of the outstanding common shares. Gannett paid a 50% stock dividend in 1981, a 50% stock dividend in 1984, and a 100% stock dividend in 1987.

Total assets: $3.8 billion
Current ratio: 1.3
Common shares outstanding: 143.2 million

		1981	1982	1983	1984	1985	1986	1987	1988	1989	1990
REVENUES (MIL.)		1,367	1,520	1,704	1,960	2,209	2,801	3,079	3,314	3,518	3,442
NET INCOME (MIL.)		173	181	192	224	253	276	319	364	398	377
EARNINGS PER SHARE		1.06	1.13	1.20	1.40	1.58	1.71	1.98	2.26	2.47	2.36
DIVIDEND PER SHARE		.53	.58	.61	.67	.77	.86	.94	1.02	1.11	1.21
PRICES	Hi	15.5	22.0	24.0	25.5	33.1	43.6	56.3	39.9	49.9	44.5
	Lo	11.3	9.9	17.1	16.8	23.5	29.6	26.0	29.3	34.5	29.5

The Gap, Inc.

One Harrison Street
San Francisco, California 94105
Tel. (415) 952-4400
Listed: NYSE
Investor contact: S.V.P. Finance & Treas. Warren R. Hashagan
Ticker symbol: GPS
S&P rating: A-

The Gap (formerly The Gap Stores) is one of America's foremost specialty apparel retailers. It operates more than 1,181 stores, including more than 836 Gap Stores (includes 27 in the U.K. and 24 in Canada), more than 206 GapKids stores (includes two in the U.K. and six in Canada), and more than 139 Banana Republic stores in the United States, Canada, and the United Kingdom.

Gap stores sell jeans, sweat suits, sweaters, shorts, and fashion tops geared to the 20–45-year-old man or woman. GapKids stores feature fashionable clothing for the 2–12 year old. A new babyGap line of clothing for infants and toddlers came on line in 1990. Banana Republic stores, acquired in 1983, retail private-label upscale casual apparel. Recently, Banana Republic has expanded into a line of fabrics versatile enough for travel, weekend, or office wear. Clothing produced by more than 500 domestic and foreign manufacturers is sold exclusively under the Gap, GapKids, and Banana Republic private labels.

The Gap's strategy is to expand both demographically and geographically. In 1991, it added about 150 stores and enlarged about 50 highly productive existing stores. It emphasizes active and casual no-frills high-quality wear at affordable prices. Sales have grown at an annual compound rate of 29% during the past decade. Profits have grown at an annual compound rate of 42% during the past five years. Sales should double to about $4.5 billion by 1995. The addition of new and larger stores and the rapid growth of GapKids, babyGap, and Banana Republic should fuel increased revenues and earnings in the years to come.

Gap is expanding at the rate of about 10 to 12 stores a year in the United Kingdom, where customers are not accustomed to its unusual attention to personal detail and satisfaction.

The Gap has paid consecutive cash dividends since going public in 1976. The Fisher family controls over 40% and institutions over 45% of the outstanding common shares. The Gap paid a 50% stock dividend in 1983; a 100% stock dividend in January, 1986; a 100% stock dividend in August, 1986; a 100% stock dividend in 1990; and a 100% stock dividend in 1991.

Total assets: $770 million
Current ratio: 1.4
Common shares outstanding: 141.8 million

		1981	1982	1983	1984	1985	1986	1987	1988	1989	1990
REVENUES (MIL.)		417	445	481	534	647	848	1,062	1,252	1,587	1,934
NET INCOME (MIL.)		12	18	22	12	34	68	70	74	98	145
EARNINGS PER SHARE		.10	.15	.16	.045	.26	.49	.49	.52	.69	1.02
DIVIDENDS PER SHARE		.019	.023	.025	.032	.035	.16	.13	.13	.17	.22
PRICES	Hi	1.2	2.8	1.5	4.0	11.5	19.5	10.6	15.4	18.1	46.3
	Lo	0.4	1.0	1.1	1.3	3.9	4.0	4.6	8.8	9.8	16.5

General Electric Company

3135 Easton Turnpike
Fairfield, Connecticut 06431
Tel (203) 373-2211
Listed: NYSE
Investor contact: Specialist Share Owner Information, Pauline M. Berardi
Ticker symbol: GE
S&P rating: A+

General Electric is a very large, diverse company of 13 separate businesses that can be classified into three major groupings: electrical equipment, technology, and financial services. The company continues to grow largely through strategic growth acquisitions and divestitures. Thus the internal structure of the company is constantly changing. General Electric maintains a leadership position in all areas of its operation. It is committed to productivity improvement through such measures as factory automation, rapid turnover of inventories, and reduction in accounts receivable.

Manufacturing operations include electrical equipment, lighting, power systems and electrical motors. Technology operations include aircraft engines, aerospace, plastics, medical systems, and factory automation. Financial services include General Electric Capital Corp., Employers Reinsurance, Kidder Peabody, and the National Broadcasting System.

In 1986 General Electric acquired RCA and its subsidiary, National Broadcasting, and in 1988 it acquired the plastics business of Borg Warner. In 1990, General Electric purchased a 51% interest in Thorn E.M.I., a British and European manufacturer and distributor of lamps.

General Electric's fastest growing segments are financial services, plastics, and medical systems. These three areas provide about 40% of the company's profits.

In 1990, aerospace operations provided 9% of revenues and 8% of profits, aircraft engines 13% of revenues and 16% of profits, broadcasting 5% of revenues and 6% of profits, industrial operations 12% of revenues and 12% of profits, appliances 9% of revenues and 6% of profits, materials 9% of revenues and 13% of profits, power systems 10% of revenues and 10% of profits, technical products 8% of revenues and 8% of profits, financial services 24% of revenues and 18% of profits, and other operations 1% of revenues and 3% of profits.

General Electric has had only one year (1975) of down earnings since 1971. It has increased its cash dividend in every year since 1975. It has paid consecutive cash dividends every year since 1899. In 1983 it paid a 100% stock dividend, and it paid another 100% stock dividend in 1987.

Total assets: $153.9 billion
Current ratio: 1.2
Common shares outstanding: 873.1 million

		1981	1982	1983	1984	1985	1986	1987	1988	1989	1990
REVENUES (MIL.)		27,854	27,192	27,681	28,936	29,272	42,013	48,158	50,089	54,574	58,414
NET INCOME (MIL.)		1,652	1,817	2,024	2,228	2,336	2,492	2,915	3,386	3,939	4,303
EARNINGS PER SHARE		1.82	2.00	2.23	2.52	2.57	2.73	3.20	3.75	4.36	4.85
DIVIDEND PER SHARE		.79	.84	.94	1.03	1.12	1.19	1.33	1.46	1.70	1.92
PRICES	Hi	17.5	25.0	29.5	29.8	36.9	44.5	66.4	47.9	64.8	75.5
	Lo	12.9	13.9	22.8	24.0	27.9	33.4	39.0	38.4	43.5	50.0

General Re Corporation

Financial Centre
695 East Main Street
Stamford,Connecticut 06904
Tel. (203) 328-5000
Listed: NYSE
Investor contact: Allen W. Rork
Ticker symbol: GRN
S&P rating: A-

> **General Re Corporation**

General Re (formerly General Reinsurance Corporation) is the nation's largest and premier reinsurance group, with operations in the United States and 30 other countries. Its largest unit is Northstar Reinsurance Corp. Gen Re is benefitting from a "flight to quality" as primary carriers seek out higher-quality long-established property and casualty reinsurance companies. Over 95% of the company's business is conducted in the United States.

Consistently, Gen Re has had lower loss and expense ratios than other large domestic reinsurers. Basically, there are two types of reinsurance, treaty and facultative. In treaty reinsurance, the reinsurance company reinsures an entire portfolio of risks, where as in facultative reinsurance, the reinsurer reviews and rates each risk individually. Increasingly, Gen Re is opting for the facultative basis. Also, most of Gen Re's business is written on an excess of loss basis, with liability phasing in only after the loss by the primary carrier exceeds a certain specified sum. The reinsurance mechanism enables primary carriers to write more risks than their surplus levels would normally allow.

In 1990, Gen Re's portfolio of risks was apportioned as follows: general liability, 42%; property and all-risk coverages, 32%; automobile coverages, 12%; workers' compensation, 8%; and other, 6%.

Gen Re is both a conservative underwriter and a conservative investor. Its investment portfolio is of the highest quality. While overseas underwriting operations are expansive, they do not represent an important part of the firm's total insurance business. Gen Re uses excess cash to repurchase its shares on the open market.

Consecutive cash dividends have been paid since 1934. Institutions control over 80% of the common shares. Gen Re paid a 100% stock dividend in 1982 and another 100% stock dividend in 1986.

Total assets: $11.0 billion
Common shares outstanding: 87.2 million

		1981	1982	1983	1984	1985	1986	1987	1988	1989	1990
REVENUES (MIL.)		1,432	1,498	1,659	1,842	2,123	3,175	3,448	2,736	2,771	2,993
NET INCOME (MIL.)		180	204	189	76	164	305	499	513	599	614
EARNINGS PER SHARE		2.06	2.30	2.10	.84	1.76	2.99	4.92	5.39	6.52	6.89
DIVIDEND PER SHARE		.44	.54	.64	.72	.78	.88	1.00	1.20	1.36	1.52
PRICES	Hi	21.9	32.4	36.5	34.1	53.1	69.5	68.9	59.4	96.3	93.3
	Lo	12.9	16.9	26.0	23.1	30.3	49.3	46.0	45.5	54.4	69.0

America's GROWTH STOCKS

Genuine Parts Company

2999 Circle 75 Parkway
Atlanta, Georgia 30339
Tel. (404) 953-1700
Listed: NYSE
Investor contact: Sr. V.P. Finance, Jerry W. Nix
Ticker symbol: GPC
S&P rating: A+

Atlanta-based Genuine Parts is a national wholesale distributor of

automotive replacement parts (and, to a much lesser extent, industrial parts) through its wholly owned subsidiary Motion Industries, and office supplies through its wholly owned subsidiary S.P. Richards. Genuine does not manufacture parts, but buys them from about 150 manufacturers. However, Genuine does have six plants which rebuild automotive parts.

Genuine owns and operates 64 of the 76 warehouse centers owned by NAPA (National Automotive Parts Association) and 616 jobbing stores. It services over 5,900 independent NAPA jobbers and stocks over 125,000 replacement parts.

In 1989 Genuine Parts formed a partnership with UAP, one of Canada's largest auto parts distributors. Genuine contributed its Western Canadian operations to the deal. UAP-NAPA will conduct the day-to-day operations of the business. UAP owns slightly more than 50% of the operation and Genuine Parts the remainder. As part of the agreement, Genuine purchased 20% of the outstanding shares of UAP.

The auto parts business is highly fragmented, and Genuine gains from aging vehicles and increased market share. The hallmarks of its success are quick service, breadth of products and inventory control.

Motion Industries distributes industrial parts such as bearings, transmission equipment, and material-handling equipment. Profitability of this operation continues to improve through stable pricing and increased operating efficiency. S. P. Richards distributes office supplies, including data processing software, furniture, and office machines.

In 1990, automotive parts provided 64% of revenues and 72% of profits; industrial parts, 20% of revenues and 15% of profits; and office products, 16% of revenues and 13% of profits.

Genuine has paid consecutive cash dividends since 1948. It has increased dividends for 35 consecutive years. It has increased earnings for 30 consecutive years. It has paid eight stock dividends since 1959, the most recent being a 50% stock dividend in 1987.

Total assets: $1.4 billion
Current ratio: 4.1
Common shares outstanding: 76.4 million

	1981	1982	1983	1984	1985	1986	1987	1988	1989	1990
REVENUES (MIL.)	1,585	1,937	2,068	2,304	2,279	2,394	2,606	2,942	3,161	3,319
NET INCOME (MIL.)	78	100	104	120	120	122	148	181	199	207
EARNINGS PER SHARE	1.23	1.23	1.27	1.47	1.49	1.52	1.88	2.35	2.58	2.68
DIVIDEND PER SHARE	.51	.58	.61	.68	.79	1.01	.92	1.04	1.20	1.38
PRICES Hi	15.9	21.0	21.5	22.5	25.5	32.3	44.4	40.9	43.3	42.8
Lo	11.5	13.3	17.1	16.0	20.1	23.6	27.3	32.5	36.0	33.1

The Gillette Company
Prudential Tower Building
Boston, Massachusetts 02199
Tel. (617) 421-7000
Listed: NYSE
Investor contact: V.P. Finance, Milton Glass
Ticker symbol: G
S&P rating: A

One of America's first safety razor companies, Gillette has expanded into toiletries, writing instruments, and other consumer products. Its major thrust of operations are razors and blades (Sensor, twin-bladed Trac II, Atra, the Daisy, Good News, and Micro Trac disposable razors; Super Stainless, Blue and Platinum Plus blades), toiletries, cosmetics and shaving cream (Adorn, Toni,  Silkience, White Rain, and Soft and Dri Shampoo; Foamy shaving cream; Right Guard, Dry Look, and Dry Idea deodorants), stationary (Papermate, Flair, Eraser Mate, and Waterman pens; Liquid Paper), Braun shavers, and small appliances and oral care, including Oral B toothbrushes, toothpastes and rinses. The restructuring of Gillette, following hostile take-over attempts, has significantly improved both productivity and profitability.

Gillette's prime successes are the Sensor Razor, the German-made Braun Flexi Control electric shaver, and Oral B oral products. The Sensor razor, with over $200 million development and roll-out costs, has exceeded all expectations. Introduced in January, 1990, the Sensor is now the largest-selling razor in the North American market with over 6% market share and an 11% share in dollar amount. The Sensor gives a much closer shave, paralleling a straight razor, and is cannibalizing the American market. Sensor profits should rapidly increase as introductory costs decline and use of the product becomes more widespread.

In early 1991, Gillette entered into a joint venture with Leninets of the Soviet Union to manufacture over 750 million razors and blades in the U.S.S.R. Also, it called its convertible preferred stock, which will increase its common shares by 12,000,000.

In 1990, sales and profits were apportioned as follows: razors and blades, 36% of sales and 60% of profits; Braun products, 25% of sales and 15% of profits; stationary items, 11% of sales and 8% of profits; and Oral B products, 6% of sales and 4% of profits.

Gillette has paid consecutive cash dividends since 1906. Institutions control over 65% of the common shares. Gillette paid a 100% stock dividend in 1986, a 100% stock dividend in 1987, and a 100% stock dividend in 1991.

Total assets: $3.7 billion
Current ratio: 1.6
Common shares outstanding: 218.4 million

	1981	1982	1983	1984	1985	1986	1987	1988	1989	1990
REVENUES (MIL.)	2,334	2,239	2,183	2,289	2,400	2,818	3,167	3,581	3,819	4,345
NET INCOME (MIL.)	124	135	146	159	160	16	230	269	285	368
EARNINGS PER SHARE	.52	.56	.60	.65	.65	.07	1.00	1.23	1.35	1.60
DIVIDEND PER SHARE	.25	.28	.29	.31	.33	.34	.37	.43	.47	.53
PRICES Hi	4.4	6.2	6.4	7.4	9.0	17.3	22.9	24.5	24.9	32.6
Lo	3.4	3.9	5.1	5.4	6.7	8.6	11.6	14.6	16.5	21.8

Handleman Company

500 Kirst Blvd.
Troy, Michigan 48084-5299
Tel. (313) 362-4400
Listed: NYSE

Investor contact: Treas. Louis A. Kircos
Ticker symbol: HDL
S&P rating: A

Handleman Company

Handleman is a wholesale distributor of recorded music, prerecorded videocassettes, hardcover and paperback books, and personal-computer software to retail chains across the United States and Canada. K-mart accounts for over 43% and Wal-Mart for about 15% of Handleman's sales. It also has extended its operations to leased departments at Sears and Montgomery Ward stores. While prerecorded music is Handleman's major item, its greatest growth is occurring in videocassettes and compact discs. In 1990 the U.S. accounted for about 93% and Canada about 7% of revenues.

Handleman's service base includes about 5,800 music departments, 5,500 video sales operations, 1,400 computer-software locations, and 2,000 book outlets. Handleman operates as a rack jobber and handles both displays and inventory at various locations. Handleman has 22 distribution centers in North America.

Handleman is a mass merchandiser. With only a 16% penetration in compact discs, this market is becoming increasingly important for mass marketing. Handleman has entered into the production of videos in a joint venture with Goodtimes Home Video.

In 1991, Handleman acquired the Sight & Sound Distributing Co. of Wilsonville, Oregon, a rack jobber of prerecorded music and videos with annual sales of about $60 million. Likewise, in 1991, Handleman acquired a portion of the assets of Lieberman Enterprises, the second-largest distributor (Handleman is first) of prerecorded music and videos to mass merchandisers.

In 1991, revenues were as follows: prerecorded music, 53.2%; prerecorded video, 38.5%; books, 7.2%; and computer software, 1.1%.

The Handleman family controls about 10% and institutions about 70% of the common shares. Handleman has paid consecutive cash dividends since 1963. It paid a 50% stock dividend in 1984, a 100% stock dividend in 1985, a 50% stock dividend in 1988, and a 50% stock dividend in 1989.

Total assets: $423.7 million
Current ratio: 1.7
Common shares outstanding: 32.8 million

	1982	1983	1984	1985	1986	1987	1988	1989	1990	1991
REVENUES (MIL.)	234	231	301	403	425	463	540	647	717	703
NET INCOME (MIL.)	8.7	9.4	16	24	25	26	36	41	37	23
EARNINGS PER SHARE	.29	.31	.51	.77	.81	.81	1.05	1.28	1.13	.72
DIVIDEND PER SHARE	.15	.15	.16	.22	.25	.25	.29	.35	.39	.40
PRICES Hi	3.3	6.1	9.1	13.4	16.9	15.3	16.0	24.0	22.8	18.8
Lo	1.6	2.6	4.8	8.6	10.3	6.0	9.1	13.8	8.1	10.3

Hannaford Bros. Co.

145 Pleasant Hill Road
Scarsborough, Maine 04074
Tel. (207) 883-2911
Listed: NYSE
Investor contact: Asst. Secy. Charles H. Crockett
Ticker symbol: HRD
S&P rating: A+

Hannaford Bros. is the premier food retailer in Northern New England. Its more than 89 supermarkets are situated throughout Maine and parts of New Hampshire, Vermont, Western Massachusetts, and upper New York State. Its supermarkets operate under the names of Shop 'n' Save, Alexander's, Martin's, and Sun Foods. Also, Hannaford owns and operates 41 drug stores under the name Wellby Super Drug. About 27 of Hannaford's supermarkets are combination grocery and drug stores. Likewise, Hannaford wholesales to more than 28 supermarkets that it does not own.

In 1990, earnings were enhanced by aggressive expansion in upper New York State and the opening of a 400,000-square-foot distribution center in Schodack, New York. The new Schodack distribution center services nine stores in New York, five in Vermont, and four in New Hampshire. Success in upper New York State is exceeding all expectations. In the second year of operation it has gained 9% of the Albany market share. In late 1990, Hannaford opened a new. 84,000-square-foot store in Utica, New York and acquired for $27 million in cash, the 11-unit supermarket chain Alexander's, located in northern Massachusetts and southern New Hampshire. In 1991, Hannaford plans to open three additional stores, two of which are in upstate New York.

Hannaford has increased profits by emphasizing higher margined and less labor intensive merchandise. It also emphasizes everyday low prices as opposed to trading stamps or other inducements. Its same-store sales volume and margins increased about 10% in 1989.

The average-sized supermarket increased in size to 25,100 square feet in 1990. Hannaford utilizes a Universal Product Code scanning checkout system, which enables it to control inventory and product marketing. Also, in 1990 Hannaford opened an additional 200,000-square-foot distribution center for general merchandise, pharmaceuticals, and health and beauty aids in Winthrop, Maine. Hannaford is steadily increasing the number of drug units in its supermarkets because the profit margin on drugs and drug sundries is much greater than that on groceries.

Hannaford has paid consecutive cash dividends since 1948 and has increased the cash dividend every year for the past 28 years. It paid a 100% stock dividend in 1983; a 50% stock dividend in February, 1985; a 50% stock dividend in August, 1985; and a 100% stock dividend in 1989.

Total assets: $629 million
Current ratio: 1.5
Common shares outstanding: 19.9 million

		1981	1982	1983	1984	1985	1986	1987	1988	1989	1990
REVENUES (MIL.)		530	559	624	707	807	899	1,033	1,261	1,520	1,688
NET INCOME (MIL.)		6.4	7.9	9.6	11	14	19	24	29	37	42
EARNINGS PER SHARE		.53	.62	.65	.71	.87	1.03	1.30	1.54	1.91	2.13
DIVIDEND PER SHARE		.13	.15	.18	.19	.24	.25	.28	.32	.36	.44
PRICES	Hi	2.8	5.1	7.0	7.3	14.1	20.3	27.4	23.6	40.8	40.6
	Lo	1.8	2.3	4.3	5.5	7.1	12.3	13.8	16.6	21.3	29.8

John H. Harland Company

2939 Miller Road
Decatur, Georgia 30035
Tel. (404) 981-9460
Listed: NYSE
Investor contact: Communications Director, Bruce Danielson
Ticker symbol: JH
S&P rating: A+

HARLAND

As stated in its 1990 Annual Report, "The John H. Harland Company is a national participant in the financial services and data collection fields." It is the second-largest check printer in the United States, with about 23% market share. "It prints magnetic ink character recognition (MICR) checks and deposit tickets for banks, savings institutions, credit unions, brokerage firms and commercial customers." Check printing provides over 80% of Harland's revenues.

Harland defines its mission as follows: "(1) to provide quality products and services to satisfy the funds transfer and other related needs of the financial community; (2) to pursue predictable repeat business utilizing the company's existing technology and resources; and (3) to seek new business with growth compatible with Harland's financial objectives."

Harland has 42 check printing plants across the country, all of which utilize offset printing technology, which increases productivity. In addition to checks, Harland provides customer-designed printed and engraved business forms, stationary, and other related printed material for accountants and banks and other financial institutions.

Scantron, acquired in 1988, produces optical character reading (OCR) equipment and supplies. Scantron is involved in data collection. To date, Scantron is primarily used to read objective test-answer forms for educational institutions, but Harland intends to expand its use for commercial markets.

Checks will continue to be the primary focus of John Harland, but at the same time it seeks to acquire compatible businesses.

Despite its heavy capital expenditures of recent years, particularly the conversion to offset printing, Harland has mounting cash reserves, which can be used either to make additional acquisitions or to repurchase its common shares.

Harland's financial position is rock solid. Sales have increased for 41 consecutive years and dividends for 36 straight years. Return on equity has exceeded 20 percent for 17 consecutive years. Institutions hold approximately 50% of the common shares and insiders 10%. Harland paid a 50% stock dividend in 1980, a 100% stock dividend in 1981, a 100% stock dividend in 1985 and a 100% stock dividend in 1987.

Total assets: $357 million
Current ratio: 4.9
Common shares outstanding: 37.6 million

		1981	1982	1983	1984	1985	1986	1987	1988	1989	1990
REVENUES (MIL.)		150	170	202	234	268	293	318	333	345	371
NET INCOME (MIL.)		14	18	22	27	33	39	47	53	58	57
EARNINGS PER SHARE		.42	.51	.62	.72	.87	1.04	1.26	1.41	1.54	1.52
DIVIDEND PER SHARE		.13	.16	.19	.23	.28	.34	.42	.58	.68	.78
PRICES	Hi	6.1	9.5	12.0	12.4	19.5	25.5	30.8	24.3	25.0	26.1
	Lo	4.4	3.9	8.9	8.1	11.9	17.1	16.4	19.3	19.5	17.1

Hechinger Company

1616 McCormick Drive
Landover, Maryland 20785
Tel. (301) 341-1000
Listed: NASDAQ
Investor contact: V.P. & Treas. Lennie H. Zaller
Ticker symbol: HECHB
S&P rating: B+

As profiled in its 1990 Annual Report, "Hechinger Company is a leading specialty retailer providing products and services for the care, repair, remodeling and maintenance of the home and garden. The company serves the growing home improvement in-

Hechinger
Company

143

dustry through three separate operations: Hechinger, consisting of 84 stores serving do-it-yourselfers from the Carolinas to Connecticut and as far west as Ohio; Home Quarters Warehouse, a major player in the popular warehouse segment of home improvement marketing with 28 stores up and down the east coast and Triangle Building Centers, with six stores covering mid-eastern Pennsylvania.

"Hechinger stores are customer-service driven, offering expert advice and a full range of building material and home improvement merchandise in facilities typically comprising 60,000 square feet of space under roof. HQ stores, with their massive merchandise presentation, follow the warehouse format, producing high volumes through low prices and excellent service. HQ stores bring a powerful assortment of building supply products to do-it-yourself and professional home repair and remodeling customers in brightly-lit uncluttered 85,000 square foot facilities.

"After listening to 3,500 D-I-Yers talk about their needs, Hechinger designed a store completely to the specifications of its customers. The result is the Hechinger Home Project Center in Glen Burnie, Maryland, which celebrated its grand opening on March 16, 1991. The new Hechinger Home Project Center's innovative floor plan is arranged by project type to allow D-I- Yers quick, direct access to everything needed for a particular project. Each home project area carries the broadest and deepest inventory available to supply that project from start to finish." Hechinger expects to continue to convert stores to this exciting and innovative format on an ongoing basis.

Hechinger's strategy is to cluster stores in a given market, where it can, through saturated advertising and promotion, gain strong market share. The company services its stores through large distribution centers such as a 781,000 square foot distribution facility in Landover, Maryland.

The company expands both by acquisition and the construction of new stores. In 1990, Hechinger opened the first two of 12–15 planned Home Quarters Warehouse Stores in the Greater Boston area. In 1988, Hechinger acquired six Triangle Building Centers in eastern Pennsylvania and seven Home Quarters stores.

Hechinger has both Class A and Class B shares. The Class B shares are controlled by the Hechinger and England families and have 10 votes per share. Consecutive cash dividends have been paid on the A shares since 1983. Hechinger paid a 50% stock dividend in 1981; a 25% stock dividend in 1982; a 50% stock dividend in January, 1983; a 25% stock dividend in November, 1983; a 25% stock dividend in 1985; and a 25%

stock dividend in 1986.

Total assets: $869.1 million
Current ratio: 2.2
Common shares outstanding: Class A 26.9 million
Class B 14.1 million

		1982	1983	1984	1985	1986	1987	1988	1989	1990	1991
REVENUES (MIL.)		211	241	309	405	479	588	725	1,019	1,230	1,392
NET INCOME (MIL.)		8.6	12	16	21	23	28	42	49	34	23
EARNINGS PER SHARE		.32	.43	.58	.74	.78	.92	1.22	1.30	.95	.65
DIVIDEND PER SHARE		.03	.04	.08	.10	.12	.15	.16	.16	.16	.16
PRICES	Hi	13.0	16.9	14.0	19.5	24.0	27.3	20.1	19.8	15.0	15.5
	Lo	4.3	9.4	9.0	12.9	15.3	15.3	15.8	11.0	6.8	6.5

H. J. Heinz Company

600 Grant Street
Pittsburgh, Pennsylvania 15219
Tel. (412) 456-5700
Listed: NYSE
Investor contact: John M. Mazur
Ticker symbol: HNZ
S&P rating: A+

Founded 120 years ago, H. J. Heinz is one of America's leading processed food companies. It manufactures soup, ketchup, baked beans, pickles, vinegar, baby food, tuna, cat food, frozen potatoes, Chico San rice cakes, and Weight Watchers and Alba diet products. Famous for ketchup, Heinz controls over 50% of the market. Ore Ida has a 48% share of the retail frozen potato

market, Star Kist tuna has a 37% market share and 9-Lives brand cat food has a 27% market share. Heinz, once known for 57 varieties, now numbers over 3,000. Over 55% of sales are generated by brands that rank first in their respective markets.

Heinz's fastest-growing division is Weight Watchers, which controls a 50% share of the domestic weight loss-services market. It has a menu of 39 frozen entrees and side dishes. The quick Success Program initiated in 1988 has experienced a 15% increase in attendance, and the Weight Watchers At Work Program is subscribed to by over 2,500 companies. Heinz expanded the Weight Watchers Program internationally so that it now accounts for 15% of total revenues.

In the period 1979-89, Heinz acquired more than 35 companies. In 1991, Heinz divested itself of the Hubinger corn milling company and acquired J. L. Foods from John Labatt Ltd. of Canada for about $500 Million. Likewise in 1991 it acquired Continental Delights, a snack food company. Marketing costs have risen to 8.3% of sales. Ketchup and tuna continue to generate increased cash, which can be used for additional acquisitions, increased dividends and common share repurchase.

About 38% of sales and 38% of income are derived from foreign operations. Foreign markets include Canada, the United Kingdom, Western Europe, Australia, and Venezuela. With such a large stake in foreign markets, Heinz's earnings are heavily dependent upon foreign currency translation.

In 1991, Heinz experienced its 27th consecutive year of sales and earnings growth. The Heinz family and trusts control about 15%, insiders about 12%, and institutions about 50% of the common stock. Heinz has paid consecutive cash dividends since 1911. It paid a 100% stock dividend in 1981, a 50% stock dividend in 1983, a 100% stock dividend in 1985, and another 100% stock dividend in 1989.

Total assets: $4.9 billion
Current ratio: 1.5
Common shares outstanding: 259.4 million

		1982	1983	1984	1985	1986	1987	1988	1989	1990	1991
REVENUES (MIL.)		3,689	3,738	3,954	4,048	4,366	4,639	5,244	5,801	6,086	6,647
NET INCOME (MIL.)		193	214	238	266	302	339	386	440	504	568
EARNINGS PER SHARE		.68	.75	.85	.96	1.10	1.24	1.45	1.67	1.90	2.13
DIVIDEND PER SHARE		.24	.27	.34	.39	.44	.50	.61	.70	.81	.93
PRICES	Hi	7.0	9.5	11.3	17.1	24.1	25.9	25.0	35.9	37.0	48.6
	Lo	4.3	6.0	8.0	10.3	14.6	16.8	18.8	22.5	27.5	31.5

Hershey Foods Corporation

100 Mansion Road East
Hershey, Pennsylvania 17033
Tel. (717) 534-4001
Listed: NYSE
Investor contact: Mgr. Investor Relations, Dianne T. Paukovits
Ticker symbol: HSY
S&P rating: A+

Hershey is the largest domestic chocolate and confectionery manufacturer and the second-largest pasta maker in the United States. Currently Hershey is building a new, state-of-the-art, chocolate manufacturing facility in Hershey, Pennsylvania. Its principal candy brands include Hershey's milk chocolate bars, Hershey's chocolate Kisses, Kit Kat wafer bars, Mr. Goodbar chocolate bars, Reese's peanut butter cups, Rolo caramels, Krackel chocolate bars, Skor toffee bars, and Hershey's chocolate milk, sold under license to dairies. Pasta products include San Giorgio, Skinner, Ronzoni, Delmonico, Light'n Fluffy, American Italian Pasta, and American Beauty.

Hershey has expanded rapidly through acquisitions and divestitures. Among recent (1990) acquisitions were American Italian Pasta and Ronzoni Foods Corp; Ludens' (cough drops and 5th Avenue candy bars) was acquired in 1986. In 1987 Hershey acquired Nabisco Brands Ltd.'s Canadian confectionery operations (Life Savers, O'Henry, Planters Nuts, and others). In 1988, it acquired Cadbury's United States confectionery operations. In 1988, Hershey divested itself of the 840-restaurant chain of Friendly Family Restaurants. While Friendly contributed about 25% of Hershey's total revenues, it had rather consistently shown poor earnings performance. In 1990, Hershey divested itself of its 17% interest in A. B. Marabou, a Swedish candy and snack-food manufacturer.

Hershey bids to become stronger both from internal economies of scale and from future acquisitions. Currently such will be attained by lower world cocoa prices. Costs of the Cadbury division are already declining as Hershey integrates Cadbury's operations into its own stream. In mid-1991, Hershey gained a foothold in the lucrative European market through the purchase of Gubor Schokoladen, a German manufacturer of confectionery products.

Hershey has increased its dividend for 17 consecutive years. It has paid consecutive cash dividends since 1930. There are both a regular and a Class B common stock issue. Institutions control about 45% of the regular shares. The Milton Hershey School controls about 30% of the regular and 99% of the Class B shares. The Class B shares are entitled to 10 votes per share, giving the Milton Hershey School effective control of the company. A 100% stock dividend was paid in 1983 and a 200% stock dividend was paid in 1986.

Total Assets $2.1 billion
Current ratio: 1.9
Common shares outstanding: 90.2 million
Class B 15.3 million

		1981	1982	1983	1984	1985	1986	1987	1988	1989	1990
REVENUES (MIL.)		1,451	1,566	1,663	1,893	1,996	2,170	2,434	2,168	2,421	2,716
NET INCOME (MIL.)		80	94	100	109	121	133	148	145	171	216
EARNINGS PER SHARE		.94	1.00	1.07	1.16	1.28	1.42	1.64	1.60	1.90	2.39
DIVIDEND PER SHARE		.29	.33	.37	.41	.48	.52	.58	.66	.74	.99
PRICES	Hi	6.9	9.9	11.8	13.8	18.4	30.0	37.8	28.6	36.9	39.6
	Lo	3.9	5.5	8.1	9.5	11.8	15.5	20.8	21.9	24.8	28.3

Hewlett-Packard Company

3000 Hanover Street
Palo Alto, California 94304
Tel. (415)857-1501
Listed: NYSE
Investor contact: Corporate Communications, Carol Parcels
Ticker symbol: HWP
S&P rating: A

Fifty-two years ago, two young electronics engineers, William Hewlett and David Packard, just out of Stanford University, started an electronic workshop in a garage. From these humble beginnings grew the electronic giant Hewlett-Packard Company. Over the years HP has grown to a company with over $13 billion in sales and a product inventory of over

12,000 electronic and computer items.

HP is number one in laser printers and electronic measurement instruments and a rising star in personal computers. The 1989 acquisition of Apollo Computer puts it in a strong position in the workstation market.

As profiled in its 1990 Annual Report, "Hewlett-Packard Company designs, manufactures and services electronic products and systems for measurement and computation. HP's basic business purpose is to provide the capabilities and support needed to help customers worldwide improve their personal and business effectiveness."

In October 1990, Hewlett-Packard began to implement a change in management structure, which enabled it to, "Simplify structure, streamline decisionmaking and give responsible managers more direct control over the technologies and sales activities required for the success of their business."

The Computer Systems Organization (CSO) brings together the workstation and multiuser systems businesses. These have been converging on a common set of capabilities—the operating system, standard-based networking user interface, and distributed-computing technolgies such as the Network Computing System (NCS) developed by the Apollo division.

The new Computer Products Organization (CPO) combines the personal computer and peripherals businesses.

The new Test and Measurement Organization (TMO) combines the activities of the Electronics, Microwave and Communications groups.

During 1990, revenues were divided as follows: measurement design, information, and manufacturing equipment, 37%; peripherals and network products, 30%; medical electronic equipment and service, 7%; analytic information and services, 4%; electronic components, 2%; and servicing sold equipment and products, 20%.

Institutions control about 50% of the common shares and the Hewlett and Packard families control another 26%. Consecutive cash dividends have been paid since 1965. HP paid a 100% stock dividend in 1981 and a 100% stock dividend in 1983.

Total assets: $11.4 billion
Current ratio: 1.5
Common shares outstanding: 250 million

	1982	1983	1984	1985	1986	1987	1988	1989	1990	1991
REVENUES (MIL.)	4,254	4,710	6,044	6,505	7,102	8,090	9,831	11,899	13,233	14,494
NET INCOME (MIL.)	383	432	665	489	516	644	816	829	739	755
EARNINGS PER SHARE	1.53	1.69	2.59	1.91	2.02	2.50	3.36	3.52	3.06	3.02
DIVIDEND PER SHARE	.12	.16	.19	.22	.22	.23	.28	.36	.42	.48
PRICES Hi	41.4	48.3	45.5	38.9	49.6	73.6	65.5	61.5	50.4	56.6
Lo	18.0	34.3	31.1	28.8	35.8	35.8	43.8	40.3	24.9	29.9

Hillenbrand Industries, Inc.

Highway 46
Batesville, Indiana 47006
Tel. (812) 934-7000
Listed: NYSE
Investor contact: Treas. Christina L. Wilkins
Ticker symbol: HB
S&P rating: A+

Hillenbrand Industries, Inc.

Hillenbrand Industries is an amalgamation of companies involved in funeral products, hospital furniture, wound therapy, life insurance, security locks, and luggage. Batesville Casket Company, the nation's largest burial casket company, makes a complete line of steel, copper, bronze, and wooden caskets. Batesville has 66 service centers across the Unites States (including Puerto Rico), Canada, and Australia from which caskets can be shipped to funeral directors.

Hill-Rom Co. makes a complete line of mechanical and electronically adjustable beds, as well as hospital furniture. A Hillenbrand subsidiary, SSI Medical Services (acquired in 1986) is the market leader in supplying beds and equipment for the bedridden patient. Usually, hospital beds are rented by the day rather than sold. SSI Medical Services also provides Clintron Therapy, an air-support system for treating wounds and Flexicair Therapy for the treatment of bedsores.

Forethought Group is a life insurance carrier designed to provide sufficient coverage for funeral expenses. This company is expected to begin making a profit in 1991.

Medco Security Locks, Inc., manufactures and markets brass and steel security locks for commercial and home use. American Tourister makes a complete line of luggage and attache cases, but is increasingly running into foreign competition.

In late 1991, Hillenbrand acquired Block Medical Inc. of Carlsbad, California, a manufacturer of home infusion therapy products.

The Hillenbrand family owns about 60% and institutions about 35% of the outstanding shares. Consecutive cash dividends have been paid since 1948. Hillenbrand paid a 100% stock dividend in 1982, a 100% stock dividend in 1984, and a 100% stock dividend in 1987.

Total assets: $1.4 billion
Current ratio: 2.2
Common shares outstanding: 36.5 million

		1981	1982	1983	1984	1985	1986	1987	1988	1989	1990
REVENUES (MIL.)		368	389	433	485	508	648	730	891	1,001	1,107
NET INCOME (MIL.)		29	31	36	38	33	50	56	66	71	76
EARNINGS PER SHARE		.72	.77	.89	.98	.85	1.30	1.47	1.77	1.92	2.05
DIVIDEND PER SHARE		.18	.20	.22	.26	.27	.28	.35	.40	.50	.55
PRICES	Hi	6.5	9.9	12.5	12.5	13.5	24.9	31.3	35.8	45.1	48.0
	Lo	3.8	5.4	9.0	8.5	9.9	12.6	19.3	22.8	26.4	30.1

The Home Depot, Inc.

2727 Paces Ferry Road
Atlanta, Georgia 30339
Tel. (404) 433-8211
Listed: NYSE
Investor contact: Treas. R.M. Brill
Ticker symbol: HD
S&P rating: B+

Home Depot is one of the most rapidly growing warehouse-type chains in the do-it-yourself home improvement market. It has only a 3% market

Home Depot, Inc.

share in a widely diffused, highly competitive market. Home Depot originated the warehouse concept, and many of its more than 145 home center warehouses are over 100,000 square feet in size. Home Depot stocks plumbing and electrical supplies, hardware, building materials, kitchen cabinet, home appliances (refrigerators, washing machines, dryers, water heaters, and stoves), garden equipment and furniture, power tools, paints, floor coverings, and wallpaper.

In recent years, Home Depot has experienced explosive growth, averaging about 40% a year. In a decade, Home Depot has become the largest home improvement retailer with over $3.5 billion in sales. Home Depot continues to increase market share both by store expansion of about 25% a year and by acquiring an increasing volume of business at the expense of smaller competitors. It plans more than 40 new stores in 1992.

Home Depot's strategy is to build large, unsophisticated warehouse centers, offer an exhaustive number of items (over 30,000) at highly competitive prices, and provide superior service.

The do-it-yourself home-improvement market is somewhat recession proof, in that homeowners seek to cut costs during an economic downturn and do many things themselves that they would otherwise hire a contractor to do.

In 1991, product sales were broken down as follows: plumbing, heating, and electrical supplies, 29%; building materials, 31%; hardware, 12%; seasonal items, 15%; and furniture and paint, 13%.

Home Depot initiated cash dividends in 1987. Institutions control over 60% and insiders over 10% of the outstanding common shares. Home Depot paid a 50% stock dividend in January, 1982; a 25% stock dividend in May, 1982; a 100% stock dividend in December, 1982; a 100% stock dividend in 1983; a 50% stock dividend in 1987; a 50% stock dividend in 1989; a 50% stock dividend in 1990; and a 50% stock dividend in 1991.

Total assets: $1.6 billion
Current ratio: 1.7
Common shares outstanding: 206.2 million

	1981	1982	1983	1984	1985	1986	1987	1988	1989	1990
REVENUES (MIL.)	52	118	256	433	701	1,011	1,454	2,000	2,759	3,815
NET INCOME (MIL.)	1	5	10	14	8	24	54	77	112	163
EARNINGS PER SHARE	.03	.05	.08	.11	.07	.18	.34	.45	.63	.90
DIVIDEND PER SHARE	—	—	—	—	—	—	.012	.024	.049	.073
PRICES Hi	2.9	6.4	5.5	4.0	4.3	8.3	9.5	17.0	29.0	55.8
Lo	0.5	2.4	2.4	2.1	2.1	3.5	5.2	8.5	15.3	23.1

Houghton Mifflin Company

One Beacon Street
Boston, Massachusetts 02108
Tel. (617) 725-5000
Listed: NYSE
Investor contact: C.F.O. S. O. Jaeger
Ticker symbol: HTN
S&P rating: A

Houghton Mifflin, a major publisher of elementary, high school, and college texts, should continue to grow over the years ahead. The outlook for Houghton Mifflin is bolstered by rising school enrollments, which are now appearing in the elementary schools. Also, Houghton Mifflin is very strong in objective test publications. School texts are sold directly to school systems.
Elementary texts emphasize the basic skills of language, reading, and arithmetic. For the secondary level, Houghton Mifflin also publishes science, social studies, and foreign language texts. College texts are distributed to both college book stores and private booksellers.

The Riverside Publishing Co., a subsidiary, is a major producer of objective and psychological tests. The wide scope of its achievement test batteries is keyed to a mastery of the subject matter they contained. Riverside also publishes textbooks and materials related to the development of skills to be tested. In addition, Riverside publishes objective tests and psychological test for college use.

153

A number of states have adopted statewide curriculum programs, particularly on the elementary level. Specifically, they adopt a defined curriculum in terms of texts and subject matter to be mastered. Also, they test the outcomes of learning with a specific test battery. Consistently, Houghton Mifflin has obtained an increasing share of this market. Its "Literary Readers" program was designed specifically to meet the requirements of California.

The trade and reference division publishes a smorgasbord of all types of books including the *American Heritage Dictionary* and software for correcting spelling and grammar usage.

In 1990, Houghton Mifflin sold its business education segment to Mac-Millan. In 1989 it had acquired Victor Gollancz, a British publishing house.

The stock price of Houghton MIfflin is somewhat volatile, due to recurring takeover rumors. Institutions hold over 50% of the common shares. It has paid a consecutive cash dividend since 1908. It paid a 100% stock dividend in 1983 and another 100% stock dividend in 1986.

Total assets: $366 million
Current ratio: 2.7
Common shares outstanding: 14.3 million

		1981	1982	1983	1984	1985	1986	1987	1988	1989	1990
REVENUES (MIL.)		184	190	219	249	278	321	343	368	404	422
NET INCOME (MIL.)		10	11	13	16	19	23	24	24	23	18
EARNINGS PER SHARE		.89	.90	1.08	1.26	1.37	1.61	1.66	1.70	1.62	1.27
DIVIDEND PER SHARE		.40	.40	.41	.45	.49	.54	.59	.63	.67	.71
PRICES	Hi	8.4	10.3	15.0	17.6	23.5	33.5	41.4	42.5	50.3	34.4
	Lo	5.9	5.4	8.9	10.5	16.5	21.0	20.8	24.4	28.1	18.4

Hubbell Incorporated
584 Derby Milford Road
Orange, Connecticut 06477-4024
Tel. (203) 799-4100
Listed: AMEX
Investor contact: Director of Public Affairs, Thomas R. Conlin
Ticker symbol: HUB.B
S&P rating: A+

Hubbell, founded in 1888 and one of America's oldest electrical equipment companies, turns out electrical and electronic products for the commercial, industrial, utility, and telecommunications markets. Likewise, it has been one of the most consistently profitable companies, having increased earnings and dividends for the past 30 years.

In the low-voltage segment, the wiring device division manufactures wiring for industrial and commercial markets. The lighting division markets all types of lighting fixtures. The industrial controls division markets items for the control of industrial machinery and processes. The Killark Electric Manufacturing subsidiary makes and markets weatherproof and explosion-proof electrical products for outside installation. The Hubbell Hermetic Refrigeration division manufactures refrigeration and air-conditioning compressors.

In 1990, Hubbell acquired Brand-Rex Telecommunications Modular Product Group (electronic components) and Marvin Electric Manufacturing Co., which manufactures lighting fixtures under the Marco Lighting name.

In the high-voltage segment, the Kerite division manufactures and markets electric power and signal cable. The Ohio Brass division manufactures products for electrical transmission.

Other products include outlet boxes and data signal processing and telecommunications equipment.

In 1990, high voltage accounted for 53% of sales and 64% of profits, low voltage for 17% of sales and 11% of profits, and other products for 30% of sales and 25% of profits.

Hubbell has both Class A and Class B shares. About 38% of the Class A shares are held by trusts for the Hubbell family. Sixty percent of the Class B shares are held by institutions, and an additional 0.72% are controlled by officers and directors of the company. Hubbell has paid consecutive cash dividends since 1934. It paid a 100% stock dividend in 1981, a 100% stock dividend in 1985, a 5% stock dividend in 1989, 1990, 1991, and 1992.

Total assets: $625 million
Current ratio: 3.4
Common shares outstanding: Class A 5.9 million
Class B 26.1 million

	1981	1982	1983	1984	1985	1986	1987	1988	1989	1990
REVENUES (MIL.)	446	419	422	467	521	559	581	614	669	720
NET INCOME (MIL.)	35	35	37	42	48	55	63	71	79	86
EARNINGS PER SHARE	1.16	1.18	1.24	1.39	1.57	1.74	1.97	2.25	2.52	2.74
DIVIDEND PER SHARE	.43	.47	.50	.55	.61	.68	.79	.87	1.12	1.32
PRICES Hi	10.2	13.6	15.4	15.1	21.8	29.9	34.5	31.9	41.8	45.1
Lo	7.0	7.0	11.6	11.9	14.4	19.9	20.9	25.0	28.7	31.9

Humana, Inc.

500 West Main Street, P.O. Box 1438
Louisville, Kentucky 40201-1438
Tel. (502) 580-1000
Listed: NYSE
Investor contact: V.P. Investor Relations, Charles E. Teeple
Ticker symbol: HUM
S&P rating: A-

Humana, Inc.

As profiled in its 1991 Annual Report, "Humana, Inc. provides an integrated system of health care services through the operation of acute-care hospitals and health benefit plans. In recent years, third party payers and private industry have initiated various measures designed to reduce both the utilization of hospital services and price paid for medically-necessary procedures. In an effort to increase hospital admissions and improve consolidated profitability, the company develops and markets health benefits and managed health care products which encourage and in certain instances require use of company hospitals. In addition, the company continuously adds new hospital services and actively pursues financial arrangements with employer groups, health maintenance organizations, and private insurers to provide hospital services at discount rates."

Humana is a private hospital chain which owns and operates 81 hospitals and has 1.7 million members in its health benefit plans. Its health maintenance organization, known as "Human Care Plus," provides a steady stream of patients to its hospitals and clinics known as "Centers of Excellence." Humana derives about 30% of its revenues from Medicare and Medicaid.

Humana's strategy is to take over hospitals (often public hospitals) which are marginally profitable and, through management efficiencies and economies of scale, return them to profitability. In early 1991, Humana acquired the 1,008-bed Michael Reese Hospital and Medical Center of Chicago and its 240,000-member health maintenance organization.

Hospital admissions in 1991 rose to 537,200 from 530,300 in 1990. In 1991, hospital operating income increased to $664 million up from $637 million in 1990. Hospital revenues paid by Humana health plans increased to $368 million in 1991 from $240 million in 1990. Humana's health plans ended 1991 with an operating profit of $110 million, up from $49 million in 1990.

Humana has paid consecutive cash dividends since 1976. Insiders control about 6% and institutions about 70% of the outstanding common shares. Humana paid a 100% stock dividend in 1981, a 50% stock dividend in 1982, a 33 1/3% stock dividend in 1983, a 20% stock dividend in 1984, and a 50% stock dividend in 1991.

Total assets: $4.4 billion
Current ratio: 1.1
Common shares outstanding: 158.2 million

	1982	1983	1984	1985	1986	1987	1988	1989	1990	1991
REVENUES (MIL.)	1,516	1,765	1,961	2,188	2,711	2,974	3,435	4,088	4,852	5,865
NET INCOME (MIL.)	127	161	193	216	54	183	227	256	310	355
EARNINGS PER SHARE	.89	1.09	1.31	1.46	.37	1.24	1.53	1.71	2.00	2.26
DIVIDEND PER SHARE	.23	.31	.38	.44	.49	.51	.55	.63	.72	.83
PRICES Hi	19.3	22.3	22.0	24.5	22.6	19.7	19.1	29.3	33.9	35.0
Lo	8.4	13.1	14.3	14.6	12.8	10.8	12.7	16.3	23.5	22.8

International Flavors & Fragrances, Inc.
521 West 57th Street
New York, New York 10019
Tel. (212) 765-5500

Listed: NYSE
Investor contact: V.P.–Treas. John P. Winandy
Ticker symbol: IFF
S&P rating: A

As profiled in its 1990 Annual Report, "IFF is a leading creator and manufacturer of flavors and fragrances used by others to impart or improve flavor or fragrance in a wide variety of consumer products.

"Fragrance products (61% of sales) are sold principally to makers of perfumes and cosmetics, hair and other personal care products, soaps, detergents, household, and other cleaning products and area fresheners.

"Flavors (39% of sales) are sold primarily to makers of dairy, meat and other processed foods, beverages, snacks and savory foods, confectionary, sweet and baked goods, pharmaceutical and oral care products, tobacco products and animal foods.

"IFF encompasses a global network with state-of-the-art manufacturing facilities, creative laboratories and sales offices in 34 countries."

The company's products utilize both natural and synthetic ingredients.

While the domestic market for flavors and fragrances is somewhat mature, the company is rapidly expanding in Western Eurpope, Eastern Europe, and the former Soviet Union.

International Flavors is financial strong with no long term debt and $8 per share in cash. It spends a great deal of money (6% of income) on research, particularly on higher priced products. Through sheer size and industry consolidation, International Flavors consistently reaps increased market share.

In 1990, 71% of sales and 75% of profits were derived from foreign markets, thus the exchange rate of the dollar can be a major factor in earnings.

International Flavors is closely held. Institutions control over 50% of the outstanding common shares. It has paid consecutive cash dividends since 1956.

Total assets: $1.1 billion
Current ratio: 5.4
Common shares outstanding: 38.2 million

	1981	1982	1983	1984	1985	1986	1987	1988	1989	1990
REVENUES (MIL.)	451	448	461	477	501	621	746	840	870	963
NET INCOME (MIL.)	66	63	68	69	70	86	107	129	139	157
EARNINGS PER SHARE	1.81	1.73	1.87	1.89	1.89	2.29	2.83	3.40	3.65	4.11
DIVIDEND PER SHARE	.96	1.02	1.05	1.09	1.13	1.18	1.33	1.60	1.92	2.16
PRICES Hi	23.0	30.0	35.8	29.3	40.0	48.9	58.0	54.5	57.5	75.1
Lo	17.9	17.4	23.8	22.9	26.0	34.5	37.3	43.1	48.5	54.6

Johnson & Johnson

One Johnson & Johnson Plaza
New Brunswick, New Jersey 08933
Tel. (201) 524-0400
Listed: NYSE
Investor contact: V.P. JoAnn H. Heisen
Ticker symbol: JNJ
S&P rating: A

Johnson & Johnson is a very large diversified company which manufactures and distributes prescription drugs, hospital supplies, and consumer products.

Johnson & Johnson's prescription drugs include Procrit, for AIDS and kidney failure (sold as Eprex overseas); Floxin, an antibiotic; Prepulsid, a gastrointestinal for ulcers; Ortho-Novum, an oral contraceptive; Retin A, for acne; and antifungals and analgesics.

Hospital supplies include such items as ligatures, diagnostic products, surgical instruments, intraocular lenses, and disposable contact lenses.

Consumer products and brands include Johnson & Johnson baby toiletries, Tylenol, Band-Aids, Stayfree, Serenity, and Reach toothbrushes.

While consumer products consistently yield high sales volume, they are most competitive and have the lowest margin of profit among Johnson & Johnson items. Ethical pharmaceuticals (prescription drugs) account for 50% of Johnson & Johnson's profits.

A 1991 appeals court rejected Genetics Institute's challenge to

Amgen's patent for Epo (Procrit), which means that Johnson & Johnson, as licensee, will have exclusive rights for the marketing of the product. Johnson & Johnson will pay a 5% royalty fee to Amgen. Johnson & Johnson's pharmaceutical sector is growing faster than its other two business, providing strong margin expansion for the company.

In 1990, foreign sales accounted for about 50% of revenues and 60% of profits. For 1990, revenues and profits were apportioned as follows: pharmaceuticals, 29% of revenues and 56% of profits; hospital supplies, 33% of revenues and 26% of profits; and consumer products, 38% of revenues and 18% of profits.

The R. W. Johnson Foundation controls 8.6% and institutions about 60% of the outstanding common shares. Johnson & Johnson has paid consecutive cash dividends since 1908. It paid a 200% stock dividend in 1981 and a 100% stock dividend in 1989.

Total assets: $9.5 billion
Current ratio: 1.8
Common shares outstanding: 333.1 million

		1981	1982	1983	1984	1985	1986	1987	1988	1989	1990
REVENUES (MIL.)		5,399	5,761	5,973	6,124	6,421	7,003	8,012	9,000	9,757	11,232
NET INCOME (MIL.)		468	523	489	515	614	330	833	974	1,082	1,143
EARNINGS PER SHARE		1.26	1.40	1.29	1.38	1.68	.93	2.42	2.86	3.25	3.43
DIVIDEND PER SHARE		.43	.49	.54	.59	.64	.69	.81	.96	1.12	1.31
PRICES	Hi	19.8	25.6	25.8	21.5	27.6	37.1	52.8	44.1	59.5	74.1
	Lo	14.1	16.3	19.5	14.0	17.6	23.6	27.5	34.6	41.5	51.1

Jostens, Inc.

5501 Norman Center Drive
Minneapolis, Minnesota 55437
Tel. (612) 830-3300
Listed: NYSE
Investor contact: V.P.–Treas. Robb L. Prince
Ticker symbol: JOS
S&P rating: A+

Jostens has a strong stake in both the school market and the rising income of young people. From humble beginnings as a jewelry store in Owatonna, Minnesota, in 1897, Jostens has become the leading purveyor of class rings, school yearbooks, recognition awards, printed apparel, and computer software for elementary schools.

JOSTENS

Jostens Scholastic division is both its largest and its oldest segment. Scholastic is involved primarily with graduation and produces such items as class rings, diplomas, caps and gowns, and announcements. The Printing and Publishing segment prints high school and college yearbooks. The Custom Sportswear division (formerly Artex) manufactures imprinted apparel and T-shirts with various logos. The Wayneco segment is a direct marketer of customized insignia items to alumni, fraternities, and sororities.

In 1990, Jostens acquired Autrey Bros. (class rings and other graduation products); Lenox Awards and Gordon B. Miller & Co. (both engaged in recognition and awards); Scholastic Pictures, Inc.; Portrait World, Inc.; and Edwards Photography.

Jostens Learning Corp., which combines the 1989 acquisition of Education Systems Corp. with Jostens Prescription Learning unit, has moved Jostens to the forefront of programmed learning, particularly in elementary schools. Jostens Learning Corp. provides computer-based learning programs in reading, writing, mathematics, and science.

Jostens recently introduced video yearbooks and has spread its wings beyond the education market to make rings for special events such as the Olympics, the Rose Bowl, the World Series, and other sporting events.

Revenues for 1991 were divided as follows: Scholastic division, 57%; Jostens Learning, 19%; recognition, 11%; sportswear, 8%; and Canada, 5%.

Earnings have increased for 34 consecutive years and dividends for 24 consecutive years. Consecutive cash dividends have been paid since 1960. A 25% stock dividend was paid in 1980, a 25% stock dividend was paid in 1981, a 50% stock dividend was paid in 1984, and a 100% stock dividend was paid in 1986.

Total assets: $530 million
Current ratio: 1.8
Common shares outstanding: 40.9 million

161

		1982	1983	1984	1985	1986	1987	1988	1989	1990	1991
REVENUES (MIL.)		364	368	381	402	449	507	576	696	788	860
NET INCOME (MIL.)		30	31	35	38	37	39	82	54	60	64
EARNINGS PER SHARE		.70	.72	.81	.86	.87	1.03	2.15	1.39	1.51	1.58
DIVIDEND PER SHARE		.29	.32	.35	.40	.44	.48	.56	.65	.72	.80
PRICES	Hi	9.8	10.0	11.4	14.9	20.3	25.0	22.8	30.4	33.0	38.6
	Lo	5.5	7.6	7.8	10.5	12.8	15.1	16.5	18.1	22.5	28.5

Kaman Corporation

1332 Blue Hill Avenue
Bloomfield, Connecticut 06002
Tel. (203) 243-8311
Listed: NASDAQ
Investor contact: R. H. Jones
Ticker symbol: KAMNA
S&P rating: A

KAMAN

Kaman (originally Kaman Aircraft), founded by Charles H. Kaman in 1945, is a combination defense contractor and distributor of industrial components, with a long history of increased earnings. Its operations are broken down as follows: diversified technologies, 15%; advanced technologies, 17%; helicopters and spare parts, 8%; aerospace subcontracting, 9%; industrial distribution, 40%; and commercial distribution (Kaman Music), 11%. Sales from distribution are now gaining the ascendancy over sales from technologies.

The technologies division manufactures helicopters and parts and components for the aerospace industry.

The distribution segment, through its bearings and supply division, markets over 500,000 industrial parts such as bearings, chains, gear reducers, sprockets, hydraulic components, and material-handling equipment through 156 service centers in 28 states and British Columbia.

Kaman does research for the Defense Department on the effects of modern warfare, both vulnerability and survivability. Also, Kaman is involved in the production of a wide range of musical instruments, especially the Ovation guitar.

In 1990, Kaman entered into an agreement with S.N.P.E. of France to form Advanced Energetic Materials Corp., a defense and industrial firm.

During 1990, diversified technologies (government contract division) provided 49% of revenues and 70% of profits; the distribution segment provided 51% of revenues and 30% of profits.

Kaman has both Class A and Class B common shares. Class A has preference over Class B for dividends but is nonvoting. Class A shares are about 40% held by institutions. Class B shares are about 73% owned by Charles H. Kaman.

Kaman has paid consecutive cash dividends since 1972. It paid a 50% stock dividend in 1981, a 100% stock dividend in 1983, a 50% stock dividend in 1985, and a 60% stock dividend in 1987.

Total assets: $444 million
Current ratio: 2.8
Common shares outstanding: Class A 17.5 million
Class B 667.8 thousand

		1981	1982	1983	1984	1985	1986	1987	1988	1989	1990
REVENUES (MIL.)		430	416	475	538	556	588	707	767	801	825
NET INCOME (MIL.)		9.0	9.3	13	17	19	20	24	25	8.7	19
EARNINGS PER SHARE		.55	.56	.76	1.01	1.11	1.16	1.37	1.42	.48	1.06
DIVIDEND PER SHARE		.13	.13	.21	.22	.26	.30	.36	.42	.44	.44
PRICES	Hi	5.1	6.3	9.8	10.4	16.6	17.5	21.4	18.5	14.9	9.5
	Lo	3.5	3.4	5.5	7.8	8.6	13.4	10.8	12.3	7.6	6.0

Kellogg Company
One Kellogg Square
P.O. Box 3599
Battle Creek, Michigan 49016-3599
Tel. (616) 961-2000
Listed: NYSE
Investor contact: J.R. Hinton
Ticker symbol: K
S&P rating: A+

Kellogg's

Kellogg is the largest producer of ready-to-eat cereals in the United States and around the world. It controls about 38% of the total domestic RTE cereal market and 50% of the foreign market. Kellogg has been in Europe for 67 years, and the European market is expanding at a much more rapid pace than the U.S. market.

Ready to eat cereal dates to 1894, when W.K. Kellogg and his brother, Dr. John Harvey Kellogg, a physician, introduced a flaked cereal to patients at the Battle Creek Sanitarium in Michigan. The product was an instant success. Then, in 1906, W.K. Kellogg formed the Battle Creek Toasted Corn Flake Company, now Kellogg Company, which has been growing ever since.

For many years Kellogg remained somewhat of a breakfast products company. Its cereal products are marketed under names such as Kellogg's Corn Flakes, Special K, Raisin Bran, Nutri-Grain, Cracklin Oat Bran, and almost 40 other ready-to-eat cereal products.

In the 1970's, Kellogg expanded beyond the cereal market and now sells such items as Mrs. Smith's Frozen Pies and Eggo Frozen Waffles.

Kellogg invests in innovative advertising and has done so since 1906. Advertising is an important factor in Kellogg Company's leadership in the cereal industry. Kellogg has now come out with its own oat cereals, Cracklin Oat Bran, Oat Bake, and Fiberwise, a psyllium-based product.

Kellogg has production facilities in 17 countries. It is constantly engaged in plant modernization and expansion. The use of new advanced technology machinery enabled Kellogg to lower production costs and at the same time expand volume.

In 1989, due to a combination of new product and marketing problems, Kellogg experienced its first earnings decline in 38 years. However, in 1990, earnings rebounded to $2.08 per share. Kellogg has paid consecutive cash dividends since 1923. The W.K. Kellogg Foundation controls about 34% of the common shares and institutions control about 33%. Kellogg declared a 2:1 stock split in 1986 and another 2:1 stock split in 1991.

Total assets: $3.7 billion
Current ratio: 0.9
Common shares outstanding: 241.6 million

	1981	1982	1983	1984	1985	1986	1987	1988	1989	1990
REVENUES (MIL.)	2,321	2,367	2,381	2,602	2,930	3,341	3,793	4,349	4,652	5,181
NET INCOME (MIL.)	205	228	243	251	281	319	396	480	470	503
EARNINGS PER SHARE	.67	.75	.80	.84	1.14	1.29	1.60	1.95	1.93	2.08
DIVIDEND PER SHARE	.36	.38	.41	.43	.45	.51	.65	.76	.86	.96
PRICES Hi	6.3	7.8	8.2	10.7	18.0	29.3	34.4	34.3	40.8	38.8
Lo	4.4	5.4	6.3	6.8	9.6	16.8	19.0	24.5	28.9	29.4

Knight-Ridder, Inc.

One Herald Plaza
Miami, Florida 33132
Tel. (305) 376-3800
Listed: NYSE
Investor contact: Mgr. Corporate Communications, Lee Ann Schlatter
Ticker symbol: KRI
S&P rating: A+

As profiled in its 1990 Annual Report, "Knight-Ridder Newspapers, Inc. is an international information and communications company engaged in newspaper publishing, business news and information services, electronic retrieval services, cable television and newsprint manufacturing. Knight-Ridder's various information services reach more than 100 million people in 135 countries."

Knight-Ridder publishes 28 daily newspapers in 15 states and three nondailies. Some of its more important newspapers include *The Miami Herald*, *Philadelphia Inquirer*, *San Jose Mercury News*, *Akron Beacon Journal*, *Detroit Free Press*, and *Wichita Eagle*. 1990 marked the first year of an operating agreement between the *Detroit Free Press* and Gannett's *Detroit News*. Knight-Ridder derives 85% of revenues and over 90% of profits from newspaper publishing.

Knight-Ridder has been engaged in restructuring both to eliminate activities which do not suit its objectives and to acquire those that do. With this in mind, Knight-Ridder sold eight TV stations and acquired

Dialog Information Services, Inc., a computer data bank.

With 1990 revenues up 14.5% and profits up 42.5%, business information is Knight-Ridder's fastest growing segment. In 1990, Dialog Information Services combined with VU/TEXT Information Services to establish the Electronic Publishing Group. Electronic Publishing has over 400 data bases. The Financial Information Group, (MoneyCenter) and American Quotation Systems, are leading vendors of real-time archival financial news, information, and analyses. The Transport Group consists of the *Journal of Commerce*, *Traffic World* and Port Import/Export Reporting Service (PIERS).

TKR Cable Co., with significant operations in New Jersey and New York, is jointly owned with Tele-Communications, Inc. Knight-Ridder also owns the Commodity Research Bureau and has a partial interest in a newsprint mill, and partial ownership of the Seattle Times Co.

Knight-Ridder has been plagued, like other newspaper companies, with a decline in advertising linage. However, with restructuring completed, Knight-Ridder should experience many economies of scale and be in the forefront of electronic communication of news and other data.

Knight-Ridder has paid consecutive cash dividends since 1969. Directors control about 25% and institutions about 70% of its common shares. It paid a 100% stock dividend in 1983.

Total assets: $2.3 billion
Current ratio: 1.2
Common shares outstanding: 49.5 million

		1981	1982	1983	1984	1985	1986	1987	1988	1989	1990
REVENUES (MIL.)		1,199	1,285	1,425	1,602	1,664	1,808	1,968	2,083	2,268	2,305
NET INCOME (MIL.)		95	96	112	131	124	133	149	147	180	149
EARNINGS PER SHARE		1.46	1.47	1.68	2.00	2.05	2.28	2.54	2.59	3.43	2.94
DIVIDEND PER SHARE		.43	.46	.58	.67	.79	.91	1.03	1.15	1.25	1.34
PRICES	Hi	20.9	25.8	30.5	31.0	41.4	57.9	61.3	47.8	58.4	58.0
	Lo	13.4	13.6	22.1	21.3	28.0	37.5	33.3	35.8	42.9	37.0

Lance, Inc.

8600 South Boulevard
(P.O. Box 32368)
Charlotte, North Carolina 28232
Tel. (704) 554-1421
Investor contact: Treas. Earl D. Leake
Ticker symbol: LNCE
S&P rating: A+

Lance and its subsidiaries Midwest Biscuit Company and Caronuts, Inc., manufacture snack foods and bakery products which are sold and distributed through the company's own sales organization to convenience stores, supermarkets, discount stores, restaurants, and similar establishments. Midwest manufactures cookies and crackers, which are sold through brokers and its own  sales organization to wholesale grocers, supermarket chains, and distributors. Caronuts, located in southeastern Virginia, is essentially a peanut acquisition agent for the company.

Lance has a strong presence in the Midwest and Southeast and operates primarily through vending machines owned and rented in 35 states and the District of Columbia. In 1990 Lance opened 89 new sales territories. Snacks include such items as corn chips, peanut butter sandwich crackers, peanuts, popcorn, and potato chips. Lance was one of the first snack food manufacturers to convert from animal fats to vegetable oils.

Midwest Biscuit Company (acquired in 1979) bakes cookies, crackers, melba toast, and breadsticks under its own Vista label and for private label brands. Midwest increased sales 6.2% in 1990. In 1990, snack items provided 77% and bread-basket items 9% of revenues.

Lance sold Hancock's Old Fashioned Country Ham in 1982, Tri Plas, Inc. (a manufacturer of molded plastic containers) in 1986, and Nutrition-Pak Corp. in 1989.

Lance has paid consecutive cash dividends since 1944 and has increased cash dividends in each of the past 16 years. It has no long-term debt. The Van Every family controls about 45% and institutions about 41% of outstanding shares. Lance paid a 50% stock dividend in 1982, a 33 1/3% stock dividend in 1985, and a 100% stock dividend in 1987.

Total assets: $288.6 million
Current ratio: 4.4
Common shares outstanding: 31.3

	1981	1982	1983	1984	1985	1986	1987	1988	1989	1990
REVENUES (MIL.)	280	292	308	337	355	367	380	408	432	446
NET INCOME (MIL.)	23	27	29	31	33	36	38	39	45	46
EARNINGS PER SHARE	.69	.81	.87	.94	1.00	1.07	1.17	1.23	1.42	1.46
DIVIDEND PER SHARE	.31	.35	.40	.43	.47	.52	.59	.66	.72	.82
PRICES Hi	6.9	10.8	11.5	11.8	16.1	20.4	26.0	21.8	25.0	27.3
Lo	5.1	5.9	9.0	9.1	11.1	15.0	16.8	16.8	17.3	19.3

Lee Enterprises Incorporated

400 Putnam Building
215 North Main Street
Davenport, Iowa 52801-1924
Tel. (319) 383-2100
Listed: NYSE
Investor contact: R. Galligan
Ticker symbol: LEE
S&P rating: A

Lee
Enterprises, Inc.

As profiled in its 1991 Annual Report, "Lee Enterprises Incorporated is in the business of communicating information and entertainment. Founded in 1890 by A. W. Lee, it has grown into a diversified media company employing over 5,000 people. Lee Enterprises publishes directly or through affiliates daily newspapers in Illinois, Iowa, Minnesota, Montana, Nebraska, North Dakota, South Dakota, Oregon, and Wisconsin; specialty publications in Illinois, Iowa, Montana, Nebraska, North Dakota, Oregon, and Wisconsin; operates or has an interest in television stations in Arizona, Hawaii, Nebraska, New Mexico, Oregon and West Virginia; markets integrated voice response systems and services through Voice Response, Inc.; markets sales and productivity systems and services through PROMO STAR; and serves the graphic arts industry through NAPP Systems Inc., the world's leading producer of photosensitive polymer printing plates for newspapers."

Lee has 19 daily and weekly newspapers and six television stations located in Midwestern and Western states. Its newspapers are located primarily in relatively small cities and towns and represent the only newspaper in each of its markets. Such newspapers are less cyclical then big city newspapers. Additionally, Lee has 32 shoppers and specialty publications. Lee has six television stations located in the growth cities of Tucson, Honolulu, Omaha, Albuquerque, Portland, and Huntington-Charlston; four are CBS affiliates.

The Media Products and Services division consists of NAPP Systems, Inc., Voice Response, and Promostar. NAPP Systems, Inc. is the worldwide market leader for photopolymer letterpress and flexographic printing plates for newspapers. In 1990, Lee purchased the remaining 50% interest in NAPP from Nippon Paint Co. of Japan. Lee is in the process of turning Promostar, a computer-based software concept combining graphic capabilities with a variety of databases, into a separate business.

In 1991, revenues and profits were apportioned as follows: newspapers, 62% of revenues and 75% of profits; broadcasting operations, 20% of revenues and 13% of profits; and media products, 18% of revenues and 12% of profits.

Lee has paid consecutive cash dividends since 1960. It paid a 100% stock dividend in 1983 and another 100% stock dividend in 1986.

Total assets: $459.3 million
Current ratio: 1.2
Common shares outstanding: 15.0 million
Class B: 8.0 million

		1982	1983	1984	1985	1986	1987	1988	1989	1990	1991
REVENUES (MIL.)		161	173	190	207	221	237	253	269	287	346
NET INCOME (MIL.)		20	23	27	31	33	42	41	43	44	32
EARNINGS PER SHARE		.71	.82	.97	1.13	1.25	1.62	1.63	1.74	1.82	1.35
DIVIDEND PER SHARE		.28	.32	.37	.45	.57	.60	.64	.68	.72	.76
PRICES	Hi	9.8	12.9	14.0	23.4	27.6	29.8	29.4	34.8	33.1	31.9
	Lo	5.8	9.3	10.1	12.9	20.5	20.0	21.8	24.8	19.8	20.1

Eli Lilly and Company

Lilly Corporate Center
Indianapolis, Indiana 46285
Tel. (317) 276-2000
Listed: NYSE
Investor contact: Robert B. Graper
Ticker symbol: LLY
S&P rating: A+

Lilly, one of the largest U.S. pharmaceutical manufacturers, is strong in the areas of antibiotics, other pharmaceuticals, medical instruments, and animal health products. Antibiotics represent about half of Lilly's drug sales, and the other half consists of drugs used to treat more-or-less chronic health problems. The strongest growth area is represented by the chronic health-care drugs. Prozac, an antidepressant first introduced in 1988, has shown an enormous increase in sales. Other important drugs to come on the market are Humulin, a genetically engineered insulin, and AXID, an antiulcer preparation.

Lilly's medical instruments operation targets the cardiovascular area. Increased sales of agricultural products, both pharmaceuticals and herbicides, have rebounded rapidly since the 1988 drought. Lilly has shifted its herbicide and agricultural chemical business to a joint venture with Dow Chemical, Dow Elanco, which is 40% owned by Lilly and 60% owned by Dow.

Lilly markets its products in more than 130 countries. International business represents 36% of sales, which means that Lilly has a strong stake in the international value of the dollar.

Lilly is a leader in the manufacture of defibralators and instruments used in angioplasty. Lilly has shifted its thrust away from injectable antibiotics toward the development of more profitable pharmaceuticals used to medicate chronic conditions.

Lilly is in superb financial shape. Long-term debt represents only 6.2% of Lilly's total capital. Lilly Endowment controls about 17% and institutions more than 70% of the outstanding shares. Lilly reported record sales and earnings for the 30th consecutive year. Lilly has paid consecutive cash dividends since 1885 and has increased them for the past 22 years. It paid a 100% stock dividend in 1986 and another 100%

stock dividend in 1989.

Total assets: $7.1 billion
Current ratio: 0.9
Common shares outstanding: 267.1 million

	1981	1982	1983	1984	1985	1986	1987	1988	1989	1990
REVENUES (MIL.)	2,773	2,963	3,034	3,109	3,271	3,720	3,644	4,070	4,176	5,192
NET INCOME (MIL.)	374	412	457	490	518	558	411	761	940	1,127
EARNINGS PER SHARE	1.24	1.36	1.54	1.69	1.85	2.01	1.42	2.67	3.20	3.90
DIVIDEND PER SHARE	.60	.65	.69	.75	.80	.90	1.00	1.15	1.35	1.64
PRICES Hi	17.3	16.4	17.1	17.0	28.0	41.8	53.9	45.9	68.5	90.4
Lo	11.4	11.4	14.3	13.3	16.1	25.1	28.9	35.4	42.4	58.8

America's GROWTH STOCKS

The Limited, Inc.

Two Limited Parkway
Columbus, Ohio 43216
Tel. (614) 479-7000
Listed: NYSE
Investor contact: V.P. Financial and Public Relations, Alfred S. Dietzel
Ticker symbol: LTD
S&P rating: A

The Limited is a very large and aggressively managed retail chain of women's apparel stores. It operates both stores and a catalog division. The Limited has more than 3,800 **THE LIMITED, INC.** stores and is constantly both adding new stores and acquiring smaller chains. Brylane, a subsidiary, is the second-largest women's fashion catalog retailer in the United States.

Some of the firm's better-known stores are the Limited and the Limited Express, a chain of more than 1,325 retail stores including about 20 superstores; Victoria's Secret, a more-than-440-store, rapidly expanding retail chain; Lerner, a more-than-850-store chain which is both the single largest women's apparel operation and appealing to the "off price" customer, selling clothing in sizes 14 and up; and Lane Bryant, a chain of more than 750 stores appealing to the large-size woman.

More recent acquisitions are the Abercrombie & Fitch chain and Henry Bendel, an upscale apparel retailer in New York City. In 1991, Limited added 600 new stores, remodeled 250 existing stores, and opened a 1.89 million square foot office and distribution center in Reynoldsburg, Ohio.

Also, Limited has entered the men's apparel business through the operation of its start-up Express Man store chain.

Limited's strategy is to move very quickly in the fast changing atmosphere of women's fashion. Its relationship with its manufacturers is one of cooperation rather than confrontation. It test-markets new styles in selected stores before each season.

Chairman and president Leslie Wexner owns about 32% and institutions about 43% of the outstanding common shares. The Limited has paid very modest cash dividends since 1970. It paid a 100% stock dividend in 1982, a 100% stock dividend in 1983, a 100% stock dividend in 1985, a 100% stock dividend in 1986, and a 100% stock dividend in 1990.

Total assets: $2.9 billion
Current ratio: 2.8
Common shares outstanding: 360.6 million

		1981	1982	1983	1984	1985	1986	1987	1988	1989	1990
REVENUES (MIL.)		365	721	1,086	1,343	2,387	3,143	3,528	4,071	4,648	5,254
NET INCOME (MIL.)		22	34	71	92	145	228	235	245	347	398
EARNINGS PER SHARE		.07	.095	.20	.26	.40	.60	.62	.68	.96	1.10
DIVIDEND PER SHARE		.007	.013	.02	.04	.054	.08	.12	.12	.16	.24
PRICES	Hi	0.8	2.1	5.2	4.7	10.6	17.3	26.4	14.0	20.0	25.6
	Lo	0.5	0.6	2.0	2.6	4.4	10.3	8.0	8.2	12.6	11.8

Liz Claiborne, Inc.

1441 Broadway
New York, New York 10018
Tel. (212) 354-4900
Listed: NYSE
Investor contact: Walter L. Krieger
Ticker symbol: LICZ
S&P rating: A-

Liz Claiborne is a designer and retailer chiefly of women's (and to a much lesser extent men's) clothing. The clothing is assembled and made by independent manufacturers both in the United States (12%) and overseas (88%). Upscale apparel is sold through more than 3,500 department and specialty stores. Liz's original and core business is sportswear.

Liz Claiborne carries a wide distribution of upscale women's apparel, designed for the career and professional woman at work and at play. The company to a lesser degree designs and retails men's clothing. The sportswear division markets a range of "better" sportswear. On the other hand, "Lizsport" and "Lizwear" offer a casual line of sportswear. In 1988, the company started a 13- (now 35-) retail-store chain of First Issue stores with apparel bearing the First Issue trademark. More expensive sportswear is sold under the "Dana Buchman" label. The menswear segment offers primarily a wide selection of separates and furnishings. Also, Liz carries a line of accessories such as fragrances, pocketbooks, belts, and scarves. The menswear segment offers primarily a wide selection of separates and furnishings. A fashion jewelry division is in the start-up phase.

In 1990, sales were divided as follows: sportswear, 56%; dresses, 9%; accessories, 9%; menswear, 7%; fragrances, 4%; and other, 15%.

In 1989, Elizabeth Claiborne Ortenburg, chairwoman and chief executive officer, and her husband Arthur Ortenburg, vice chairman, retired from active management but remain as directors of the company.

Consecutive cash dividends have been paid since 1964. Institutions control 75% of the outstanding common shares. Liz Claiborne paid a 50% stock dividend in 1982, a 100% stock dividend in 1983, a 100% stock dividend in 1984, a 100% stock dividend in 1986, and a 100%

stock dividend in 1987.

Total assets: $985 million
Current ratio: 3.5
Common shares outstanding: 85.5 million

		1981	1982	1983	1984	1985	1986	1987	1988	1989	1990
REVENUES (MIL.)		117	166	229	391	557	813	1,053	1,184	1,411	1,729
NET INCOME (MIL.)		10	14	22	42	61	86	114	110	165	206
EARNINGS PER SHARE		.13	.17	.27	.50	.71	1.00	1.32	1.26	1.87	2.37
DIVIDEND PER SHARE		—	—	—	.047	.081	.12	.16	.18	.19	.24
PRICES	Hi	1.4	2.6	4.8	6.8	12.5	24.3	39.1	20.0	27.8	35.0
	Lo	0.9	1.0	2.0	3.1	5.9	11.9	12.3	12.8	16.5	20.3

Luby's Cafeterias, Inc.
2211 Northeast Loop 410
P.O. Box 33069
San Antonio, Texas 78265
Tel. (512) 654-9000
Listed: NYSE
Investor contact: Treas. J. E. Curtis,Jr.
Ticker symbol: LUB
S&P rating: A

Luby owns and operates a chain of more than 150 cafeterias in Texas, Oklahoma, New Mexico, Arizona, Arkansas, Florida, and more recently Louisiana. However, well over a hundred of the cafeterias are in Texas. Some cafeterias are located in shopping malls, and a number are freestanding. The menu is not uniform but varies to local tastes and market availability. During the day Luby's caters to shoppers, retail store personnel, and office employees. In the evening, it caters to families for dinner. Luby's gears its facilities toward children. All restaurants are carpeted, air-conditioned, and open seven days a week.

With its restaurants concentrated in the energy belt, Luby's has experienced a drop in customer traffic of between 1.5–2.0%. This has had a negative impact on the earnings increases to which Luby stockholders had been accustomed. However, Luby's continues to increase earnings by a combination of new stores and price increases.

Luby's is experimenting with a number of future possibilities. One is the expansion of take-out service, which to date has been minimal. Another is an expanded restaurant size. Luby's offers minimum growth near-term and excellent growth long-term.

Officers and directors own about 16% and institutions about 37% of the common shares. Consecutive cash dividends have been paid since 1973. Luby's paid a 25% stock dividend in 1980, a 50% stock dividend in 1981, a 25% stock dividend in 1983, a 33 1/3 stock dividend in 1984, a 50% stock dividend in 1986, and a 50% stock dividend in 1990.

Total assets: $260.7 million
Current ratio: 0.5
Common shares outstanding: 27.4 million

		1982	1983	1984	1985	1986	1987	1988	1989	1990	1991
REVENUES (MIL.)		127	141	171	196	215	233	254	283	311	328
NET INCOME (MIL.)		12	14	17	20	22	24	28	30	32	32
EARNINGS PER SHARE		.45	.51	.63	.71	.80	.87	1.01	1.08	1.17	1.18
DIVIDEND PER SHARE		.13	.16	.20	.24	.27	.30	.34	.39	.44	.46
PRICES	Hi	10.9	12.9	14.3	18.6	19.4	21.9	17.2	18.9	21.3	20.8
	Lo	6.6	9.3	10.5	11.9	15.0	13.3	13.5	15.4	15.6	12.0

Marion Merrell Dow, Inc.

9300 Ward Parkway
Kansas City, Missouri 64114-0480
Tel. (816) 966-4000
Listed: NYSE
Investor contact: V.P. Communications and Investor Relations,
Larry W. Wheeler
Ticker symbol: MKC
S&P rating: A+

175

Marion Merrell Dow, Inc.

Marion Merrell Dow was founded in 1988 by the merger of Marion Laboratories with Merrell Dow, a former subsidiary of Dow Chemical. Marion's strength is in cardiovascular, antihistamine, and peptic ulcer medications.

Marion's primary pharmaceutical is Cardizem, used in the treatment of angina pectoris and other cardiovascular disorders. In fact, Cardizem accounts for more than 50% of Marion's revenues. Sales reached $700 million in 1990. While the patent on Cardizem expires in November 1992, Marion plans to market a number of product extensions to counter generic competition.

Marion's second-most-important drug is Seldane, an antihistamine used in the treatment of respiratory disorders. The chief advantage of Seldane over competing products is that Seldane does not cause drowsiness. In 1990, sales of Seldane were more than $500 million.

Marion Manufactures and sells more than 50 products. In addition to Cardizem and Seldane, some of its more important products are Carafate, used in the treatment of peptic ulcers; Rifadin, an antibiotic; Nitro-Bid, a nitroglycerin product used in the treatment of heart attacks; Gaviscon, an antacid; Ditropan, a urological product; Os-Cal, a calcium supplement; Nicorette, which helps break addiction to tobacco; and Lorlco, an anticholesterol drug.

In early 1991, Marion entered into an agreement with Hoffman-La Roche for the development and marketing of a new calcium blocker heart drug. Marion faces the prospect of several of its very important pharmaceuticals losing patent protection in a few years. However, Marion has a number of new drugs in regulatory approval channels and is seeking new uses for its current medications.

Dow Chemical owns about 69% of the outstanding Marion shares. Marion has paid consecutive cash dividends since 1957. It paid a 100% stock dividend in 1983, a 100% stock dividend in 1985, a 100% stock dividend in 1986, and a 100% stock dividend in 1987.

Total assets: $2.2 billion
Current ratio: 2.0
Common shares outstanding: 276 million

	1981	1982	1983	1984	1985	1986	1987	1988	1989	1990
REVENUES (MIL.)	119	153	181	226	296	399	597	752	930	2,462
NET INCOME (MIL.)	8	9	15	24	36	55	97	150	211	487
EARNINGS PER SHARE	.06	.07	.10	.16	.24	.35	.61	.96	1.46	1.72
DIVIDENDS PER SHARE	.04	.04	.04	.049	.064	.088	.15	.26	.34	.70
PRICES Hi	1.9	3.5	6.0	5.5	11.9	25.0	41.5	27.9	36.5	36.3
Lo	1.3	1.5	2.9	3.5	5.3	11.3	18.6	14.6	19.8	21.0

Marriott Corporation

10400 Fernwood Road
Bethesda, Maryland 20058
Tel. (301) 380-9000
Listed: NYSE
Investor contact: Laura Paugh
Ticker symbol: MHS
S&P rating: A

Marriott is one of the largest operators of lodging facilities and is strong in food contract services and a major factor in both the franchising and the operation of restaurants. Marriott has a very aggressive management that acquires businesses and, if they don't work out, disposes of them. It operates more than 640 hotels under the  Marriott, Courtyard, Residence Inn, and Fairfield Inn names. Marriott is directed toward the higher-priced markets. Both Courtyard and Fairfield Inns are directed toward the lower-priced markets. Marriott also operates the Residence Inn chain, directed toward the long-stay client. Also, it operates 13 retirement facilities for the elderly. Marriott's strategy is to build hotels, sell the hotels and real estate to investors, and then manage and operate the hotels.

Marriott is a large contract caterer to businesses, hospitals, and educational institutions. However, it has sold its In-Flight food service unit for $600 million because it didn't fit well into Marriott's structure. Marriott has acquired Corporate Food Services, which provides contract

177

dining services for law firms, banks, and corporations. Marriott has also entered into a joint agreement with Adachi Enterprises Group for the purchase of nine hotels in Europe, including the United Kingdom, for $400,000,000.

Marriott intends to divest itself of most of its retail restaurant operations. It sold its 600-unit Roy Rogers fast-food chain to Hardee's Food System, Inc., for $350 million. Its more than 430 family restaurants operating under the names of Bob's Big Boy, Wag's, Howard Johnson's, Allie's, and Bickford's are up for sale. It intends to retain airport and plaza operations and the Hot Shoppes in the District of Columbia area.

Marriott has paid consecutive cash dividends since 1975. The Marriott family controls about 25% and institutions control about 35% of the outstanding common shares. It paid a 400% stock dividend in 1986.

Total assets: $6.9 billion
Current ratio: 0.9
Common shares outstanding: 95.1 million

	1981	1982	1983	1984	1985	1986	1987	1988	1989	1990
REVENUES (MIL.)	2,000	2,541	3,037	3,525	4,242	5,266	6,522	7,370	7,536	7,646
NET INCOME (MIL.)	86	94	115	135	167	192	223	232	181	47
EARNINGS PER SHARE	.64	.69	.83	1.00	1.24	1.40	1.67	1.95	1.62	.46
DIVIDEND PER SHARE	.051	.064	.076	.094	.11	.14	.17	.21	.25	.28
PRICES Hi	9.5	12.5	16.3	16.0	23.4	39.0	43.8	33.4	41.3	33.6
Lo	5.9	6.5	10.0	11.8	14.8	20.6	24.0	26.3	29.8	8.4

Marshall & Ilsley Corp.

770 North Water Street
Milwaukee, Wisconsin 53202
Tel (414) 756-7801
Listed: NASDAQ
Investor contact: Secy. M.A. Hatfield
Ticker symbol: MRIS
S&P rating: A

Marshall & Ilsley, a large bank holding company, owns Marshall &

Ilsley Bank (Wisconsin's third largest) and 39 other banks in Wisconsin and one in Arizona. Marshall & Ilsley has 132 banking offices in Wisconsin, 14 banking offices in Arizona, and a trust operation in Florida.

Marshall & Ilsley Corporation

Marshall & Ilsley is very aggressive on the acquisition front. In 1990, it acquired Central Federal Savings & Loan of Ripon with $90 million of deposits, Rosendale State Bank with $31.5 million of deposits, and Barneveld State Bank with $16 million of deposits. In 1989, it acquired the First National Bank of Cudahy with assets of $42 million and Scottscom Bancorp. with assets of $44 million. In 1988, it acquired Central Wisconsin Bankshares, Inc., with assets of $800 million. That same year it also acquired Greater Milwaukee Bank, Hartland National Bank, and the Village Bank of Elm Grove, with total assets of $115 million.

Also, Marshall & Ilsley is engaged in a number of bank-related activities such as trust services, discount brokerage, investment management, mortgage banking, and data services.

In 1990, net income fell to $71.3 million due to losses both in its lead Marshall & Ilsley Bank and in its Arizona operation. Also, in 1990 Marshall & Ilsley settled, for $5 million, a long-standing claim of the Pension Benefit Guaranty Corporation.

In 1990, loans of $4.8 billion were divided as follows: commercial, financial and agricultural, 34.3%; revenue bonds, 1.5%; construction, 3.9%; residential mortgage, 25.4%; commercial mortgage, 18.3%; personal, 12.1%; and lease financing, 4.5%.

In 1990, income of $833.3 million was apportioned as follows: interest on loans, 60.1%; investment securities, 16.9%; and other, 23.0%.

Founded in 1847, Marshall & Ilsley has paid consecutive cash dividends since 1938. Northwestern Mutual Life owns 11.8% and the Marshall & Ilsley Trust 10.2% of the outstanding common shares. A 100% stock dividend was paid in 1978, and a 200% stock dividend was paid in 1986.

Total assets: $7.1 billion
Common shares outstanding: 22 million

	1981	1982	1983	1984	1985	1986	1987	1988	1989	1990
NET INCOME (MIL.)	20	26	32	35	43	55	58	76	85	71
EARNINGS PER SHARE	1.55	2.02	2.18	2.21	2.66	2.95	3.16	3.48	3.84	3.25
DIVIDEND PER SHARE	.56	.60	.65	.70	.74	.79	.83	.93	1.05	1.17
PRICES Hi	8.3	11.5	16.8	17.5	27.5	38.8	33.0	30.5	38.0	35.5
Lo	6.5	6.5	11.3	13.1	16.9	25.6	24.3	27.3	28.0	23.3

Masco Corporation

21001 Van Born Road
Taylor, Michigan 48180
Tel. (313) 274-7400
Listed: NYSE
Investor contact: Treas. John C. Nicholls, Jr.
Ticker symbol: MAS
S&P rating: A -

Masco Corporation

Masco, known for the washerless faucet, has expanded broadly over the years to all types of plumbing supplies and home furnishings. It is significant that all of Masco's forays into the various home plumbing, fixtures, kitchen cabinets, and furniture markets have met with huge success, yet not one of the products is sold under the Masco label.

For example, Masco markets faucets and bathroom fixtures under the names of Delta, Peerless, Delex, Artistic Brass, Epic, Damixa, American Bath, Mariani, and Mixet. It manufactures kitchen cabinets under the names of Merilatt and Fieldstone and plumbing supplies under the names of Brass-Craft and Plumb Shop. It manufactures kitchen appliances under the names of Thermador and Waste King. Bathroom tubs and showers are manufactured under the names of Aqua Glass and Hot Springs Spas. Finally, locks and building supplies are marketed under the Weiser and Baldwin names.

In 1984, Masco restructured its operations and spun off to

shareholders the industrial-products segment of its business under the name of Masco Industries. Masco retained a 40% interest in Masco Industries.

More recently Masco has been expanding into the home-furnishings business. In July, 1986 it acquired Henredon Furniture. In October, 1986 it acquired Drexel Heritage (another furniture manufacturer). In September, 1987 it acquired Lexington Furniture. With the May 1989 acquisition of Universal Furniture Ltd., Masco became the largest furniture manufacturer in the United States, with about a 10% market share.

In 1990, building products provided 54% of sales and 72% of profits. Home furnishings provided 46% of sales and 28% of profits.

The Manoogian family controls about 7% and institutions about 55% of the common shares. Masco has paid consecutive cash dividends since 1944. A 100% stock dividend was paid in 1982 and another 100% stock dividend was paid in 1986.

Total assets: $3.8 billion
Current ratio: 2.5
Common shares outstanding: 147.8 million

		1981	1982	1983	1984	1985	1986	1987	1988	1989	1990
REVENUES (MIL.)		877	856	1,059	1,020	1,154	1,452	2,023	2,439	3,151	3,209
NET INCOME (MIL.)		88	78	107	116	164	203	219	288	221	139
EARNINGS PER SHARE		.87	.75	.97	1.00	1.28	1.56	1.65	2.10	1.42	.91
DIVIDEND PER SHARE		.18	.20	.22	.25	.29	.34	.38	.44	.50	.54
PRICES	Hi	10.6	14.4	18.5	16.9	21.3	34.5	40.9	30.4	31.1	26.8
	Lo	7.0	6.9	12.5	11.4	13.0	19.5	18.8	22.0	23.8	14.3

America's GROWTH STOCKS

The May Department Stores Company

611 Olive Street
St. Louis, Missouri 63101
Tel. (314) 342-6300
Listed: NYSE
Investor contact: Director Corporate Communications, Sharon L. Bateman
Ticker symbol: MA
S&P rating: A+

The May Department Stores Company operates 328 department stores and a national self-service shoe chain. Its department stores operate under such well-known names as the May Company (in California and Ohio), Lord & Taylor, G. Fox, Hecht's, Foley's, and Filene's. Its self-service shoe operation, Payless ShoeSource, is the nation's largest shoe chain with more than 3,000 shoe stores. May owns a 50% interest in May Center Associates, which is involved in the development and operation of shopping malls. The other 50% is owned by The Prudential Life Insurance Company and Melvin Simon & Associates.

In 1990, May acquired the Richmond, Virginia-based Thalhimers department store (25 stores) from Carter Hawley Hale for $317 million. Also in 1990, May spun off to shareholders its 79-store Venture discount chain based in the Midwest. In 1989, it sold Loehmann's and Caldor, a 119-store discount chain in the Northeast. The reason for the divestitures is that May wants to focus on operations and expansion of its higher-return and faster-growing businesses—department stores and specialty shoe stores. Most of the $1.5 billion derived from these sales was used to buy back stock or reduce debt.

May's five-year plan is to add 88 new department stores and 1,325 additional Payless ShoeSource outlets.

In fiscal 1990, department stores represented 86% of sales and 85% of operating earnings, and specialty shoe stores provided 14% of sales and 15% of operating earnings.

May has paid consecutive cash dividends since 1911. Institutions hold approximately 65% of the common shares. May paid a 50% stock dividend in 1984 and a 100% stock dividend in 1986.

Total assets: $8.3 billion
Current ratio: 2.5
Common shares outstanding: 122.9 million

		1981	1982	1983	1984	1985	1986	1987	1988	1989	1990
REVENUES (MIL.)		4,913	5,205	5,815	6,361	6,825	7,437	7,480	8,874	9,602	10,066
NET INCOME (MIL.)		192	217	297	327	347	381	444	534	498	500
EARNINGS PER SHARE		1.32	1.45	1.94	2.11	2.21	2.41	2.89	3.62	3.52	3.74
DIVIDEND PER SHARE		.56	.60	.65	.78	.92	1.02	1.12	1.25	1.39	1.54
PRICES	Hi	10.7	16.4	21.0	24.2	32.5	44.1	50.9	40.0	52.6	60.4
	Lo	7.8	7.7	14.8	15.0	21.0	31.9	22.3	28.8	34.6	37.4

McDonald's Corporation

McDonald's Plaza
Oak Brook, Illinois 60521
Tel. (708) 575-3000
Listed: NYSE
Investor contact: V.P. Sharon Vuinovich
Ticker symbol: MCD
S&P rating: A+

Since the late Roy Kroc opened the doors of the first McDonald's in 1955, McDonald's has expanded both nationally and internationally. The hallmark of McDonald's success has been aggressive expansion and creative merchandising. McDonald's emphasizes quality, service, cleanliness and value. It serves 22 million customers a day  in more than 10,720 fast-food restaurants in 50 countries. Seventy-five percent of its fast-food outlets are in the United States and 25% in other countries, predominantly Canada (500), Japan (500), the United Kingdom (300), West Germany (300), and Australia (200).

Most McDonald's are franchise operations. The investor is required to put up around $500,000, 60% of which may be borrowed. Most franchise arrangements are for 20 years. The McDonald company wants investors who will be active owners of the operation. The franchisee must adhere to rigid specifications and pay the McDonald Company a fee based on a percentage of sales.

McDonald's offers a fairly uniform menu including burgers, fries, fish, chicken, salads, beverages, and desserts. When the price of beef went up, McDonald's introduced chicken nuggets. It is now testing pizza in selected restaurants.

McDonald's is expanding both by increasing sales at existing restaurants and by adding more than 600 new restaurants a year. The most rapid expansion is occurring overseas, which offers an unexploited market and unlimited growth. McDonald's controls a 36% market share of the fast-food restaurant business.

In 1990, the United States represented 58% of sales and 62% of profits, Europe 25% of sales and 20% of profits, Canada 10% of sales and 8% of profits, and other countries 7% of sales and 10% of profits.

In 1990, the McDonald Company owned and operated 2,643 restaurants, franchisees owned and operated 8,131, and affiliates owned and operated 1,029.

McDonald's has increased earnings and cash dividends each year since 1976. It paid a 50% stock dividend in 1982, a 50% stock dividend in 1984, a 50% stock dividend in 1986, a 50% stock dividend in 1987, and a 100% stock dividend in 1989.

Total assets: $10.7 billion
Current ratio: 0.5
Common shares outstanding: 359.2 million

		1981	1982	1983	1984	1985	1986	1987	1988	1989	1990
REVENUES (MIL.)		2,477	2,715	3,001	3,366	3,695	4,144	4,853	5,521	6,065	6,640
NET INCOME (MIL.)		265	301	343	389	433	480	549	646	727	802
EARNINGS PER SHARE		.65	.74	.85	.98	1.11	1.24	1.45	1.72	1.95	2.20
DIVIDEND PER SHARE		.094	.12	.14	.17	.20	.22	.24	.27	.30	.33
PRICES	Hi	7.3	9.8	11.1	12.5	18.3	25.6	30.6	25.5	34.9	38.5
	Lo	4.8	5.8	8.1	9.1	11.4	16.3	15.8	20.4	23.0	25.0

McGraw-Hill, Inc.

1221 Avenue of the Americas
New York, New York 10020
Tel. (212) 512-2000
Listed: NYSE
Investor contact: V.P. (Public Affairs) Donald S. Rubin
Ticker symbol: MHP
S&P rating: NR
Duff & Phelps A+

McGraw-Hill is a 102-year-old multimedia, publishing, and information services company serving worldwide markets in education, business, industry, the professions, and government.

McGraw-Hill changed from a media to a market orientation in 1985.

Today, the company is organized in to 14 market focus groups. Among some of the recognized names within these groups are *Aviation Week & Space Technology* magazine (Aviation Week Group); *Business Week* magazine and *Business Week International* (Business Week Group); *Byte* magazine and Datapro Research Corpora-

tion (Computers and Communications Group); F.W. Dodge Company and Sweet's (Construction Information Group); *Chemical Engineering* and *Modern Plastics* magazines (Science & Technology Group); Shepherd's/McGraw-Hill (Legal Information Group); moreover, the company has groups for Standard & Poor's Ratings (with ratings offices in London, Tokyo, Stockholm, Melbourne, Paris, San Francisco, and New York); S&P Information (including Compustat, Platt's Energy Services, and MMS International); DRI/McGraw-Hill (advisory and consulting services); Kenny S&P (information to the securities markets, particularly municipal securities); the trade and logistics services of the Tower Group; and a group for the company's four U.S. Television stations. McGraw-Hill also has the Education Group and Professional Publishing Group serving needs in those markets.

Education and professional publishing has always been a McGraw-Hill mainstay. The company is the nation's second-largest college textbook publisher. It combined its elementary and high school publishing business with Macmillan in 1989, and the resulting joint venture— Macmillan/McGraw-Hill School Publishing Company—is now the nation's largest el-hi publisher. McGraw-Hill also publishes a variety of professional and reference books, which are distributed through bookstores, and book clubs and by direct mail. Besides the McGraw-Hill imprint, other well-known ones are TAB Books and Osborne computer titles. The company also produces Primis custom-published texts for the college market through an electronic system which has applications to other publishing markets as well.

For financial reporting purposes, the market focus groups are divided into four segments. The first is Information and Publication Services (which includes the Aviation Week Group, the Business Week Group, the Computers and Communications Group, the Construction Information Group, and the Science and Technology Group). This segment provided 39% of the company's operating revenue in 1990, and 35% of its operating profit.

Educational and Professional Publishing, the second segment, includes groups for Education, Professional Publishing, and Legal Information. This segment provided 28% of the company's operating revenue in 1990, and 22% of its operating profit.

The third segment is Financial Services (which include the S&P Ratings Group, S&P Information Group, Tower Group, DRI/McGraw-Hill, and Kenny S&P Group.) This segment provided 28% of the company's operating revenue in 1990, and 34% of its operating profit.

Broadcasting Group comprises the fourth financial reporting segment. This segment provided 5% of the company's operating revenue in 1990, and 9% of its operating profit.

McGraw-Hill has paid consecutive cash dividends since 1936. The company's board of directors approved a two-for-one stock split in 1983.

Total assets: $2.5 billion
Current ratio: 1.1
Common shares outstanding: 51.5 million

		1981	1982	1983	1984	1985	1986	1987	1988	1989	1990
REVENUES (MIL.)		1,007	1,087	1,178	1,276	1,360	1,428	1,600	1,674	1,789	1,939
NET INCOME (MIL.)		98	110	126	144	147	154	165	186	48	172
EARNINGS PER SHARE		1.97	2.20	2.52	2.86	2.92	3.04	3.27	3.83	.98	3.53
DIVIDEND PER SHARE		.84	.94	1.08	1.24	1.40	1.52	1.68	1.84	2.00	2.16
PRICES	Hi	28.0	40.5	53.9	48.8	52.0	64.0	84.5	76.0	86.1	61.1
	Lo	19.7	22.4	35.0	34.0	39.8	46.5	43.0	46.8	53.5	39.9

Medtronic,Inc.

7000 Central Avenue N.E.
Minneapolis, Minnesota 55432
Tel. (616) 574-4000
Listed: NYSE
Investor contact: Director Investor Relations, Elizabeth Combs
Ticker symbol: MDT
S&P rating: A

Medtronic is the world's primary manufacturer of implantable and non-implantable cardiac pacemakers. Medtronic enjoys a market share of more than 45% for electronic pacemakers. Pacemakers are usually implanted under the skin in the chest and generate an electrical impulse, which is carried to the heart through a lead. More recently Medtronic has introduced, outside the United States, a pacemaker cardioverter defibrillator device used in the treatment of tacharrhythmia or

rapid heartbeat. PCDs can be adjusted by a physician to control the intensity, duration, and rate of the patient's heartbeat. The PCD will be commercially launched in the United States market following FDA approval.

In addition to pacemakers, Medtronic manufactures and distributes other cardiopulmonary products such as heart valves, oxygenators, coronary catheters, and implantable electrodes.

Medtronic's leading new product is the Elite rate-responsive pacer, which weighs 39 grams (about 1.4 oz.) and which Medtronic is selling in more than 80 countries. In 1990, Medtronic acquired Bio-Medicus, a leading manufacturer of centrifugal pumps used in open-heart surgery.

In 1991, pacemakers represented 65%, cardiovascular products 22%, and other products 13% of total sales. Foreign revenues are 42% of total sales, which means that exchange rates can be a major factor in earnings. However, Medtronic maintains an active hedging program.

Prospects for Medtronic are very bright. One note of caution is that there is always the possibility of failure or defect in a product, which could result in a large number of lawsuits. However, Medtronic remains one of the largest and most successful medical products companies.

Medtronic has paid consecutive cash dividends since 1977. Institutions control over 70% of the outstanding shares. Medtronic paid a 100% stock dividend in 1989 and a 100% stock dividend in 1991.

Total assets: $1.0 billion
Current ratio: 2.1
Common shares outstanding: 59.3 million

		1982	1983	1984	1985	1986	1987	1988	1989	1990	1991
REVENUES (MIL.)		318	353	391	370	412	515	670	766	866	1,021
NET INCOME (MIL.)		48	55	60	38	54	75	87	100	113	133
EARNINGS PER SHARE		.72	.81	.87	.58	.87	1.25	1.46	1.73	1.93	2.25
DIVIDEND PER SHARE		.14	.16	.18	.19	.20	.22	.26	.30	.35	.41
PRICES	Hi	14.1	15.0	11.2	11.0	23.2	27.2	25.0	35.5	46.0	94.3
	Lo	8.3	10.2	6.2	6.4	10.8	16.0	17.2	19.3	29.5	38.5

Melville Corporation

1 Theall Road
Rye, New York 10580
Tel. (914) 925-4000
Listed: NYSE
Investor contact: Exec. V.P. C.F.O., Robert D. Huth
Ticker symbol: MES
S&P rating: A+

MELVILLE CORPORATION What started out as a Thom McAn retail shoe chain has expanded into an enormous retail entity selling everything from wearing apparel to toys. Melville has expanded because of a combination of acquisitions and new stores. In 1990, it acquired the 330-store Circus World Toy Stores, as well as Peoples Drug Stores, with more than 490 stores. In 1988, it acquired the Berman's Specialty Stores leather goods chain (190 stores). Melville builds approximately 200–300 new stores a year. If a store doesn't live up to expectations, then Melville gets rid of it.

Wearing apparel is sold through Marshall's more than 340 stores (a name-brand cut-rate operation), Chess King's more than 545 off-price men's stores, and Wilson's more than 500 leather apparel stores.

Footwear is sold through the Thom McAn chain of more than 950 stores and Fan Club, consisting of more than 100 athletic shoe stores. In addition, footwear under the Meldico label is sold through more than 2,150 leased shoe departments in KMart stores.

Drug, health, and beauty aids are sold through more than 775 CVS (Consumer Value Stores) and more than 25 Freddy's deep-discount drug stores.

Toys are sold through more than 775 Kay-Bee Toy & Hobby Centers.

Household furnishings are sold through Linens 'n Things (more than 150 stores selling towels and bath items) and Prints Plus (more than 70 stores), a California chain selling prints and posters.

In 1990, apparel accounted for 35% of sales and 34% of profits; footwear, 20% of sales and 21% of profits; drug, health, and beauty aids,

31% of sales and 27% of profits; and toys and household items, 14% of sales and 18% of profits.

Melville has paid consecutive cash dividends since 1916. It has increased earnings for 15 consecutive years. It paid a 100% stock dividend in 1983 and another 100% stock dividend in 1989.

Total assets: $3.7 billion
Current ratio: 1.8
Common shares outstanding: 102.9 million

		1981	1982	1983	1984	1985	1986	1987	1988	1989	1990
REVENUES (MIL.)		2,761	3,262	3,923	4,423	4,775	5,262	5,930	6,780	7,554	8,687
NET INCOME (MIL.)		136	142	176	190	220	238	285	355	398	385
EARNINGS PER SHARE		1.32	1.37	1.68	1.80	2.04	2.20	2.63	3.26	3.56	3.59
DIVIDEND PER SHARE		.45	.51	.55	.66	.72	.78	.88	1.05	1.30	1.42
PRICES	Hi	12.0	19.1	23.9	22.8	26.5	36.9	42.0	38.4	53.6	57.6
	Lo	8.9	9.3	15.3	15.4	17.6	24.6	22.1	26.6	36.9	32.6

Mercantile Bankshares Corporation

2 Hopkins Plaza
Baltimore, Maryland 21203
Tel. (301) 237-5900
Listed: NASDAQ
Investor contact: S.V.P. Treas. Charles C. McGuire, Jr.
Ticker symbol: MRBK
S&P rating: A

As stated in its Annual Report, "Mercantile Bankshares Corporation is a multi-bank holding company with headquarters in Maryland. Each affiliated bank is a community bank, maintaining a high degree of autonomy and community identification. Each operates under its own name, management and board of directors. Affiliate banks, because of their association with Mercantile Bankshares Corporation, are able to offer their customers the more sophisticated services and financial strength of a major banking organization."

Mercantile Bankshares is the holding company for 19 commercial banks with more than 140 retail banking offices in three states, a mortgage company (Mercantile Mortgage corporation), an insurance agency (MBC Agency, Inc.), and a realty company (MBC Realty, Inc.) Its lead bank is Mercantile–Safe Deposit and Trust Company with 16 offices in the Baltimore area. Chairman Baldwin states that Mercantile consists of locally managed community banks, "A structure which enables us to bring local knowledge to customer relationships. We have never sought size for its own sake. Nor do we seek combinations to achieve efficiencies of scale. Our geographic expansion occurs through affiliation with quality banks in contiguous communities."

In 1990, Mercantile acquired Baltimore Trust Company, a $203 million asset bank in Selbyville, Delaware, and Farmers & Merchants Bank, a $132 million asset bank in Olney, Virginia.

In 1990, return on assets was a high 1.6% and return on equity a strong 14.7%. Loans were apportioned as follows: commercial and agricultural, 34.5%; mortgages, 37.9%; installment, 17.9%; and construction, 9.7%. Deposits of $3.7 billion were divided as follows: savings, 20%; money market, 14%; CDs, 48%; and non-interest demand, 18%. Revenues were divided as follows: interest on loans, 77%; return on investment securities, 20%; and other, 3%.

Consecutive cash dividends have been paid since 1909. Dividends have been increased for the past 14 years. Mercantile paid a 100% stock dividend in 1986 and a second 100% stock dividend in 1989.

Total assets: $4.9 billion
Common shares outstanding: 25.7 million

		1981	1982	1983	1984	1985	1986	1987	1988	1989	1990
NET INCOME (MIL.)		20	25	30	34	37	40	46	53	62	70
EARNINGS PER SHARE		.98	1.11	1.21	1.29	1.45	1.56	1.80	2.08	2.40	2.32
DIVIDEND PER SHARE		.30	.32	.35	.38	.44	.50	.56	.63	.73	.82
PRICES	Hi	4.3	6.1	8.8	11.3	18.5	23.6	22.6	19.8	27.6	26.5
	Lo	3.5	3.9	5.3	8.0	10.5	17.3	14.0	16.3	17.5	13.3

Mercantile Stores Company, Inc.

1100 North Market Street
Wilmington, Delaware 19801
Tel. (302) 575-1816
Listed: NYSE
Investor contact: Controller, William A. Carr
Ticker symbol: MST
S&P rating: A

Mercantile Stores is a department store chain with more than 80 stores in 16 states of the South and Midwest. Mercantile operates the stores under 12 local names such as McAlpin's of Cincinnati; Knot Dry Goods of Nashville; Gayfers of Mobile, Alabama; Bacon's of Louisville; and The Jones Store Co. of Kansas City, Missouri. Mercantile sold its Canadian operation in 1988. Also, Mercantile has 14 freestanding beauty parlors and a joint partnership in six shopping malls.

Mercantile offers a fairly wide assortment of merchandise. It markets both private label and name-brand goods. It is gradually edging into higher-quality merchandise. Most of Mercantile's stores are suburban rather than downtown, and the suburban stores accounted for 92% of sales.

Mercantile's strategy is to expand and upgrade existing stores and to add new stores. It is totally remodeling and reallocating space at about ten stores a year. Also, its plans call for four new stores to be opened in the next few years. In order to cut overhead, Mercantile is installing a new computer system in all its stores. Mercantile is not as heavily leveraged as most department stores and can finance a large portion of its remodeling, expansion and computerization by means of a strong cash flow.

Management controls about 40% and institutions about 40% of the common shares. Mercantile has paid consecutive cash dividends since 1940. Mercantile paid a 150% stock dividend in 1983 and another 150% stock dividend in 1987.

Total assets: $1.6 billion
Current ratio: 6.1
Common shares outstanding: 36.8 million

	1982	1983	1984	1985	1986	1987	1988	1989	1990	1991
REVENUES (MIL.)	1,269	1,428	1,626	1,707	1,880	2,028	2,156	2,266	2,313	2,367
NET INCOME (MIL.)	58	70	83	85	102	111	130	144	130	124
EARNINGS PER SHARE	1.57	1.90	2.26	2.30	2.78	3.01	3.52	3.92	3.54	3.36
DIVIDEND PER SHARE	.27	.32	.40	.46	.51	.58	.68	.78	.89	.96
PRICES　Hi	19.5	30.3	23.6	31.3	46.9	53.4	46.5	50.5	45.4	42.5
Lo	8.5	15.9	16.1	21.9	29.1	30.6	34.8	37.5	24.3	26.8

Merchants Bank of New York

434 Broadway
New York, New York 10013
Tel. (212) 669-6600
Listed: NASDAQ
Investor contact: Chairman, Spencer B. Witty
Ticker symbol: MBNY
S&P rating: A

Merchants Bank of New York

Merchants Bank of New York and its six branches provide commercial banking services in Manhattan. It offers the usual banking services such as checking and thrift accounts, certificates of deposit, and money market accounts. It provides commercial and installment loans.

Founded in 1874 as Markel Brothers Private Bankers, Merchants primarily serves small to medium-sized businesses and individuals. In its early history, Merchants catered to the diamond, jewelry, and watch trades. These businesses still account for 36% of Merchant's loans and 25% of its deposits. Also, Merchant's is a depository for the U.S. Government, the State of New York, and the City of New York.

Merchant's has an FDIC-insured money market fund that attracts outside funds and a Personal Loan Department which offers quick action on billpayer, vacation, and low-cost auto loans. Likewise, Merchants offers lease security accounts for landlords, whereby the bank holds the tenants' security deposits and keeps the owner's records.

In early 1991, consistent with its strong conservative policy, Merchants increased its holdings of U.S. Government securities to $178 million. Over 55% of the investment securities held by the bank are those of the U.S. Government and federal agencies.

In 1990, loans of $301.9 million were divided as follows: commercial, 95.2%; installment, 3.4%; and mortgage, 1.4%. Deposits of $564.3 million were divided as follows: time, 42.1%; demand, 35.2%; money market, 20.4%; and savings, 2.3%.

Revenues of $61.0 million were divided as follows: interest on fees and loans, 54.0%; investment securities, 35.3%; service fees, 7.3%; deposits, 1.6%; and other interest, 1.8%.

Merchants has paid consecutive cash dividends since 1932. Officers and directors control more than 15% of the common shares. Merchants has no long term debt or senior securities. It paid 10% stock dividends in 1980, 1981, 1982, 1983, 1984, and 1985. It paid a 20% stock dividend in 1987, a 25% stock dividend in 1988, and a 50% stock dividend in 1990.

Total assets: $671.4 million
Common shares outstanding: 4.7 million

		1981	1982	1983	1984	1985	1986	1987	1988	1989	1990
NET INCOME (MIL.)		3.7	4.3	4.7	5.4	6.7	5.4	9.2	10	11	8.1
EARNINGS PER SHARE		1.49	1.72	1.89	2.17	2.69	3.38	3.73	4.17	4.22	3.25
DIVIDEND PER SHARE		.28	.30	.33	.37	.40	.45	.51	.63	1.43	1.50
PRICES	Hi	—	17.8	26.0	30.3	51.0	70.3	107.8	136.0	110.0	68.6
	Lo	—	13.9	11.8	27.5	30.3	47.2	67.2	90.7	62.6	42.0

Merck & Co., Inc.
126 East Lincoln Avenue
Rahway, New Jersey 07065
Tel. (908) 594-4000
Listed: NYSE

Investor contact: Director Investor Relations, Gary L. Sender
Ticker symbol: MRK
S&P rating: A+

Merck is both the world's largest and its premier pharmaceutical firm with over 7,000 salesmen worldwide. Merck is not a household name because it is predominantly an ethical (prescription) drug manufacturer. Recently, Merck entered into an arrangement with Johnson & Johnson whereby Johnson & Johnson will market over-the-counter drugs developed by Merck.

The strengths of Merck are strong management, a superb international marketing system, and an excellent balance sheet. Merck is a leader in both human and animal pharmaceuticals. Drugs developed since 1984 represent about 52% of Merck's total sales. Excellent earnings are being produced by Vasotec (a cardiovascular medication), Mevacor (a cholesterol-lowering drug), Primaxin (an antibiotic), Pepcid (an ulcer agent), and Ivermectin (an antiparasitic for cattle).

Merck's strategy for success is research and development. Merck spends over 10% of gross sales a year and employs almost 5,000 people in research. Merck has a large number of pharmaceuticals wending their way through the FDA regulatory process. One of the more promising ones is Prosear, which is designed to treat enlargement of the prostate.

The specialty chemicals segment consists of Calgon Corp. and Kelco. Calgon Corp. is engaged in water purification, and Kelco is involved in the manufacture of paints, paper, food additives, and cleaning products.

In 1990, Merck entered into a joint pharmaceutical agreement with DuPont. The combined efforts are expected to yield over $700 million in sales the first year.

In 1990, human and animal health products represented 92% of sales and 97% of profits, and specialty chemicals represented 8% of sales and 3% of profits.

In February 1991, Merck announced that it would repurchase up to $1 billion worth of its common shares. No specific amount of time to complete the program has been disclosed.

Merck has paid consecutive cash dividends since 1939. It paid a 100% stock dividend in 1986 and a 200% stock dividend in 1988.

Total assets: $8.0 billion
Current ratio: 1.3
Common shares outstanding: 386.6 million

	1981	1982	1983	1984	1985	1986	1987	1988	1989	1990
REVENUES (MIL.)	2,929	3,063	3,246	3,560	3,548	4,129	5,061	5,939	6,550	7,672
NET INCOME (MIL.)	398	415	451	493	540	676	906	1,207	1,495	1,781
EARNINGS PER SHARE	.89	.94	1.02	1.12	1.26	1.62	2.23	3.05	3.78	4.56
DIVIDEND PER SHARE	.44	.47	.48	.51	.55	.67	.90	1.38	1.72	2.02
PRICES Hi	17.3	14.8	17.5	16.4	23.0	43.3	74.4	59.6	80.8	91.1
Lo	12.8	10.8	13.6	13.0	15.0	22.5	40.8	48.0	56.3	67.0

NBD Bancorp, Inc.

611 Woodward Avenue
Detroit, Michigan 48226
Tel. (313) 225-1000
Listed: NYSE
Investor contact: Second V.P. M. Renee Ahee
Ticker symbol: NBD
S&P rating: A

NBD Bancorp is the holding company for NBD Bank, formerly National Bank of Detroit. NBD Bank is a large, consistently profitable bank, which in recent years has expanded largely by acquisitions within Michigan and out of state in Illinois, Indiana, Ohio and Florida.

NBD Bank was formed in 1990 by the consolidation of a 17 subsidiary banks in Michigan, the largest of which was the National Bank of Detroit, established in 1933. During 1990, NBD Bancorp acquired three failed thrift institutions and in October 1991 acquired FNW Bankcorp, a $1.4 billion asset holding company for eight banks in Illinois. In early 1992, NBD Bancorp will complete the acquisition of Gainer Corporation, a $1.5 billion asset one-bank holding company for the Gainer Bank National Association of Gary, Indiana.

NBD is a conservative bank with a large stake in lower-yielding government bonds. Its problem loans are less than 2% of total loans, a ratio much below that of competing banks. The Michigan-based core bank (NBD Bank) contributes over 80% of total earnings. NBD has an excellent balance between corporate and retail customers. Its loan quality is superb.

NBD has nine nonbank subsidiaries. It has a large trust operation. It is also engaged in mortgage banking, consumer credit processing, check clearing, CIRRUS automatic teller operations, insurance, and discount brokerage operations.

In 1990, NBD's loan portfolio was broken down as follows: commercial, 56%; real estate, 17%; consumer, 20%; and international, 7%. Sources of funds were time deposits, 51%; demand deposits, 14%; savings deposits, 13%; short-term borrowings, 12%; and other, 10%.

NBD has paid consecutive cash dividends since 1935. Institutions control over 45% of the outstanding common shares. It declared a two-for-one split in 1985, and three-for-two splits in 1986, 1989, and 1992.

Total assets: $26.8 billion
Common shares outstanding: 109.5 million

		1981	1982	1983	1984	1985	1986	1987	1988	1989	1990
NET INCOME (MIL.)		65	82	82	95	118	146	162	227	259	275
EARNINGS PER SHARE		.79	.99	1.00	1.17	1.42	1.72	1.54	2.14	2.39	2.50
DIVIDEND PER SHARE		.23	.31	.32	.43	.30	.47	.53	.61	.75	.89
PRICES	Hi	4.3	4.7	6.7	7.7	11.9	16.7	17.9	17.7	23.6	23.9
	Lo	3.3	2.9	4.3	5.9	7.4	11.1	11.4	13.4	16.1	16.2

NCNB Corporation
One NCNB Plaza
Charlotte, North Carolina 28255
Tel. (704) 374-5000
Listed: NYSE
Investor contact: Senior V.P., Russell J. Page

Ticker symbol: NCB
S&P rating: A

Originally the North Carolina National Bank, NCNB has, through numerous acquisitions, become the largest superregional bank in the Southeast.

NCNB Corporation

NCNB has more than 900 full-service banking offices in North Carolina, South Carolina, Florida, Maryland, Virginia, and Texas. It closed its bank in Atlanta, Georgia, and moved it to North Carolina.

NCNB, which originally took a 20% interest in the failed First Republic Bank of Texas, then raised it to a 49% interest, purchased the remaining 51% from the Federal Deposit Insurance Corporation in 1989. The NCNB–Texas National Bank is the largest banking enterprise in Texas, and it is proving itself to be a very profitable one. The FDIC agreed to assume an unlimited number of bad loans in 1989 and up to $750 million in bad loans in 1990. In mid-1990, NCNB acquired the nine failing banks of San Antonio–based National Bancshares Corp. of Texas.

In mid-1991, NCNB announced a merger agreement with C&S/Sovran, forming the new NationsBank with $118 billion in assets and 1,900 full-service banking offices in nine states and the District of Columbia. NCNB agreed to exchange 0.84 shares of NCNB stock for each share of C&S/Sovran. NationsBank will be the third largest in the United States, behind Citicorp and the new Chemical Bank. The combined entity will have market capitalization of about $6.8 billion, ranking it behind only J. P. Morgan and BankAmerica. The new bank will be headquartered in Charlotte, North Carolina. The NationsBank franchise extends from Maryland to Florida and west to Tennessee and Texas. Dilutions because of the stock swap will be reduced by the elimination of administrative and back-office redundancies and the consolidation of overlapping offices. The consolidation will result in cost savings of $350 million and a loss of 4,800 to 6,000 jobs.

Institutions control about 50% of the outstanding common shares. NCNB has paid consecutive cash dividends since 1903. NCNB paid a 100% stock dividend in 1986.

197

Total assets: $65.3 billion
Common shares outstanding: 115.3 million

		1981	1982	1983	1984	1985	1986	1987	1988	1989	1990
NET INCOME (MIL.)		55	76	92	119	164	199	167	252	447	366
EARNINGS PER SHARE		1.33	1.59	1.84	2.04	2.30	2.53	2.03	2.90	4.62	3.40
DIVIDEND PER SHARE		.41	.46	.52	.59	.69	.78	.86	.94	1.10	1.42
PRICES	Hi	9.0	10.4	14.9	18.3	23.6	27.8	29.1	29.3	55.0	47.3
	Lo	6.5	5.9	9.3	11.5	16.9	20.0	15.5	17.5	27.0	16.9

National Medical Enterprises, Inc.

2700 Colorado Avenue
Santa Monica, California 90404
Tel. (213) 315-8000
Listed: NYSE
Investor contact: Sr. V.P. Investor Relations, Paul J. Russell
Ticker symbol: NME
S&P rating: A-

National Medical Enterprises is one of America's leading hospital management companies. Currently it operates 35 acute-care and 115 specialty hospitals, which provide psychiatric care, substance-abuse treatment, and physical rehabilitation.

In January 1990, it spun off to Hillhaven 86% of its nursing home subsidiary, including 104 of its 227 long-term care nursing homes. It leased the remaining nursing homes to Hillhaven with an option for Hillhaven to purchase them at a later date. Essentially, National Medical Enterprises has interests in three types of hospitals: acute-care hospitals, specialty hospitals, and long-term nursing homes. Its long-term strategy is to pare down its acute-care (general) hospitals and its nursing homes and expand its much more profitable specialty hospital operations. Its specialty hospitals consist of 86 psychiatric and 29 rehabilitative hospitals. While about half of its operations are in California, National Medical Enterprises has facilities in more than 40 states and in England and Singapore.

Because of changes in medical insurance and improved medical technology, the occupancy rate of the acute-care hospitals has remained about 50%, whereas the occupancy rate of its specialty hospitals is about 75%, believed to be the highest in the industry. Since the spin-off of Hillhaven, returns on equity and assets have reached new highs, although revenues declined slightly as a result.

During fiscal 1991, National Medical Enterprises had 6,591 licensed beds in 35 acute-care hospitals. Medicare produced 31.8%, Medicaid 6.0%, and private payers 62.2% of acute-care hospital revenues. It had 6,953 licensed beds in 86 psychiatric and substance abuse hospitals and 2,474 licensed beds in 29 physical rehabilitation hospitals.

In 1991, acute-care hospitals provided 50% of revenues and 38% of operating profits; specialty hospitals 46% of revenues and 55% of operating profits; and lease and other income (nursing homes) 4% of operating revenues and 7% of operating profits.

National Medical Enterprises paid consecutive and annually increased cash dividends since 1973. Institutions control over 65% of the outstanding common shares. National Medical Enterprises paid a 25% stock dividend in 1983 and a 100% stock dividend in 1991.

Total assets: $4.1 billion
Current ratio: 1.6
Common shares outstanding: 157.4 million

		1982	1983	1984	1985	1986	1987	1988	1989	1990	1991
REVENUES (MIL.)		1,019	1,531	1,756	2,190	2,577	2,881	3,202	3,676	3,935	3,806
NET INCOME (MIL.)		76	92	115	144	117	141	170	193	242	277
EARNINGS PER SHARE		.60	.66	.77	.94	.74	.92	1.15	1.29	1.52	1.73
DIVIDEND PER SHARE		.16	.19	.22	.25	.28	.30	.32	.34	.36	.40
PRICES	Hi	11.9	16.2	12.8	16.4	13.4	15.4	12.4	19.5	20.1	25.8
	Lo	4.9	10.1	8.8	9.4	9.6	8.1	8.8	10.7	14.6	12.6

National Service Industries, Inc.

1420 Peachtree Street N.E.
Atlanta, Georgia 30309
Tel. (404) 892-2400
Listed: NYSE
Investor contact: Chairman, Erwin Zaban
Ticker symbol: NSI
S&P rating: A+

As profiled in its 1990 Annual Report, "National Service Industries, Inc., is a diversified manufacturing and service company with operations in seven industries. Its three core businesses—lighting equipment, textile rental, and specialty chemicals—account for more than three-fourths of revenues and operating profits. The companies that form NSI are strong competitors in their markets, holding leading positions or special niches.

"NSI's balanced diversification has resulted in a record of consistent growth and profitability. The company has reported increased income and earnings per share in 28 of the last 29 years, and return on stockholders' equity has averaged 17 percent over the past ten years. Dividends have been paid without a decrease every year since 1937. The company is virtually debt free. NSI ranked 255th in sales among the largest U.S. industrial companies in the latest Fortune 500 list. Headquartered in Atlanta, NSI employs 21,800 people and operates in all 50 states.

"Lithonia Lighting is the nation's largest manufacturer of lighting equipment. The company's nine product groups include fluorescent fixtures; high-intensity discharge fixtures; outdoor lighting; downlighting; track lighting; vandal-resistant fixtures; emergency lighting; lighting and dimming controls; and manufactured wiring systems.

"National Linen Service, NSI's original business, serves four markets: linen supply (restaurants and lodging), healthcare (hospitals, clinics, and nursing homes), industrial (uniforms and shop towels), and dust control (mats and mops).

"The Chemical Division, which includes Zep Manufacturing Company, Selig Chemical Industries, Zep Manufacturing Company of Canada and National Chemical, is a leading producer of specialty chemicals for maintenance, sanitation, and water treatment."

Other operations are insulation (North Bros. Co.), envelopes (Atlantic Envelope Company), records storage and filing systems (ATENCO), carpet merchandising (Marketing Services Division), and men's apparel (Block Industries).

In 1991, lighting equipment accounted for 41% of revenues and 28% of profits, textile rental for 27% of revenues and 35% of profits, chemicals for 15% of revenues and 29% of profits, and other sources 17% of revenues and 8% of profits.

National Service Industries paid a 33⅓% stock dividend in 1983, a 50% stock dividend in 1984, a 33⅓% stock dividend in 1986, and a 50% stock dividend in 1987.

Total assets: $962 million
Current ratio: 4.3
Common shares outstanding: 49.6 million

	1982	1983	1984	1985	1986	1987	1988	1989	1990	1991
REVENUES (MIL.)	885	936	1,073	1,191	1,283	1,327	1,414	1,540	1,648	1,602
NET INCOME (MIL.)	51	55	62	68	71	76	86	95	100	32
EARNINGS PER SHARE	1.02	1.12	1.25	1.37	1.45	1.54	1.75	1.92	2.02	.65
DIVIDEND PER SHARE	.36	.39	.43	.49	.54	.62	.73	.82	.90	.95
PRICES　Hi	9.5	14.4	14.9	19.8	26.5	28.6	24.5	30.4	28.8	28.3
Lo	5.8	8.9	10.5	13.4	19.4	16.5	18.3	21.4	22.1	19.0

Neutrogena Corporation

5760 West 96th Street
Los Angeles, California 90045
Tel. (213) 642-1150
Listed: NASDAQ
Investor contact: V.P. Treas. Dasha Lewin
Ticker symbol: NGNA
S&P rating: A-

Neutrogena Corporation, headquartered in Los Angeles, manufactures and sells high-quality, premium-priced specialty skin care and hair care

Neutrogena Corporation

products. While Neutrogena's products are directed toward an upscale market, they are mass merchandised in drug stores, convenience food stores, and other retail outlets in the United States and countries throughout the world.

Neutrogena soaps are mild and translucent. The soaps are manufactured for individual skin types. There are both scented and nonscented formulations. They are marketed under such names as Neutrogena Original Formula, Dry Skin Formula, Baby Cleansing Formula, Oily Skin Formula, and Cleansing Bar for Acne-prone skin.

Once again Neutrogena's specialty skin-care products are formulated for individual skin types, they include products such as Liquid Neutrogena. Neutrogena Norwegian Formula Hand Cream, Neutrogena Natural Sesame Body Oil, Neutrogena Moisture, Neutrogena Acne Mask, Neutrogena Body Lotion, and Neutrogena Eye Cream. Also, Neutrogena skin-care products division markets a prescription product Melanex Topical Solution for the removal of dark skin spots.

Hair-care products play an increasing role in Neutrogena's operations. Hair-care items include Neutrogena Shampoo, Neutrogena Conditioner, Neutrogena Shampoo for Permed and Color Treated Hair, Neutrogena Conditioner for Permed and Color Treated Hair, and various Neutrogena T/Gel formulas for the treatment of dandruff, psoriasis, and seborrheic dermatitis of the scalp.

International operations account for 15% of sales. In 1990, skin-care products accounted for 70% and hair-care products for 30% of sales. Neutrogena has increasingly targeted skin-care products as offering the greatest opportunity for future growth.

Neutrogena has no long-term debt. The Cotsen family controls 44% of the common shares. Consecutive cash dividends have been paid since 1976. Neutrogena paid a 100% stock dividend in 1981, a 10% stock dividend in 1982, a 100% stock dividend in 1984, a 50% stock dividend in 1985, a 50% stock dividend in 1986, a 50% stock dividend in 1987, a 50% stock dividend in 1988, and a 25% stock dividend in 1989.

Total assets: $132.1 million
Current ratio: 2.1
Common shares outstanding: 26.8 million

	1982	1983	1984	1985	1986	1987	1988	1989	1990	1991
REVENUES (MIL.)	39	46	59	75	96	135	179	203	210	231
NET INCOME (MIL.)	3.1	3.2	4.2	6.2	8.1	15	23	27	17	21
EARNINGS PER SHARE	.11	.12	.16	.24	.30	.55	.85	1.00	.65	.80
DIVIDEND PER SHARE	.09	.02	.02	.03	.04	.06	.11	.16	.20	.20
PRICES Hi	2.8	3.3	6.1	10.0	15.5	29.6	35.6	29.8	29.3	27.5
Lo	2.0	2.3	2.9	5.0	7.4	11.6	18.3	20.8	10.0	10.5

New England Business Service, Inc.

500 Main Street
Groton, Massachusetts 01471
Tel. (508) 448-6111
Listed: NASDAQ
Investor contact: Treas. Thomas W. Freeze
Ticker symbol: NEBS
S&P rating: A

New England Business Service (NEBS) designs, manufactures, and sells business forms and related printed products to small businesses in the United States, Canada, and the United Kingdom. NEBS usually focuses on businesses with 20 or fewer employees. It is almost exclusively a mail-order operation, so its geographic distribution is very wide. The company generates about 60,000 orders a week. NEBS sends out millions of catalogs and advertising circulars to existing and potential customers.

> **New England Business Service, Inc.**

NEBS spends a great deal of money on market and product research. In 1990, it introduced some 100 new products. It targets potential customers by occupational classification: for example proprietors of gas stations, fuel-oil dealers, dentists, attorneys, and physicians.

The company's products include more than 600 items such as continuous forms, standardized forms, check-writing systems, and forms holders. Through mail order and a toll-free telephone number, NEBS serves more than a million customers. More than three million orders a year are shipped, generally within six days of receipt.

During 1989, NEBS sold its Devoke Company subsidiary, because Devoke did not fit the company's commitment to small businesses and the business-forms market.

Officers and directors control about 25% and institutions about 70% of the common shares. NEBS has paid consecutive quarterly cash dividends since 1965. It paid a 50% stock dividend in 1981, a 100% stock dividend in 1983, and a 100% stock dividend in 1986.

Total assets: $134 million
Current ratio: 3.6
Common shares outstanding: 16.4 million

	1982	1983	1984	1985	1986	1987	1988	1989	1990	1991
REVENUES (MIL.)	92	103	127	143	159	173	202	226	233	232
NET INCOME (MIL.)	7.6	9.7	13	13	17	19	22	22	21	20
EARNINGS PER SHARE	.45	.57	.77	.76	.99	1.12	1.30	1.29	1.26	1.24
DIVIDEND PER SHARE	.16	.18	.22	.25	.29	.44	.54	.66	.76	.80
PRICES Hi	9.6	17.5	17.5	17.0	30.3	26.8	27.5	23.8	19.8	20.3
Lo	6.1	9.5	13.4	11.6	15.5	16.8	19.5	17.0	10.5	12.3

New York Times Company

229 W. 43rd Street
New York, New York 10036
Tel. (212) 556-1234
Listed: AMEX
Investor contact: Director of Corporate and Public Affairs, Nancy Nielson
Ticker symbol: NYT
S&P rating: A

The *New York Times* has been printing "all the news that's fit to print" since 1851. Not only does it publish the *Times* but also 26 smaller-city daily newspapers, six weekly newspapers, and 17 magazines. It also owns five TV stations, one radio station, and a substantial interest in three Canadian and newsprint mills and one in Maine.

The flagship *New York Times* has 1.15 million daily and 1.7 million Sunday circulation. It circulates in 50 states and 66 foreign countries. The *New York Times* has eight satellite printing plants across the United States, and page images are beamed by satellite from New York to these eight plants. However, 70% of *New York Times* circulation is confined to New York City and its suburbs.

𝕮𝖍𝖊 𝕹𝖊𝖜 𝖄𝖔𝖗𝖐 𝕮𝖎𝖒𝖊𝖘

Its daily newspapers, except for one in California and one in Maine, are based primarily in rapidly growing cities of the Southeast. Of its 17 magazines, *Family Circle* with six million circulation and *McCalls*, purchased in 1989, are the best known. Its T.V. stations are located in Pennsylvania, Illinois, Alabama, Tennessee, and Arkansas.

$420 million cash from the sale of a cable TV franchise has been used for both debt reduction and re-investment in plant and acquisition.

In 1990, the New York Times Company sold three newspapers in Kentucky and Tennessee. Its color printing plant in Edison, New Jersey is scheduled to come on line in early 1992.

In 1990, newspapers provided 77%, magazines 19%, and broadcasting 4% of revenues.

There are two classes of common stock, Class A and Class B shares. The founding Ochs family holds 85% of the Class B shares and thus controls the company. Consecutive cash dividends have been paid on the A and B shares since 1958. The New York Times Company paid a 200% stock dividend in 1983 and a 100% stock dividend in 1986.

Total assets: $2.2 billion
Current ratio: 0.8
Common shares outstanding: Class A 76.8 million
Class B 440.5 thousand

	1981	1982	1983	1984	1985	1986	1987	1988	1989	1990
REVENUES (MIL.)	840	925	1,091	1,230	1,394	1,565	1,690	1,700	1,769	1,777
NET INCOME (MIL.)	50	54	79	100	116	132	160	161	68	65
EARNINGS PER SHARE	.67	.72	1.01	1.27	1.45	1.63	1.96	2.00	.87	.85
DIVIDEND PER SHARE	.18	.20	.22	.25	.29	.33	.40	.46	.50	.54
PRICES Hi	6.5	9.6	15.4	19.5	25.5	42.0	49.6	32.8	34.6	27.5
Lo	4.5	5.5	9.0	10.9	17.5	23.3	24.8	24.4	24.4	16.9

Newell Co.

29 East Stephenson Street
Freeport, Illinois 61032
Tel. (815) 235-4171
Listed: NYSE
Investor contact: V.P. W. T. Alldredge
Ticker symbol: NWL
S&P rating: A

The newell Group. Illinois-based Newell Co. is a combination of houseware, hardware, industrial packaging, and closure businesses. Its very strong management acquires, restructures, and rapidly assimilates companies into its own operations. Newell's major acquisition was its 1987 purchase of Anchor Hocking for $332 million. Anchor Hocking is a major producer of glassware, hardware, packaging, and plastic products.

Through its Amerok division, Newell markets cabinet, window, and bath hardware. Also Newell, through its Mirro/Foley unit, manufactures aluminum cookware, bakeware, and kitchen utensils. Through such branded products as Mirro, Wearever, and Rena, Newell controls about 50% of the North American market for aluminum cookware.

Newell Window Furnishings makes and markets drapery hardware, window shades, and blinds. A new product, Spectrim Blinds, makes use of a machine that allows retailers such as J.C. Penney to provide customers with cut-to-measure blinds. Newell controls a minimum of 30% of the domestic market for cabinet and window hardware. The Anchor Hocking division manufactures and sells table-top glassware, oven bakeware, and plastic microwave cookware. The EZ Painter division controls about 25% of the domestic market for paint brushes and rollers. Also, Newell makes and markets propane Bernz-Omatic torches and Counselor bath scales. Newell distributes its products widely through discount, variety, hardware, and houseware stores and through chain home-improvement stores.

Newell's industrial products division consists primarily of packaging and closures. Its 1989 purchase of the closure business of Owen

Illinois put Newell into the forefront of the packaging industry. It is now a major contender in tamper-proof packaging for the pharmaceutical industry.

In 1990, hardware and housewares provided 75% of sales and 79% of profits and industrial products provided 25% of sales and 21% of profits.

Consecutive cash dividends have been paid since 1946. Institutions control about 60% of the outstanding common shares. Newell paid a 100% stock dividend in 1983, a 100% stock dividend in 1988, and a 100% stock dividend in 1989.

Total assets: $871 million
Current ratio: 2.1
Common shares outstanding: 59.6 million

	1981	1982	1983	1984	1985	1986	1987	1988	1989	1990
REVENUES (MIL.)	170	178	237	308	350	401	720	988	1,123	1,073
NET INCOME (MIL.)	10	8	13	14	19	24	37	61	85	101
EARNINGS PER SHARE	.38	.34	.38	.41	.53	.55	.69	1.09	1.41	1.67
DIVIDEND PER SHARE	.11	.13	.13	.13	.13	.19	.21	.28	.43	.50
PRICES Hi	2.5	4.0	5.9	4.5	5.8	9.3	10.8	14.9	25.3	35.5
Lo	1.5	1.6	3.4	3.4	3.9	5.3	5.4	6.9	12.8	17.8

Nordstrom, Inc.

1501 Fifth Avenue
Seattle, Washington 98101-1603
Tel. (206) 628-2111
Listed: NASDAQ
Investor contact: Treas. John A. Goesling
Ticker symbol: NOBE
S&P rating: A+

As profiled in its 1991 Annual Report, "Nordstrom is a fashion specialty retailer offering a wide selection of fine quality apparel, shoes, and accessories for men, women, and children. The company was founded by John W. Nordstrom in 1901, in Seattle, Washington. Today, Nordstrom

Nordstrom, Inc.

operates 46 large specialty stores in Washington, Oregon, California, Utah, Alaska, and New Jersey; five smaller specialty stores (Plate Two fashion shops); 12 clearance stores (Nordstrom Rack discount stores); and leased shoe departments in 11 department stores in Hawaii. Managed by the third generation of the family, Nordstrom remains committed to its founding principles of quality, selection, value, and service.

"Nordstrom has experienced tremendous growth since its establishment in 1901. Then a single shoe store with just two employees, the company now has approximately 30,000 employees—the majority of whom work on the sales floor.

"Because of their sheer number and critical role in the company, salespeople are second in importance only to customers in the Nordstrom organizational structure. This system of management resembles an inverted pyramid, with customers—who always come first—at the top, immediately followed by salespeople and support staff. The next level of the pyramid include department managers, store managers, buyers, regional managers, and the Board of Directors. The sales staff holds this prominent position because they are closest to the customers, and are therefore largely responsible for the company's ongoing success."

Nordstrom is one of the nation's premier upscale department stores catering to middle and upper-income clientele. Nordstrom is noted for its wide apparel selection and its excellent customer service.

In 1991, Nordstrom opened new stores in Oak Brook, Illinois, Riverside, California; Edison, New Jersey; and Bethesda, Maryland.

In 1991, women's apparel represented 39% of sales; women's accessories, 20%; shoes, 19%; men's apparel and furnishings, 16%; children's apparel and accessories, 4%; and other, 2% of sales.

Except for 1990 and 1991, Nordstrom increased earnings every year since going public in 1971. The Nordstrom family controls about 39% and institutions about 40% of the common shares. Nordstrom paid a 100% stock dividend in 1983, a 100% stock dividend in 1986, and a 100% stock dividend in 1987.

Total assets: $1.9 billion
Current ratio: 2.0
Common shares outstanding: 81.7 million

	1982	1983	1984	1985	1986	1987	1988	1989	1990	1991
REVENUES (MIL.)	512	599	769	959	1,302	1,630	1,920	2,238	2,671	2,894
NET INCOME (MIL.)	25	27	40	41	50	73	93	123	115	116
EARNINGS PER SHARE	.35	.38	.54	.54	.65	.91	1.13	1.51	1.41	1.42
DIVIDEND PER SHARE	.055	.063	.07	.10	.11	.13	.18	.22	.28	.30
PRICES Hi	6.5	11.6	9.8	13.3	25.6	40.8	34.0	42.5	39.3	53.0
Lo	2.5	5.9	6.8	7.1	11.9	15.8	19.8	29.8	17.3	22.0

Old Kent Financial Corporation

One Vandenberg Center
Grand Rapids, Michigan 49503
Tel. (616) 771-5000
Listed: NASDAQ
Investor contact: Vice Chairman & Treas. B. P. Sherwood III
Ticker symbol: OKEN
S&P rating: A+

As described in its 1990 Annual Report, "Old Kent Financial Corporation is a bank holding company headquartered in Grand Rapids, Michigan, with total assets of $8.2 billion. Old Kent is engaged in the business of commercial banking and related services through its 19 banking subsidiaries and 4 non-banking subsidiaries. Old Kent's principal markets for financial services are communities within Michigan and Illinois, where its 200 banking offices are located."

> **Old Kent Financial Corporation**

During 1990, Old Kent acquired the St. Charles Federal Savings Association in St. Charles, Illinois, from the Resolution Trust Corp. In 1991, it acquired six branches of the First Federal Savings Bank & Trust of Pontiac, Michigan.

Old Kent has streamlined its 182 banking offices in Michigan for reciprocal banking. This means that a customer can do business with any Old Kent banking office as his account is available on computer line. In addition to Michigan and Illinois, Old Kent is weighing acquisition possibilities in Indiana, Ohio, and Wisconsin.

In a July, 1989 Olson Research Associates study, Old Kent Financial was ranked the top bank holding company in the United States. Holding companies were ranked by a complex formula that included 125 evaluations of profitability, safety, soundness, and the ability to generate sustained above-average earnings.

Income for 1990 came from interest on fees and loans, 66%; interest on investment securities, 18%; interest on deposits, 3%; other interest income, 1%; trust income, 4%; and other non-interest income, 8%.

Old Kent called its Series A Convertible Preferred Stock for redemption on April 1, 1990, and at the same time authorized the purchase of its common stock, not to exceed $50 million. "The purpose of the stock repurchase program is to acquire shares of common stock to be issued to holders of the preferred stock upon conversion."

1990 marked the 18th consecutive year that Old Kent has increased net income and dividends. Consecutive cash dividends have been paid on the common stock since 1937. Old Kent paid a 5% stock dividend in 1980, a 5% stock dividend in 1981, a 50% stock dividend in 1984, and a 50% stock dividend in 1986.

Total assets: $8.2 billion
Common shares outstanding: 26.6 million

		1981	1982	1983	1984	1985	1986	1987	1988	1989	1990
NET INCOME (MIL.)		20	23	32	45	49	61	63	77	86	88
EARNINGS PER SHARE		1.22	1.35	1.69	2.33	2.55	2.69	2.76	2.95	3.23	3.29
DIVIDEND PER SHARE		.43	.45	.47	.54	.68	.75	.82	.96	1.09	
PRICES	Hi	5.9	7.1	10.9	15.5	26.0	26.6	26.9	25.1	29.6	28.9
	Lo	4.9	4.8	6.4	9.3	14.6	20.9	18.0	18.6	22.4	18.3

PNC Financial Corp.
Fifth Avenue & Wood Street
Pittsburgh, Pennsylvania 15222
Tel. (412) 762-2666
Listed: NYSE
Investor contact: V.P. Sheila S. Fischl

Ticker symbol: PNC
S&P rating: B+

PNC Financial is the product of a 1983 merger of Pittsburgh National Corp. and Provident National Corp. Since the merger, PNC has acquired some 23 commercial banking subsidiaries including Northeastern Bancorp, Marine Bancorp, Hershey Bank, Citizen's Fidelity Bank, Central Bancorp, and the Bank of Delaware. PNC subsidiary banks have more than 510 banking offices in Pennsylvania, New Jersey, Delaware, Ohio, Kentucky, and southern Indiana.

PNC FINANCIAL

Additional wholesale banking offices are operated in 19 states and nine foreign countries.

PNC has an increasing stream of earnings from nonbanking sources such as trust, money management, and credit card processing. Its trust operation manages over $80 billion. It has a family of mutual funds with more than $19 billion under management. It has an investment banking division which services medium-sized companies in raising capital.

In early 1991, PNC acquired from the Resolution Trust Corp. $2.4 million of performing assets of the Pittsburgh-based First Federal Savings & Loan. Also in 1991, PNC acquired the $695 million asset, Erie-based, First National Pennsylvania Corp. for $80 million in stock.

In 1990, earnings assets of $42.5 billion were divided as follows: commercial loans, 36%; consumer loans, 15%; real estate loans, 13%; foreign loans, 1%; investment securities, 32%; and other investments, 3%.

In 1990, sources of funds of $28.8 billion were divided as follows: demand and savings deposits, 26%; time deposits, 42%; short-term borrowing, 22%; equity, 6%; and other, 4%.

Consecutive cash dividends have been paid by the predecessor banking companies since 1860. A 100% stock dividend was paid in 1985.

Total assets: $4.5 billion
Common shares outstanding: 95.8 million

	1981	1982	1983	1984	1985	1986	1987	1988	1989	1990
NET INCOME (MIL.)	57	62	117	143	188	286	256	443	377	71
EARNINGS PER SHARE	2.32	2.49	2.83	3.26	3.88	4.44	3.00	5.09	3.98	.73
DIVIDEND PER SHARE	.81	.91	1.01	1.11	1.28	1.47	1.64	1.83	2.06	2.12
PRICES Hi	14.1	18.9	23.1	23.5	35.6	51.0	51.0	46.5	49.0	44.1
Lo	11.0	11.5	15.8	18.1	22.9	34.9	33.3	36.5	38.5	15.8

Pall Corporation

2200 Northern Boulevard
East Hills, New York 11548
Tel. (516) 484-5400
Listed: AMEX
Investor contact: Director Investment Communications, Marcia A. Fulton
Ticker symbol: PLL
S&P rating: A+

Pall Corporation, founded by Dr. David B. Pall in 1946, is the leading fluid filtration manufacturer in the world. Pall manufactures filters for the removal of contaminants from liquids and gasses. Pall's products are used in the health-care, aeropower (includes aerospace, military, and fluid power), and fluid processing industries.

Large manufacturing facilities are located in New York, Florida, Puerto Rico, and the United Kingdom. Smaller facilities are located in Connecticut and California. Pall also manufactures in Japan and has facilities in Korea.

Pall's health-care segment is its largest and fastest growing. In this segment, Pall markets a wide variety of biomedical filters used for the protection of patients during blood transfusions, surgical procedures, and the administration of breathing gasses and intravenous fluids. In 1990, Pall entered into an agreement with Cutter Biological, a division of Miles, Inc., under which Pall's leukocyte-depleting blood-transfusion filters are combined with Cutter's disposable blood-processing products, including blood bags, tubing, and connectors, and marketing to the blood banking community. Also included in Pall's health-care segment are filters used in the manufacture of pharmaceuticals, food, and beverages, as well as filter media used in the diagnostics industry.

For the aeropower market, Pall manufactures lube oil, hydraulic oil, fuel and air filters for manufacturers of military and commercial airframes and engines, combat vehicles, and vessels. Also included in this segment are industrial customers such as those which manufacture or use fluid power equipment in steel, paper, plastic, automobile, and other manufacturing.

Pall's fluid processing business involves the removal of contaminants from liquids and gasses in the manufacture of microelectronic components, magnetic or optical recording and transmission tape, film, fiber, paint, chemicals, petrochemicals, gas, oil, and electric power.

In 1990, health-care sales accounted for 38% of total revenues and 47% of operating profits. Aeropower represented 34% of sales and 35% of operating profits, and fluid processing accounted for 28% of sales and 18% of operating profits. Pall has duplicate manufacturing facilities in the United States and England. In addition to serving as a dual source of supply to its customers, this benefits Pall by reducing the risk of currency fluctuation and guarding against protectionism of the U.S. and European communities. Approximately 60% of Pall's revenues are derived from outside the United States.

About 8.0% of Pall's outstanding common shares are owned by directors, and institutions hold about 55%. Pall has increased earnings for 20 consecutive years and has paid consecutive cash dividends since 1974. Since 1981, Pall has paid stock dividends as follows: 33⅓% in 1982, 50% in 1985, 33⅓ in 1986, 50% in February of 1991, and 50% in December 1991.

Total assets: $786 million
Current ratio: 1.6
Common shares outstanding: 87.0 million

		1981	1982	1983	1984	1985	1986	1987	1988	1989	1990
REVENUES (MIL.)		169	196	215	242	276	332	390	434	497	564
NET INCOME (MIL.)		22	25	28	31	34	41	48	57	58	66
EARNINGS PER SHARE		.28	.31	.35	.38	.42	.50	.57	.67	.67	.76
DIVIDEND PER SHARE		.06	.07	.08	.09	.10	.12	.15	.17	.21	.24
PRICES	Hi	6.6	5.8	9.3	8.6	9.0	14.9	15.5	15.7	15.2	16.6
	Lo	4.4	4.1	4.6	6.1	7.2	8.0	10.8	8.7	11.1	13.4

Pep Boys—Manny, Moe & Jack

3111 West Allegheny Avenue
Philadelphia, Pennsylvania 19132
Tel. (215) 229-9000
Listed: NYSE
Investor contact: Treas. M. J. Holden
Ticker symbol: PBY
S&P rating: A+

PEP BOYS 😃😃😃 Pep Boys is a large retail chain of automotive part and accessory stores. It also provides automotive maintenance, service, and installation of parts through its more than 310 retail shops in 16 states in the Mid-Atlantic and Southeast regions, Southern California, and the Southwest. Additional new stores are being opened in Charlotte, North Carolina, Oklahoma City, and the Texas Rio Grande. Long-term earnings growth can be attributed to a combination of expanding earnings in existing markets, increasing prices, and the constant expansion in the number of new shops.

The typical full service Pep Boys shop is about 19,500 square feet including its automotive service bays. About 80% of the stores are owned, the remainder are leased. Much of the expansion is financed with internal cash flow as well as outside borrowings. Pep Boys is increasing the number of national brands at its stores. The company employs about 10,000 people and labor costs are about 20% of sales. Sales volume varies both with the time of year and weather patterns. The company is to a certain degree recession-proof, because customers tend to retain older cars during an economic downturn.

Products are essentially the same at each store, except that inventory is varied to match the types of cars registered in a given area. During 1989, Pep Boys opened a new distribution center in Mesquite, Texas. Each store stocks more than 10,000 items. Products include tires, batteries, and new and rebuilt automotive parts such as radiators, cylinders, oil filters, belts, hoses, and brake linings. Chemicals include such items as antifreeze, coolants, polishes, and gasoline additives. Accessories include such items as seat belts, radios, alarms, mirrors, and floor mats.

About 15% of the common shares is closely held and another 55% is controlled by institutions. Pep Boys has paid consecutive cash dividends since 1950. Pep Boys paid a 6% stock dividend in 1979, a 6% stock dividend in 1980, a 6% stock dividend in 1981, a 100% stock dividend in 1982, a 200% stock dividend in 1983, a 100% stock dividend in 1985, and a 200% stock dividend in 1987.

Total assets: $8.19 million
Current ratio: 1.5
Common shares outstanding: 55.6 million

		1982	1983	1984	1985	1986	1987	1988	1989	1990	1991
REVENUES (MIL.)		233	265	306	348	389	486	554	656	799	885
NET INCOME (MIL.)		11	12	16	18	21	28	34	38	35	38
EARNINGS PER SHARE		.25	.27	.33	.39	.43	.52	.62	.68	.63	.67
DIVIDEND PER SHARE		.033	.043	.049	.059	.065	.073	.078	.09	.11	.12
PRICES	Hi	3.5	5.8	5.5	9.5	16.1	18.9	15.9	17.3	17.3	19.5
	Lo	1.6	3.1	3.9	4.9	8.5	9.5	10.4	10.5	8.5	8.4

PepsiCo, Inc.

World Headquarters
Purchase, New York 10577
Tel. (914) 253-2000
Listed: NYSE
Investor contact: V.P., Margaret D. Moore
Ticker symbol: PEP
S&P rating: A

PepsiCo is the world's second-largest producer of soft drinks, with more than 1,000 bottlers, and it is the world's largest seller of salty snacks. Basically, PepsiCo operates in three areas: soft drinks, snack foods, and restaurants. Its soft drinks include PepsiCola, Diet Pepsi, Teem, Slice,

Diet Slice, and Mountain Dew. In 1986, it acquired the international business of Seven Up. Its Frito Lay snack foods division includes such brands as Lay's potato chips, Doritos, Ruffles, and the cookies Walker Crisps and Smiths Crisps. Its quick-service restaurant operations include Pizza Hut, KFC (formerly Kentucky Fried Chicken), and Taco Bell. In 1990, the three chains had over 19,000 units, of which over 4,500 were located outside the United States. Over the past five years, PepsiCo has spent over $8 billion in acquisitions.

PepsiCo opened some 300 restaurants internationally in 1991 and expects to be selling snack foods in over 40 countries by 1995. Cost reductions should drive up domestic soft-drink profits, while volume expansion should fuel PepsiCo international operations in high-profit-margin European and Asian countries. Future dramatic growth in revenues and earnings is expected to take place in overseas markets. Additional major snack food acquisitions are expected to take place abroad.

Recent revenue enhancement innovations include new chicken-based products at Taco Bell, home delivery service at Pizza Hut, and lower-calorie "Lite 'n' Crispy" chicken at KFC.

While PepsiCo lost the fountain business at Burger King in 1990, it became the exclusive fountain supplier for a 120-unit chain of Howard Johnson's restaurants in early 1991. Also, it gained the fountain business of Marriott's hotel and food-service operations and acquired 209 domestic Kentucky Fried Chicken restaurants from Collins Foods.

In 1990, soft drinks provided 37% of revenues and 35% of profits, snack foods provided 28% of revenues and 42% of profits, and restaurants provided 35% of revenues and 23% of profits. Overseas operations accounted for 21% of revenues and 17% of profits.

PepsiCo has paid consecutive cash dividends since 1952. Institutions control more than 60% of the common shares. PepsiCo paid a 200% stock dividend in 1986 and another 200% stock dividend in 1990.

Total assets: $17.1 billion
Current ratio: 0.9
Common shares outstanding: 863.1 million

	1981	1982	1983	1984	1985	1986	1987	1988	1989	1990
REVENUES (MIL.)	7,027	7,499	7,896	7,699	8,057	9,291	11,485	13,007	15,242	17,803
NET INCOME (MIL.)	333	224	284	207	420	458	605	762	901	1,091
EARNINGS PER SHARE	.40	.27	.33	.24	.50	.58	.77	.97	1.13	1.37
DIVIDEND PER SHARE	.16	.18	.18	.19	.20	.21	.22	.27	.32	.38
PRICES Hi	4.4	5.6	4.5	5.1	8.4	11.9	14.1	14.6	21.9	27.9
Lo	3.0	3.5	3.6	3.8	4.5	7.3	8.5	10.0	12.6	18.0

Pfizer, Inc.

235 East 42nd Street
New York, New York 10017
Tel. (212) 573-2323
Listed: NYSE
Investor contact: Director Investor Relations, Rebecca Schiff
Ticker symbol: PFE
S&P rating: A+

Pfizer is one of America's premier pharmaceutical manufacturers of both ethical
and over-the-counter drugs. Also, it is a purveyor of hospitals supplies, animal-health
pharmaceuticals, drug sundries, specialty
chemicals, and minerals.

Health-care products include antiinfec-
tives such as Diflucan and Unasyn, car-
diovascular drugs such as Procardia XL, and antiinflamatories such as
Feldene. It produces a number of hospital products, including implantable medical devices. Animal-health products include feed additives and
antibiotics. Drug sundries include Ben-Gay, Visine eye drops, Desitin
diaper ointment, and Coty fragrances. Specialty chemicals and minerals
include bulk antibiotics, ingredients for the food industry, and mineral-
based products for industrial uses.

Pfizer's big profit leaders are ethical pharmaceuticals Procardia XL,
Diflucan, and Feldene. In 1990, the FDA approved Pfizer's antihyperten-
sion drug Cardura. Pfizer has six additional drugs going through the FDA
regulatory process, several of which are now being sold on the international market.

In 1990, 46% of Pfizer's sales and 34% of its profits were from
overseas operations. Thus currency exchange can play a major role in
Pfizer's earnings.

In 1990, health care provided 68% of sales and 82% of profits, consumer products 10% of sales and 4% of profits, animal health 8% of
sales and 8% of profits, specialty chemicals 9% of sales and 3% of
profits, and specialty minerals 5% of sales and 3% of profits.

For 30 years, Pfizer's earnings have increased every year but one.

Pfizer has paid consecutive cash dividends since 1902 and has increased its dividend annually for the past two decades. Institutions control about 65% of the outstanding common shares. Pfizer paid a 100% stock dividend in 1983 and a 100% stock dividend in 1991.

Total assets: $9.1 billion
Current ratio: 1.4
Common shares outstanding: 230.9 million

		1981	1982	1983	1984	1985	1986	1987	1988	1989	1990
REVENUES (MIL.)		3,250	3,454	3,750	3,855	4,025	4,476	4,920	5,385	5,671	6,406
NET INCOME (MIL.)		274	333	447	508	580	660	690	791	681	801
EARNINGS PER SHARE		.91	1.07	1.37	1.54	1.72	1.95	2.04	2.35	2.02	2.39
DIVIDEND PER SHARE		.40	.46	.58	.66	.74	.82	.90	1.00	1.10	1.20
PRICES	Hi	13.8	20.2	22.4	21.2	28.1	36.4	38.5	30.1	37.9	40.9
	Lo	10.0	12.4	16.8	14.7	18.8	23.1	20.6	23.7	27.0	27.3

Philip Morris Companies, Inc.

120 Park Avenue
New York, New York 10017
Tel. (212) 880-5000
Listed: NYSE
Investor contact: Financial Communications, Nicholas M. Rolli
Ticker symbol: MO
S&P rating: A+

Philip Morris, one of America's leading consumer products companies, has essentially three operations: tobacco, packaged foods, and beverages.

Philip Morris is the largest cigarette company in the United States. It has doubled its share of the cigarette market in the past ten years, marketing its cigarettes in more than 100 countries. With such brands as Marlboro, Benson & Hedges, and Virginia Slims, it controls 42% of the domestic market and 7.5% of the world market. Philip Morris is the largest exporter of cigarettes to the rapidly expanding Japanese market. A ruling in a Federal District Court (not involving Philip Morris) that only one plaintiff could receive punitive damages in a successful product-liability case bodes well for the tobacco industry.

Thanks to the 1985 acquisition of General Foods and the 1988 acquisition of Kraft, Philip Morris has become the largest and most diversified food company in the United States. General Foods supplies such products as Post Cereals, Entenman's baked goods, Birdseye frozen foods, and Maxwell House Coffee. Kraft adds such products as Velveeta cheese, Miracle Whip, Parkay margarine, and Breyers dairy products.

Miller Brewing is the second-largest brewer, behind Anheuser Busch. Its brand include Miller High Life, Lowenbrau, Meisterbrau, and Milwaukee's Best.

In 1990, tobacco accounted for 41% of sales and 68% of profits, food accounted for 51% of sales and 27% of profits, brewing accounted for 7% of sales and 3% of profits, and real estate accounted for 1% of sales and 2% of profits.

In September 1990, Philip Morris acquired, for $3.8 billion in cash, the $3.6 billion operations of the Swiss chocolate and coffee giant Jacobs Suchard A.G.

Consecutive cash dividends have been paid since 1928. There have been 26 dividend boosts in the past 23 years. Earnings have increased for the past 17 years. Institutions hold about 65% of the common shares. Philip Morris paid a 100% stock dividend in 1979, a 100% stock dividend in 1986, and a 300% stock dividend in 1989.

Total assets: $46.6 billion
Current ratio: 1.0
Common shares outstanding: 926.8 million

		1981	1982	1983	1984	1985	1986	1987	1988	1989	1990
REVENUES (MIL.)		8,307	9,102	9,466	10,138	12,149	20,681	22,279	25,860	39,011	44,323
NET INCOME (MIL.)		676	782	904	889	1,255	1,478	1,842	2,064	2,946	3,540
EARNINGS PER SHARE		.68	.78	.90	.91	1.31	1.55	1.94	2.22	3.18	3.83
DIVIDEND PER SHARE		.25	.30	.36	.43	.50	.62	.79	1.01	1.25	1.55
PRICES	Hi	6.9	8.5	9.1	10.4	11.9	19.5	31.1	25.5	45.8	52.0
	Lo	5.3	5.5	6.8	7.8	9.0	11.0	18.1	20.1	25.0	36.0

America's GROWTH STOCKS

Pitney Bowes, Inc.

World Headquarters
Stamford, Connecticut 06926-0700
Tel. (203) 356-5000
Listed: NYSE
Investor contact: Investor Relations, Ernest J. Johnson
Ticker symbol: PBI
S&P rating: A+

Pitney Bowes, based in Stamford, Connecticut, began as a postage-meter manufacturer. It has expanded into a wide range of office equipment and supplies. Today it is the largest postage-meter company in the United States; in addition, it has a complete line of business equipment, supplies, and financial services (leasing business equipment and financing sales of new business equipment).

Pitney Bowes offers complete mailing systems, including postage meters, scales, inserting systems, parcel registers, and shipping systems. Currently, Pitney's fastest growing segment is facsimile machines. Since 1982, Pitney has led the pack with machines manufactured by Matsushita of Japan. Its facsimile machines vary from low-cost personal models to high-speed commercial varieties. Its dictaphone division has a 45% market share of the worldwide voice-processing market. Pitney has about a 3% market share in the highly competitive copying machine market.

Pitney's business supplies segment, through its Data Documents System, provides bar-coded labels. Its Monarch Marking subsidiary provides price marking and product identification items to both retail and industrial customers. It is selling its Wheeler Group catalog of business supplies and has acquired Pandich Tech, which specializes in reprographics and mailroom services.

Pitney Bowes financing services segment has low delinquency and default rates. During times of rising interest rates, it often experiences a profit squeeze but during declining rates, it is quite profitable.

In 1990, business equipment provided 72% of revenues and 54% of profits, business supplies and services provided 11% of revenues and 8% of profits, and financial services provided 17% of revenues and

38% of profits.

Institutions control about 80% of the shares. Pitney Bowes has paid consecutive cash dividends since 1934. It paid a 100% stock dividend in 1983 and another 100% stock dividend in 1986.

Total assets: $6.1 billion
Current ratio: 0.6
Common shares outstanding: 78.9 million

		1981	1982	1983	1984	1985	1986	1987	1988	1989	1990
REVENUES (MIL.)		1,414	1,455	1,606	1,732	1,832	1,987	2,251	2,650	2,876	3,196
NET INCOME (MIL.)		70	83	118	138	145	166	199	237	180	207
EARNINGS PER SHARE		.95	1.08	1.51	1.76	1.83	2.10	2.53	3.00	2.27	2.60
DIVIDEND PER SHARE		.40	.40	.45	.52	.60	.66	.76	.96	1.04	1.20
PRICES	Hi	8.9	12.1	18.4	18.1	24.9	38.3	50.3	47.5	54.8	53.5
	Lo	5.5	5.5	10.5	13.4	16.9	22.8	29.6	33.8	40.9	27.0

Policy Management Systems Corporation

One PMS Center
Blythewood, South Carolina 29016
Tel. (803) 735-4000
Listed: NYSE
Investor contact: Asst. V.P., John Hutto
Ticker symbol: PMS
S&P rating: B+

As described in its 1990 Annual Report, "Policy Management Systems Corporation revenues are generated primarily by licensing standardized insurance software systems and providing related automation support and information services to the insurance industry.

"As part of its systems licensing arrangement, the Company provides customers with enhancements to and maintenance of most of its systems. Generally, license agreements extend for a minimum of six years and provide for both an initial license charge and an ongoing monthly license charge.

"Most customers licensing the Company's software systems also utilize the Company's professional support services, including systems implementation and integration assistance and consulting and educational service, which are normally provided under services and charged separately.

"The Company provides a wide range of information services to the entire insurance industry, most of which can be ordered and received on an automated basis through the Company's nationwide telecommunications network. These services include motor vehicle reports, individual driver information, claims histories, credit reports and histories, property inspection and valuation reports, property claims estimating, premium audits, attending physician statements and personal medical history interviews."

Most of its customers are small to medium-sized companies, although PMSC has a strong penetration in the top 50 property and casualty insurers in the United States PMSC developed, at tremendous cost, its Series III computer software systems, which are the ultimate in insurance applications and are designed around IBM's leading technologies such as imaging and cooperative processing.

In 1991, PMSC acquired Management Data Communications Corp., a provider of software and processing to group health insurers; in 1990, it purchased PMS, Inc., a provider of personal medical information to life and health insurers.

Growth prospects are excellent with only 30% domestic insurer and a smaller international market penetration. In 1989, IBM purchased a 20% interest in the company with the option to acquire up to an additional 10% interest. In 1990, an agreement was reached with IBM whereby IBM designated PMSC as IBM's Insurance Applications Affiliate, the only such company to receive this designation.

No cash dividends have ever been paid. Institutions, including IBM, control about 75% of the common shares. PMSC paid a 100% stock dividend in 1983.

Total assets: $508 million
Current ratio: 5.4
Common shares outstanding: 19.4 million

	1981	1982	1983	1984	1985	1986	1987	1988	1989	1990
REVENUES (MIL.)	32	44	62	85	103	151	180	217	266	346
NET INCOME (MIL.)	3.8	6.6	9.7	14	14	14	17	21	27	37
EARNINGS PER SHARE	.28	.44	.63	.85	.89	.85	1.05	1.30	1.60	1.92
DIVIDEND PER SHARE	—	—	—	—	—	—	—	—	—	—
PRICES Hi	9.3	21.4	35.1	31.0	34.8	24.5	30.3	26.0	37.3	43.5
Lo	8.0	8.1	18.0	22.0	16.5	15.0	15.3	18.8	21.8	30.0

Potomac Electric Power Company

1900 Pennsylvania Avenue N.W.
Washington, D.C. 20068
Tel. (202) 872-2000
Listed: NYSE
Investor contact: V.P. James S. Culp
Ticker symbol: POM
S&P rating: A

As profiled in its 1990 Annual Report, "Potomac Electric Power Company (PEPCO) provides retail electric service to 1.85 million people in a 640-square-mile service territory in the Washington metropolitan areas, including the District of Columbia and major portions of Montgomery and Prince George's counties in Maryland.

> **Potomac Electric Power Company**

"PEPCO's unique service territory, with virtually no heavy industry, benefits from economic stability and low unemployment. The Washington metropolitan area remains one of the nation's major markets with a well-educated and affluent population."

In 1990, prime fuels for electric generation were coal, 77%; oil and gas, 10%; and purchased power, 13% (Ohio Edison). Potomac has no nuclear investment. In 1991, Potomac added combustion turbines producing 380 megawatts of power. It plans to bring on stream in 1992 another combustion turbine producing 138 megawatts, the first element of a planned and licensed 788 megawatts of a combined cycle installation. In addition, PEPCO plans to purchase power from a variety of supply sources and implement major conservation programs to meet future energy needs.

Potomac Electric Power owns a nonregulated finance subsidiary, Potomac Capital Investment Corporation, the major assets of which are a combination of an investment-grade marketable securities portfolio and an equipment-leasing business. The investment objective of the subsidiary is to provide a supplement to utility earnings and to build long term-value for PEPCO shareholders.

In 1990, Potomac's revenues were divided as follows: commercial, 48%; residential, 28%; federal government, 15%; local government, 3%; and wholesale, 6%.

Potomac has paid consecutive cash dividends since the public company was organized in 1947, and over the past 16 years has shown a strong pattern of increasing dividends. Institutions control about 25% of the outstanding common shares. Potomac split its stock two-for-one in 1987.

Total assets: $5.7 billion
Current ratio: 0.3
Common shares outstanding: 105.6 million

	1981	1982	1983	1984	1985	1986	1987	1988	1989	1990
REVENUES (MIL.)	1,001	1,095	1,170	1,198	1,316	1,371	1,332	1,350	1,395	1,412
NET INCOME (MIL.)	110	119	140	168	184	206	208	211	215	170
EARNINGS PER SHARE	1.07	1.14	1.33	1.61	1.79	2.06	2.11	2.14	2.16	1.62
DIVIDEND PER SHARE	.79	.84	.89	.97	1.08	1.18	1.30	1.38	1.46	1.52
PRICES Hi	7.8	9.4	11.1	12.8	17.4	29.6	27.4	24.0	24.3	24.0
Lo	5.9	6.9	8.6	9.6	12.4	16.9	18.0	19.3	19.3	18.0

Premier Industrial Corporation

4500 Euclid Avenue
Cleveland, Ohio 44103
Tel. (216) 391-8300
Listed: NYSE
Investor contact: V.P. Secy, Grant C. Grinnell

Ticker symbol: PRE
S&P rating: A

PREMIER INDUSTRIAL CORPORATION

Premier Industrial is essentially engaged in two operations, as a distributor of electronic and electrical components and as a manufacturer and distributor of industrial and maintenance products, including high-performance firefighting equipment.

Premier is a market leader in the distribution of more than 100,000 electrical and electronic components to manufacturers of computers, data-processing hardware, communications products, and industrial controls. Also, it sells electrical and electronic components to those engaged in the repair and maintenance of such equipment. Its products include microprocessors, capacitors, resistors, connectors, and electrical terminals. Its large volume of business with those engaged in the repair and maintenance of equipment tends to stabilize its business as compared with those engaged exclusively in original-equipment sales.

The industrial-products segment includes a large array of products such as lubricants, auto and truck parts, welding equipment, protective coatings for asphalt surfaces, degreasers, cleaning chemicals, and firefighting equipment such as nozzles and valves.

Premier has more than 330 branches worldwide. It markets industrial products to both original equipment manufacturers and secondary, largely maintenance, users. It sells to industrial, construction, commercial, institutional, and municipal markets.

Premier has paid consecutive cash dividends since 1950. Insiders control more than 60% of the outstanding common shares. Premier paid a 50% stock dividend in 1985, a 50% stock dividend in 1988, and a 50% stock dividend in 1990.

Total assets: $349 million
Current ratio: 7.2
Common shares outstanding: 58.2 million

		1982	1983	1984	1985	1986	1987	1988	1989	1990	1991
REVENUES (MIL.)		332	317	378	432	435	459	528	596	626	637
NET INCOME (MIL.)		35	31	38	39	41	48	64	70	75	75
EARNINGS PER SHARE		.49	.44	.55	.58	.62	.73	.98	1.13	1.29	1.30
DIVIDEND PER SHARE		.11	.12	.13	.15	.17	.19	.23	.29	.36	.42
PRICES	Hi	9.3	11.5	11.0	13.0	15.9	21.6	22.1	25.5	27.5	33.1
	Lo	5.3	7.9	7.5	8.4	11.3	12.9	15.5	16.9	21.0	22.3

Price Company

2657 Ariane Drive
San Diego, California 92186-5466
Tel (619) 581-4600
Listed: NASDAQ
Investor contact: V.P. Daniel T. Carter
Ticker symbol: PCLB
S&P rating: B+

Price operates a chain of wholesale membership clubs in Arizona, California, Colorado, Connecticut, Maryland, New Jersey, New Mexico, New York, Virginia, British Columbia, Ontario, and Quebec. During fiscal 1991, Price opened 13 new Price Clubs and expects to open 16 more in fiscal 1992. Price has entered into a joint venture with Commercial Mexicana, a leading retailer in Mexico, to open Price Clubs in Mexico. Price operates close to 70 clubs in the United States and Canada.

Price wholesales directly from its warehouses to its membership. Membership is offered to small businesses, government employees, credit union employees, and the like. There are basically two types of membership. Gold Star membership is offered to those in preferred occupations. Business membership is for businesses or individuals who purchase for resale. There are now about 2.0 million Gold Star members and approximately 1.25 million business members. Membership requires a $25.00 fee. Price has a very high renewal rate.

Warehouses vary in size from 96,000 to 135,000 square feet. Price merchandises a variety of brand-name items, including durable goods, food, liquor, furnishings, home and office furniture, and sundries. It plans to introduce meat and bakeries at a number of locations. An independent Price Club distributor is engaged in the cost-effective distribution of merchandise to warehouses. Price Club Industries manufactures and processes items for sale in club stores. Its operations include central photo processing, a central optical laboratory, optical dispensing at most Price Club locations, a ground-meat packaging plant, and the packaging of selected food products. The Price Club Realty is both a source of income and affords another way to leverage down Price Club's occupancy cost.

In 1990, Price purchased from Steinberg the 50% interest in six Price Clubs of Canada, which it did not already own.

Price paid a one-time cash dividend of $1.50 a share in July 1989. Institutions control about 60% of the outstanding common shares. Price paid a 200% stock dividend in 1984 and a 100% stock dividend in 1986.

Total assets: $1.8 billion
Current ratio: 1.3
Common shares outstanding: 48.7 million

		1982	1983	1984	1985	1986	1987	1988	1989	1990	1991
REVENUES (MIL.)		370	641	1,158	1,871	2,648	3,306	4,140	5,012	5,412	6,756
NET INCOME (MIL.)		—	15	29	46	59	73	95	117	125	134
EARNINGS PER SHARE		.20	.34	.64	1.01	1.25	1.50	1.93	2.30	2.47	2.68
DIVIDEND PER SHARE		—	—	—	—	—	—	—	1.50	—	—
PRICES	Hi	12.3	20.8	24.5	36.1	55.8	52.5	42.3	49.5	48.3	65.3
	Lo	3.0	9.6	11.9	20.4	28.3	23.5	31.0	34.8	26.5	37.8

The Procter & Gamble Company

One Procter & Gamble Plaza
Cincinnati, Ohio 45202
Tel. (513) 983-1100
Listed: NYSE
Investor contact: Mgr. Shareholder Services, R. J. Thompson
Ticker symbol: PG
S&P rating: A

Procter & Gamble is America's preeminent consumer products company. It markets soap, detergents, cosmetics, foods, beverages, disposable diapers, drugs, and health-care products. Some of its better known products include detergents such as

227

Bold, Cheer, and Oxydol; soaps such as Ivory, Zest, and Safeguard; dish cleaners such as Dawn and Cascade; household cleaners such as Comet; shampoos such as Head & Shoulders and Prell; diapers such as Pampers; tissue products such as White Cloud; cooking fats such as Crisco; food products such as Citrus Hill orange juice, Jif peanut butter, and Folgers coffee; cosmetics such as Cover Girl and Old Spice. Procter & Gamble expands through intensive marketing, new products, acquisitions, and geographic expansion.

In 1985, Procter & Gamble acquired the drug firm Richardson Vicks. Other major acquisitions include Blendex, a German manufacturer of toothpaste and toiletries; Noxell, the maker of Noxzema and Cover Girl cosmetics; the exclusive U.S. marketing and distribution of Rorer's line of OTC drugs such as Maalox, an antacid, Ascriptin pain reliever and Perdiem laxative; a toiletries line from American Cyanamid; the Sundor Group, a manufacturer of Sunny Delight citrus juices; Speas Farm and Lincoln apple juices; Sun Sip fruit juices; Del Monte's Hawaiian Punch; and, more recently, Revlon's Max Factor cosmetics and Beatrix fragrances divisions.

Disposable diapers are Procter & Gamble's most important single product, with annual sales of more than $4 billion, two-thirds of which is from abroad. Health care is its most rapidly growing product line. It markets such well-known over-the-counter drugs as Vicks, Pepto Bismol, and Metamucil. Prescription drug sales are now over $300 million a year. Editronate, effective in the treatment of osteoporosis, is now being marketed in France and the Netherlands and is awaiting FDA approval in the United States. Also on the FDA list is Olestra, a zero-calorie fat substitute with wide market potential.

In 1991, revenues and profits were apportioned as follows: laundry products, 32% of sales and 35% of profits; personal care products, 49% of sales and 55% of profits; food and beverages, 13% of sales and 2% of profits; and pulp and chemicals, 6% of sales and 8% of profits. Foreign operations provided 45% of sales and 28% of profits.

Procter & Gamble has paid consecutive cash dividends since 1891. Institutions control over 45% of the common shares. Procter & Gamble split its stock 2 for 1 in 1983 and 2 for 1 in 1989.

Total assets: $20.5 billion
Current ratio: 1.3
Common shares outstanding: 338 million

	1982	1983	1984	1985	1986	1987	1988	1989	1990	1991
REVENUES (MIL.)	11,994	12,452	12,946	13,552	15,439	17,000	19,336	21,398	24,081	27,026
NET INCOME (MIL.)	777	866	890	635	709	327	1,020	1,206	1,602	1,773
EARNINGS PER SHARE	2.35	2.61	2.68	1.90	2.10	.94	2.98	3.56	4.49	4.92
DIVIDEND PER SHARE	1.03	1.13	1.20	1.30	1.31	1.35	1.38	1.50	1.75	1.95
PRICES Hi	30.8	31.6	30.0	35.9	41.3	51.8	44.0	70.4	91.3	95.4
Lo	19.5	25.3	22.9	25.3	31.9	30.0	35.4	42.1	61.8	76.0

The Quaker Oats Company

Quaker Tower
321 North Clark Street, P.O. Box 9001
Chicago, Illinois 60610
Tel. (312) 222-7818
Listed: NYSE
Investor contact: Director, Investor & Corporate Communications
Margaret Eichman
Ticker symbol: OAT
S&P rating: A

Quaker Oats is a worldwide producer of packaged foods and pet foods. Its food segment includes such well-known brands as Quaker hot and dry cereals, Aunt Jemima pancakes, and Celeste frozen pizza. Grocery products include Golden Grain products, Rice-A-Roni, and pet foods such as Ken-L-Ration, Puss'n Boots, and Gaines Burgers.

Grocery specialities include Van Camp's Beans and Gatorade. Fisher-Price, Inc., a manufacturer of toys and juvenile products, was spun off to shareholders in June 1991, on the basis of one share of Fisher-Price for every five shares of Quaker Oats.

Chicago-based Quaker is one of the nation's largest food operations. It has facilities in 16 states, Canada, Latin America, and Western Europe. Foreign sales represent 30% of revenues.

Since the 1987 acquisition of Gaines, Quaker has had problems with the profitability of its pet-food segment. The pet population remains static and the market highly competitive. Quaker closed down a domestic pet-food operation and, despite extensive marketing and advertising, does not seem able to increase market share. Unlike the United States market, the European pet food market is growing at a 4–5% per year. Quaker's European pet foods are in a number two market position and are growing in line with the market.

In 1991, the United States and Canada provided 70% of sales and 80% of profits and international grocery products provided 30% of sales and 20% of profits.

Institutions control over 45% of the outstanding common shares. Consecutive cash dividends have been paid since 1906. Quaker paid 100% stock dividends in 1964 and 1986 and distributed Fisher-Price shares to its shareholders in a spin-off transaction effective June 28, 1991.

Total assets: $3.0 billion
Current ratio: 1.4
Common shares outstanding: 76.3 million

		1982	1983	1984	1985	1986	1987	1988	1989	1990	1991
REVENUES (MIL.)		2,115	2,172	2,831	2,926	2,969	3,824	4,508	4,879	5,031	5,491
NET INCOME (MIL.)		97	57	139	157	180	244	256	203	169	206
EARNINGS PER SHARE		1.19	.66	1.67	1.88	2.24	3.10	3.20	2.56	2.15	2.65
DIVIDEND PER SHARE		.45	.50	.55	.62	.70	.80	1.00	1.20	1.40	1.56
PRICES	Hi	10.9	12.9	16.1	26.1	39.8	57.6	57.1	66.3	68.9	75.8
	Lo	7.8	8.8	10.6	14.8	23.5	32.6	31.0	42.6	45.1	44.4

RPM, Inc.
2628 Pearl Road, P.O. Box 777
Medina, Ohio 44258
Tel. (216) 225-3192
Listed: NASDAQ
Investor contact: V.P. & Treas. R. E. Klar
Ticker symbol: RPOW
S&P rating: A+

RPM is a widely diversified manufacturer of coatings (corrosion control and waterproofing), specialty chemicals, wall coverings, and hobby items. RPM began in 1947 as a one-product manufacturer of a liquid aluminum compound used as a protective coating in a process and product known as Alumination.

RPM has expanded over the years, largely because of the acquisition of a large number of relatively small niche companies. In almost all of the acquired companies, the existing management remained intact with a minimum of control by RPM executives. The common thread among most of these companies is that the product is some form of protective coating such as paint, sealant, membrane, furniture, and automobile touch-ups.

RPM has made about 25 acquisitions in the past two decades. About 65% of sales are to industrial customers and 35% are to consumers.

Coatings, sealants, and anticorrosion products are sold under such trade names as Alumination, Mohawk, Permaroof, Bondex, Testor, and Zinseer.

Wall coverings and fabrics are sold in the United States under the trade names Design/Craft fabrics and Thibaut Wall Coverings.

The hobby segment includes furniture repair kits, painting-by-number sets, and the like.

In 1991, RPM acquired Rust-Oleum International, which manufactures and markets rustproof compounds and industrial coatings in Europe. In 1990, it purchased Kop-Coat, Inc., a national brand company selling coatings for the marine, deck, and swimming-pool markets. Also in 1990, it acquired Paramount Technical Products, a waterproofing concern, and sold a 50% interest in Euclid to Holderchem, a huge European cement manufacturer.

RPM has achieved higher sales and earnings in each of the past 43 years. RPM has paid consecutive cash dividends since 1969 and has increased dividends in each of the past 16 years. It paid a 25% stock dividend in 1983, a 25% stock dividend in 1984, a 50% stock dividend in 1987, and a 25% stock dividend in 1990.

Total assets: $375 million
Current ratio: 2.9
Common shares outstanding: 31.1 million

	1981	1982	1983	1984	1985	1986	1987	1988	1989	1990
REVENUES (MIL.)	119	125	131	154	203	251	291	342	376	445
NET INCOME (MIL.)	5.8	6.7	7.2	8.4	11	13	16	21	24	28
EARNINGS PER SHARE	.35	.39	.42	.46	.55	.56	.62	.76	.86	.98
DIVIDEND PER SHARE	.13	.16	.19	.22	.27	.32	.37	.43	.48	.53
PRICES Hi	4.8	5.8	7.1	7.5	10.3	12.8	13.8	14.4	16.0	18.3
Lo	2.9	3.0	5.0	5.3	7.1	9.4	8.6	10.9	12.3	12.4

Rubbermaid Incorporated

1147 Akron Road
Wooster, Ohio 44691
Tel. (216) 264-6464
Listed: NYSE
Investor contact: V.P. Investor Relations and Corporate
Communications Richard D. Gates
Ticker symbol: RBD
S&P rating: A+

Rubbermaid, which started as a balloon manufacturer in 1920, has expanded to become the nation's largest manufacturer of household plastic and rubber products. Rubbermaid has grown rapidly in recent years, by both new products and acquisitions.

It acquired Eldon Industries (office accessories) in 1990, SECO Industries (floorcare products) and Micro Computer Accessories (products for personal computers and word processors) in 1988, Viking Brush in 1987, Gott Corporation (thermos containers) in 1985, Little Tykes (toys) in 1984, and Con-Tact Brand (decorative coverings in 1981.

In 1991, Rubbermaid merged its Rubbermaid Office Products Division with Eldon Industries to form Rubbermaid Office Products Group.

The Specialty Products Division includes such products as planters, bird feeders, and gasoline containers.

The office products segment includes such products as chair mats, waste baskets, and WorkManager computer work-station furniture.

Although Rubbermaid has sales offices in Canada, Europe, and Hong Kong, only about 13% of total sales are to foreign markets, and 50% of foreign sales are to Canada.

The highly volatile cost of resin is a major factor in Rubbermaid's profit margin.

Rubbermaid has undertaken a joint venture with the Dutch chemical company, DSM, whereby the latter makes and markets rubber and plasta houseware products in Europe, the Middle East, and North Africa.

Rubbermaid has paid consecutive cash dividends since 1941. In 1990, Rubbermaid increased its cash dividend for the 36th consecutive year. It paid a 100% stock dividend in 1982, 1985, 1986, and 1991.

Total assets: $1.1 billion
Current ratio: 2.6
Common shares outstanding: 160.2 million

	1981	1982	1983	1984	1985	1986	1987	1988	1989	1990
REVENUES (MIL.)	357	376	436	566	671	795	1,015	1,194	1,344	1,534
NET INCOME (MIL.)	26	28	36	47	57	70	85	99	116	144
EARNINGS PER SHARE	.21	.23	.29	.35	.40	.48	.58	.68	.79	.90
DIVIDEND PER SHARE	.068	.079	.088	.098	.11	.13	.16	.19	.23	.27
PRICES Hi	2.6	4.0	6.3	5.7	8.8	14.3	17.5	13.5	18.4	22.5
Lo	1.5	2.3	3.7	4.1	5.4	8.3	9.5	10.5	12.5	15.5

America's GROWTH STOCKS

Russell Corporation

1 Lee Street
Alexander City, Alabama 35010
Tel. (205) 329-4000
Listed: NYSE
Investor contact: Asst. Treas. K. Roger Holliday
Ticker symbol: RML
S&P rating: A+

As profiled in its 1990 Annual Report, "Russell Corporation (formerly Russell Mills), founded in 1902, is a vertically integrated international

Russell Corporation

designer, manufacturer and marketer of leisure apparel, activewear, athletic uniforms and a comprehensive line of lightweight, yarn-dyed woven fabrics. The company's manufacturing operations include the entire process of converting raw fibers into finished apparel and fabrics. Russell's products are marketed primarily through three sales divisions—Athletic, Knit Apparel, and Fabrics—as well as Cross Creek Apparel, Inc., (acquired 1988) and Russell Corp. UK Limited (acquired 1989), two wholly owned subsidiaries that manufacture and market complementary apparel products.

"Apparel is marketed to sporting goods dealers, department and specialty stores, mass merchandisers, golf pro shops, college book stores, screen printers, distributors and mail order houses. The Company believes it is the largest manufacturer of athletic uniforms in the United States.

"During 1990, a new knit complex was completed at Cross Creek's Mt. Airy, North Carolina facility. Additionally, the Lafayette, Alabama, fine-count spinning plant began operation, and construction started on an additional spinning plant in Wetumpka, Alabama, scheduled to begin operation in late 1991.

"Today, RUSSELL ATHLETIC is the world's leading teamwear apparel manufacturer and one of the most recognized brands in the men's and women's athletics team uniform business."

Russell Athletic manufactures and markets athletic uniforms and activewear. Knit apparel manufactures and markets knitted apparel such as T-shirts, pullovers, fleece sweaters, and lightweight sportswear under both the Jerzees brand and private labels. The fabrics division manufactures and markets quality woven fabrics and Cross Creek produces and sells quality knit products such as placket shirts (golf shirts) and turtlenecks. Russell Corp. UK produces T-shirts and fleece for the European market.

Russell Corp. has paid consecutive cash dividends since 1963. The Russell family controls over 45% and institutions about 40% of the outstanding common shares. Russell paid a 100% stock dividend in 1981, a 60% stock dividend in 1983, and a 100% stock dividend in 1986.

Total assets: $794.5 million
Current ratio: 4.0
Common shares outstanding: 41.4 million

	1981	1982	1983	1984	1985	1986	1987	1988	1989	1990
REVENUES (MIL.)	270	275	319	353	385	438	480	531	688	714
NET INCOME (MIL.)	24	21	27	28	30	43	46	54	64	67
EARNINGS PER SHARE	.64	.56	.67	.70	.74	1.08	1.17	1.36	1.57	1.65
DIVIDEND PER SHARE	.12	.13	.14	.15	.15	.16	.19	.23	.28	.32
PRICES Hi	5.2	7.7	9.4	9.0	10.0	19.6	20.5	17.8	26.5	31.0
Lo	3.2	3.8	6.3	5.6	6.8	9.3	10.6	11.4	15.6	16.0

Safety-Kleen Corp.

777 Big Timber Road
Elgin, Illinois 60123
Tel. (708) 697-8460
Listed: NYSE
Investor contact: Sr. V.P. Finance, Robert W. Willmschen
Ticker symbol: SK
S&P rating: A

Safety-Kleen is basically in the business of recycling liquid hazardous waste materials. It provides a variety of services to about 475,000 businesses that generate hazardous wastes such as auto repair shops, dry cleaners, and manufacturing plants. It has expanded from its original solvent business to include sludge, solids, and flammable and chlorinated solvents. In the case of solvents, such as mineral spirits and dry cleaning fluid, it collects and recycles the waste and then sends it back to the customer for reuse.

Safety-Kleen's core business is its parts cleaner service. The familiar "red sink on a drum" containing solvents for cleaning was first offered to service stations, repair garages, auto dealers, and truck fleets in 1969. In 1990, the parts cleaner service had 425,000 customers worldwide, served by the company's network of 273 branches. In 1990, the parts cleaner service accounted for 55% of Safety's revenues.

Safety-Kleen provides clean pads and a paint spray gun to 11,000 autobody shops. It picks up the pads and used solvent on a regular basis for recycling.

The rapid growth of Safety-Kleen's services has paralleled the increase of government regulations regarding the disposal of hazardous wastes.

In 1987, Safety-Kleen acquired Breslube Enterprises of Ontario, Canada. Breslube is the largest refiner of motor oils in North America. Oil Collection and reprocessing has grown from 30 million gallons in 1987 to more than 100 million gallons in 1990.

Safety-Kleen has had 20 years of consecutive earnings increases. It has paid consecutive cash dividends since 1979. It paid a 100% stock dividend in 1980, a 50% stock dividend in 1982, a 50% stock dividend in 1984, a 50% stock dividend in 1985, a 50% stock dividend in 1987, and a 50% stock dividend in 1991.

Total assets: $719 million
Current ratio: 1.7
Common shares outstanding: 56.7 million

		1981	1982	1983	1984	1985	1986	1987	1988	1989	1990
REVENUES (MIL.)		135	149	163	186	221	255	334	417	478	589
NET INCOME (MIL.)		11	13	16	19	24	28	35	42	46	55
EARNINGS PER SHARE		.24	.29	.34	.41	.49	.57	.71	.85	.91	1.05
DIVIDEND PER SHARE		.026	.045	.059	.089	.13	.14	.16	.20	.24	.27
PRICES	Hi	4.6	5.8	9.3	8.3	12.1	17.3	28.4	23.5	25.0	29.7
	Lo	3.0	2.6	5.1	5.9	7.1	11.4	14.8	14.5	15.0	18.3

Sara Lee Corporation
3 First National Plaza
Chicago, Illinois 60602
Tel. (312) 726-2600
Listed: NYSE
Investor contact: V.P. Investor Relations, Janet Bergman

Ticker symbol: SLE
S&P rating: A+

SARA LEE CORPORATION

Based in Chicago, the Sara Lee Corporation, formerly Consolidated Foods, has become a major factor in the quality consumer packaged goods industry. Sara Lee has both strong management and a favorable degree of pricing flexibility. Its products include packaged meats, frozen bakery products, coffee, personal products, and household and personal-care items. Continual growth has been achieved through internal expansion, acquisitions, and divestitures.

Packaged foods include Ball Park Hot Dogs, Jimmy Dean Sausage, Hillshire packaged meats, Sara Lee frozen baked goods, and Douwe Egberts coffee. Food-service operations include PYA/Monarch, a leading supplier of food to institutions in the Southeast United States. Consumer products include Hanes pantyhose and underwear, L'Eggs pantyhose, Bali foundations, Coach leatherwear, and Kiwi shoe polish.

Sara Lee operates in about 40 countries and derives about 30% of sales abroad which means that currency exchange rates can have a major impact on Sara Lee's earnings, although the company hedges to reduce exposure to fluctuating rates.

Acquisitions in fiscal 1991 included Henson Kickernick, a premier U.S. manufacturer of foundations; the Sans Group, Spain's leading underwear manufacturer; and the Linter textiles group, Australia's largest apparel manufacturer. Sara Lee also acquired a majority interest in Compack Trading and Packing, the largest coffee roaster in Hungary.

In 1991, packaged meats and bakery items accounted for 41% of sales and 21% of profits; coffee and grocery products accounted for 16% of sales and 23% of profits; personal products accounted for 33% of sales and 44% of profits; and household and personal-care items accounted for 10% of sales and 12% of profits.

Earnings have increased for 14 consecutive years. Sara Lee has paid consecutive cash dividends since 1946. It paid a 100% stock dividend in 1983, a 100% stock dividend in 1986, and a 100% stock dividend in 1989.

Total assets: $8.1 billion
Current ratio: 1.2
Common shares outstanding: 232.7 million

	1982	1983	1984	1985	1986	1987	1988	1989	1990	1991
REVENUES (MIL.)	6,039	6,572	7,000	8,117	7,938	9,115	10,424	11,718	11,606	12,381
NET INCOME (MIL.)	157	171	188	206	223	267	325	410	470	535
EARNINGS PER SHARE	.68	.72	.82	.91	1.01	1.01	1.42	1.75	1.91	2.15
DIVIDEND PER SHARE	.26	.28	.32	.35	.39	.48	.58	.69	.81	.92
PRICES Hi	6.0	6.8	8.8	13.0	18.5	24.5	25.8	33.8	33.4	58.1
Lo	3.8	4.8	6.3	7.8	11.8	13.3	16.5	21.5	24.1	29.6

Schering-Plough Corporation

One Giralda Farms
Madison, New Jersey 07940
Tel. (201) 822-7000
Listed: NYSE
Investor contact: V.P. Investor Relations, Geraldine U. Foster
Ticker symbol: SGP
S&P rating: A+

Schering-Plough is a strong leader in the manufacture and sale of anti-infective, anticancer, dermatological, respiratory, and cardiovascular ethical pharmaceuticals. Also it has a large over-the-counter array of medications and drug sundries. Likewise, Schering-Plough has been quite successful in taking off-patent prescription drugs to the over-the-counter drug market. A recent example is Gyne-Lotrimin, an anti-yeast vaginal medication.

Schering is very active in the development, licensing, and marketing of biotech products. It manufactures some of its own biotech products through its wholly owned DNAX Research Institute. In early 1991, the FDA approved Intron A, or alpha interferon, an anti-hepatitis pharmaceutical licensed from Biogen. Other new drugs in the pipeline include Claratin, a nonsedating antihistamine currently with expanding sales in Europe and awaiting FDA approval; Leucomax, a white blood cell stimulator with broad anti-infective properties; and Uni-Dur, a once-a-day anti-asthma medication.

Schering has an extensive array of ethical pharmaceuticals such as Provential for asthma and emphysema, Lotrisone for dermatological fungus, Eulexin for prostate cancer, and Normozide for cardiovascular problems.

When Schering merged with Plough in 1971, Plough had an extensive number of over-the-counter drugs, to which Schering has added a large number of products over the years. Some of the more important over-the-counter items include Coppertone, DiGel, Chlor-Trimeton, Coricidin, and Fibre Trim. Scholl's foot care is a wholly owned subsidiary of Schering. In late 1990, Schering sold its Maybelline cosmetics subsidiary.

In 1990, pharmaceuticals accounted for 78% of revenues and 82% of profits and consumer products 22% of sales and 18% of profits. Also, in 1990 international sales accounted for 41% of sales and 30% of profits.

Schering has paid consecutive cash dividends since 1952. Institutions own more than 60% of the outstanding shares. Schering paid a 100% stock dividend in 1987 and another 100% stock dividend in 1990.

Total assets: $4.1 billion
Current ratio: 1.3
Common shares outstanding: 218 million

		1981	1982	1983	1984	1985	1986	1987	1988	1989	1990
REVENUES (MIL.)		1,809	1,818	1,809	1,874	1,927	2,399	2,699	2,969	3,158	3,323
NET INCOME (MIL.)		179	184	179	177	193	266	316	390	471	565
EARNINGS PER SHARE		.83	.85	.85	.88	.95	1.09	1.37	1.74	2.09	2.50
DIVIDEND PER SHARE		.42	.42	.42	.42	.42	.45	.51	.70	.89	1.07
PRICES	Hi	10.8	11.0	12.1	10.0	16.8	22.0	27.6	29.8	43.0	50.8
	Lo	6.3	6.6	9.3	8.3	8.9	14.0	15.6	22.6	27.8	37.0

Service-Master Limited Partnership

One Service-Master Way
Downers Grove, Illinois 60515
Tel. (708) 964-1300
Listed: NYSE

Investor contact: Maureen Gettings
Ticker symbol: SVM
S&P rating: A+

Service-Master L.P. provides housekeeping, kitchen, and maintenance services to hospitals, schools, health care facilities, and residential, commercial, and industrial customers. In addition, Service-Master is engaged in pest and termite control and in radon testing.

Service-Master acquired Terminix and American Food Management in 1966. It also acquired Merry Maids, a housekeeping organization. More recently it acquired American Home Shield, which markets home service warranty contracts.

Management services include plant maintenance, cafeteria services, laundry, equipment maintenance, and home health care.

Consumer services include grounds care, both residential and industrial; cleaning; housekeeping; and pest control.

In 1990, Service-Master provided services to about 2,000 customers in 49 states, the District of Columbia, Canada, Japan, and the Middle East.

In 1990, Service Master entered into an agreement with Waste Management to form a new venture, Service-Master Consumer Services, Ltd. Service-Master contributed its SVM cleaning service, Terminix, Merry Maids and American Home Shield to the venture. Waste Management contributed its TRU Green lawn-care service and WMX pest control. Service-Master retains 80.1% ownership in the company.

Also in 1990, Service-Master acquired Classic Care of America, a residential and outside household cleaning company with 24 franchises in 18 states.

In 1990, management services provided 79% of sales and 70% of profits and consumer services 21% of sales and 30% of profits.

Service-Master is a limited partnership, which means that profits flow directly to the shareholder without a corporate income tax. It in effect avoids double taxation first to the company and then to the shareholder.

Institutions control about 20% of the common shares. Consecutive cash dividends have been paid since 1962. Service-Master paid a 50% stock dividend in 1980, 1981, 1983, 1985, and 1992.

Total assets: $797 million
Current ratio: 1.5
Common shares outstanding: 48.0 million

	1981	1982	1983	1984	1985	1986	1987	1988	1989	1990
REVENUES (MIL.)	502	595	701	850	1,022	1,123	1,425	1,531	1,609	1,826
NET INCOME (MIL.)	18	22	26	31	33	33	60	65	68	83
EARNINGS PER SHARE	.37	.43	.52	.62	.67	.67	1.27	1.35	1.40	1.75
DIVIDEND PER SHARE	.25	.31	.39	.46	.53	.68	1.05	1.13	1.17	1.23
PRICES Hi	8.7	12.6	20.5	16.3	17.0	18.3	21.3	18.9	16.2	15.9
Lo	6.7	7.0	11.5	11.9	11.7	13.2	13.7	14.6	13.9	13.2

Sherwin-Williams Company

101 Prospect Avenue N.W.
Cleveland, Ohio 44115
Tel. (216) 566-2000
Listed: NYSE
Investor contact: V.P.–Treas. Conway G. Ivy
Ticker symbol: SMW
S&P rating: A

Sherwin-Williams is North America's largest manufacturer and retailer of paint and wall coverings. Consistent with its trademark, Sherwin-Williams does truly "cover the earth" with more than 2,075 retail paint stores in North and Central America, joint ventures in 3 foreign countries, and licensees in 30 foreign  countries. In addition, Sherwin-Williams has 150 automotive coatings outlets. Coatings include paint, varnishes, and lacquers.

Its products include such well-known brands as Dutch Boy, Kem-Tone, Martin-Senour, Sherwin-Williams, Cuprinol, and some private labels. Also, Sherwin-Williams markets all types of related products such as wall and floor coverings, industrial finishes, brushes, rollers, spray equipment, chemical and industrial coatings, and Krylon and Dupli-

Color spray paints for touch-ups.

Sherwin-Williams supplies its stores and direct customers through 40 distribution warehouses. It expands by adding new large direct accounts, by opening about 40 to 100 new stores each year, and by acquisition. In 1989, it opened 48 new stores.

In 1990, Sherwin-Williams opened 44 new stores and completed its acquisition of DeSoto's architectural coatings and Krylon. Desoto is a private-label paint manufacturer with over $170 million in annual sales. Krylon is a leading aerosol brand of touch-up paints with annual sales of $95 million.

In 1991, Sherwin-Williams opened 50 new stores and remodeled 32 existing stores. In 1991, Sherwin-Williams completed the purchase of Cuprinol, a leading brand of stains, preservatives, and liquid sealers. At the time of acquisition, Cuprinol had annual sales of over $20 million. Also in 1991, Sherwin-Williams completed the purchase of an aerosol packaging plant in Holland, Michigan.

In 1990, retail paint stores accounted for 63% of sales and 39% of profits; coatings for 36% of sales and 59% of profits; and other activities for 1% of sales and 2% of profits.

Sherwin-Williams has posted increased earnings in each of the past 15 years. After a hiatus of several years, Sherwin-Williams restored its cash dividend in 1979. Cash dividends have increased in each of the past eleven years. Institutional investors hold about 60% of the common shares. Sherwin-Williams paid a 100% stock dividend in 1983, a 100% stock dividend in 1986, and a 100% stock dividend in 1991.

Total assets: $1.5 billion
Current ratio: 1.9
Common shares outstanding: 86.7 million

		1981	1982	1983	1984	1985	1986	1987	1988	1989	1990
REVENUES (MIL.)		1,537	1,852	1,973	2,075	2,195	1,553	1,793	1,950	2,123	2,267
NET INCOME (MIL.)		31	43	55	65	75	96	94	101	109	123
EARNINGS PER SHARE		.39	.51	.58	.71	.81	1.05	1.05	1.15	1.26	1.41
DIVIDEND PER SHARE		.10	.13	.15	.19	.23	.25	.28	.32	.35	.38
PRICES	Hi	3.0	6.3	7.9	8.1	11.8	16.1	19.3	15.8	17.9	21.0
	Lo	2.1	2.3	4.6	5.6	7.0	10.7	10.1	12.0	12.5	15.1

Sigma-Aldrich Corporation

3050 Spruce Street
St. Louis, Missouri 63103
Tel. (314) 771-5765
Listed: NASDAQ
Investor contact: V.P.–Treas. P. A. Gleich
Ticker symbol: SIAL
S&P rating: A+

Sigma-Aldrich is basically in two distinct businesses. Its core operation is the manufacture and distribution of some 51,000 biochemicals used in laboratory research and medical diagnosis. Its second operation, B-Line systems, manufactures steel and aluminum components for the strut-cable tray-and-pipe support systems.

Sigma-Aldrich is a major factor in the manufacture and distribution of both organic and inorganic chemicals for diagnostic and research testing. Its chemicals are used in biochemistry, synthetic chemistry, immunology, hematology, pharmacology, and endocrinology.

On some 51,000 products Listed: in Sigma-Aldrich's catalogue, 21,000 are manufactured by Sigma and the remainder are bought from other manufacturers. However, the 21,000 manufactured by Sigma accounted for 44% of sales.

In 1989, Sigma-Aldrich completed its acquisition of Fluka Chemie A.G. Buchs of Switzerland. Fluka sells about 12,000 chemicals in Europe, and about 7,000 of these chemicals are duplicates of Sigma-Aldrich's offerings. Thus, Sigma should be able to realize a number of economies of scale. The acquisition will add about $60 million to Sigma's sales.

In 1990, B-Line Systems purchased Kin-Line, Inc., a West Coast manufacturer and distributor of strut systems.

In 1990, members of the founding families and related trusts sold 1.9 million common shares to the public at $56 a share.

The Bader, Boida, and Fischer families control 16% and institutional investors 60% of the outstanding common shares. Consecutive cash dividends have been paid since 1970. Sigma paid a 100% stock dividend in 1982, a 200% stock dividend in 1986, and a 100% stock dividend in 1991.

Total assets: 546.0 million
Current ratio: 3.7
Common shares outstanding: 49.7 million

		1981	1982	1983	1984	1985	1986	1987	1988	1989	1990
REVENUES (MIL.)		123	136	151	180	215	253	305	375	441	529
NET INCOME (MIL.)		16	17	20	24	29	34	42	57	64	71
EARNINGS PER SHARE		.32	.33	.38	.47	.57	.69	.85	1.15	1.30	1.44
DIVIDEND PER SHARE		.061	.069	.076	.088	.11	.13	.15	.17	.19	.21
PRICES	Hi	5.4	6.8	8.6	8.6	14.2	20.1	25.3	25.6	29.8	35.9
	Lo	4.2	4.2	6.4	7.2	8.6	13.4	15.1	19.9	21.9	25.0

The J.M. Smucker Company

Strawberry Lane
Orrville, Ohio 44667
Tel. (216) 682-3000
Listed: NYSE
Investor contact: Secy. Steven J. Ellcessor
Ticker symbol: SJM
S&P rating: A

Smucker is a leading manufacturer of jams, jellies, orange marmalades, and preserves. It has expanded into related products such as pancake syrup, ice-cream toppings, fruit butters, fruit purees, fruit syrups, ketchup, peanut butter, and fruit juices. It markets its products under such labels as Smucker's, Dickenson's, R. W. Knudsen Family, Magic Shell, Mary Ellen, Good Morning, Goober Jelly, and private-label brands. In addition, it markets jelly and dairy fillings to the bakery trade. Smucker has about 38% market share of the jelly and preserve trade.

Smucker dominates the jam market and is able to continually increase market share against competitors such as Kraft. Its primary preserve and jelly plant is in Orrville, Ohio. It also has a specialty jam and jelly manufacturing plant in Ripon, Wisconsin, and satellite manufacturing facilities in Salinas, California; Memphis, Tennessee; Elsenham, England; and Kyabram, Victoria, Australia. Peanut butter is processed in Bethlehem, Pennsylvania. Fruit processing is undertaken at two plants in California, one in Oregon, and one in the state of Washington. Juices are produced in Chico, California.

In 1989, Smucker introduced a line of fruit spreads under the brand name Simply Fruit. Also in 1989, Smucker introduced a peanut butter and jelly item under the name Goober Snack Pack. In 1989, Smucker acquired the Vitari product line of a frozen whipped fruit-flavor dessert which it is marketing under the name of "Smucker's Fruitage." Also in 1989, Smucker purchased the Australian Henry Jones line of jams, preserves, and honey and is now marketing it under the name of "IXL."

The Smucker family controls about 27% and institutions about 50% of the outstanding common shares. Consecutive cash dividends have been paid since 1949. Smucker paid a 100% stock dividend in 1983, a 100% stock dividend in 1985, a 100% stock dividend in 1990, and one Class B (nonvoting) common share for each share of Class A in 1991.

Total assets: 252.4 million
Current ratio: 2.8
Common shares outstanding: Class A 14.8 million
Class B 14.8 million

		1982	1983	1984	1985	1986	1987	1988	1989	1990	1991
REVENUES (MIL.)		191	200	215	230	263	288	314	367	422	455
NET INCOME (MIL.)		11	12	14	16	16	18	23	28	30	32
EARNINGS PER SHARE		.37	.42	.47	.54	.54	.60	.78	.94	1.03	1.08
DIVIDEND PER SHARE		.08	.09	.10	.12	.14	.16	.19	.23	.28	.35
PRICES	Hi	4.7	5.8	7.0	12.9	12.5	15.0	15.7	19.5	23.2	38.9
	Lo	2.0	3.8	4.5	6.5	9.3	9.8	11.7	14.4	16.1	20.0

Society Corporation

800 Superior Avenue
Cleveland, Ohio 44114-2692
Tel. (216) 689-3000
Listed: NASDAQ

Investor contact: S.V.P. Eric P. Rasmussen
Ticker symbol: SOCI
S&P rating: A+

As profiled in its 1990 Annual Report, "Society Corporation is a financial services company focussed on the Great Lakes Basin of the United States and based in Cleveland, Ohio. At December 31, 1990, Society Corporation had an asset base of $15.1 billion, over 350 banking offices in Ohio, Indiana and Michigan, and a trust subsidiary in Florida. Society's major business activities include providing traditional banking and associated financial services to consumer, business and commercial markets. The Corporation also offers customers a variety of complementary services, either directly or through its nonbank subsidiaries. Society operates the Green Machine automated teller machine (ATM) network with more than 850 ATMs in the region and additional access through regional and international ATM networks.

"Society Corporation serves its customers principally through five regional banks headquartered in Ohio, Indiana, and Michigan and a trust subsidiary in Florida." With the early 1990 acquisition of Trustcorp, Inc., of Toledo, Society became the third-largest bank holding company in Ohio. Its banking units include Society National of Cleveland; Society Bank & Trust, Toldeo; Society Bank National Association, Dayton; Society Bank, Indiana; and Society Bank, Michigan. Its banks are supported by credit-life, mortgage, and credit-card services provided by Society Corporation subsidiaries.

In September 1991, Society acquired Cleveland rival Ameritrust Corp., in a stock-swap deal valued at nearly $1.2 billion. Ameritrust has banking offices in Ohio and Indiana. While Ameritrust has substantial loan losses, it has a very strong trust department. The merger will create a huge banking company with more than $26 billion in assets and more than 500 banking offices in Ohio, Indiana, Michigan, and Connecticut. The combined banking company will retain the name Society Corp.

In 1990, loans of $10.1 billion were apportioned as follows: commercial, financial, and agricultural, 31.1%; real estate construction, 5.4%; real estate residential, 15.2%; real estate commercial, 13.8%; consumer, 30.8%; lease financing, 3.5%; and foreign, 0.2%.

Society has paid consecutive cash dividends since 1963. Institutions control about 35% of the common shares. It paid a 100% stock dividend in 1987.

Total assets: 15.1 billion
Common shares outstanding: 33.4 million

		1981	1982	1983	1984	1985	1986	1987	1988	1989	1990
NET INCOME (MIL.)		23	27	29	44	80	84	91	100	110	158
EARNINGS PER SHARE		1.77	2.09	2.27	2.72	3.01	3.43	3.75	4.19	4.63	4.71
DIVIDEND PER SHARE		.72	.76	.80	.85	.92	.96	1.20	1.36	1.60	1.76
PRICES	Hi	9.6	12.3	15.1	18.3	27.5	35.8	40.0	37.8	40.5	35.3
	Lo	7.5	7.1	10.8	14.3	17.8	27.0	26.5	31.0	33.0	24.0

SouthTrust Corporation

420 N. 20th Street
Birmingham, Alabama 35203
Tel. (205) 254-5509
Listed: NASDAQ
Investor contact: Treas. Aubrey D. Barnard
Ticker symbol: SOTR
S&P rating: A

Based in Birmingham, Alabama, South-Trust is a rapidly growing commercial bank, which consistently acquires small-sized banks in the Southeast. It is the second-largest bank in Alabama. At last count it operated 27 banks in Alabama, nine in Florida, three in Georgia, two in South Carolina, and one in Tennessee as well as

> **SouthTrust Corporation**

eight banking affiliates. These banks have a total of more than 265 banking offices. During 1989, SouthTrust opened banking offices in Sarasota, Florida, and Charleston, South Carolina. It is contemplating an acquisition in North Carolina.

SouthTrust consistently increased its fee income and mortgage business. Its trust business is very strong.

In 1990, deposits of $6.5 billion were divided as follows: time deposits, 73.1%; demand deposits, 22.0%; and savings 4.9%.

In 1990, loans of $5.6 billion were divided as follows: commercial, financial, and agricultural, 34%; real estate construction, 9%; commercial mortgage, 20%; residential mortgage, 18%; and consumer, 19%.

In 1990, income of $867.7 million was earned as follows: interest and fees on loans, 64.3%; investment securities, 25.7%; trust, 1.1%; fees and charges, 6.3%; and other income, 2.6%.

Institutions control about 30% of the outstanding common shares. Consecutive cash dividends have been paid since 1944. SouthTrust paid a 50% stock dividend in 1983, a 66 2/3% stock dividend in 1985, a 4% stock dividend in 1989, and a 50% stock dividend in 1992.

Total assets: $9.0 billion
Common shares outstanding: 40.9 million

		1981	1982	1983	1984	1985	1986	1987	1988	1989	1990
NET INCOME (MIL.)		20	23	28	35	44	54	60	68	73	70
EARNINGS PER SHARE		.69	.81	.94	1.14	1.27	1.45	1.57	1.71	1.82	1.71
DIVIDEND PER SHARE		.26	.28	.31	.34	.39	.44	.51	.56	.64	.69
PRICES	Hi	3.6	3.8	6.7	8.9	12.3	16.5	15.9	14.2	16.8	15.5
	Lo	2.9	2.6	3.8	5.7	8.6	12.2	10.3	11.2	13.1	8.6

Student Loan Marketing Association

1050 Thomas Jefferson Street N.W.
Washington, D.C. 20007
Tel. (202) 333-8000
Listed: NYSE
Investor contact: V.P. Beth Van Houton
Ticker symbol: SLM
S&P rating: A

Student Loan Marketing (Sallie Mae) is a quasi-governmental federally charted corporation, established by Congress in 1972 to provide a liquid market for student loans originated by banks and educational institutions. The president of the United States appoints the chairperson and 7 members to the 21-member board.

Sallie Mae makes a secondary market in federally guaranteed loans made to students by lenders participating in the Guaranteed Student Loan Program and the Health Education Assistance Loan Program. The federal government pays 3.25% over the federal 91-day bill rate plus an allowance on these loans while the student is still in school. After graduation, the student becomes obligated to start repayment of principle and interest. It is at the point of the student's graduation that Sallie Mae purchases most of the loans.

SallieMae

Although, because of demographics, the student population is declining, Sallie Mae continues to expand for a number of reasons. First, the cost of an education continues to rise. Second, more older people are showing up on campuses. Third, the sheer complexity of the government requirements makes it easier to sell the loans to Sallie Mae, which is technically geared to handle a large volume of loans.

Sallie Mae has upward of 33% of the market for student loans. Sallie Mae's loan processing system, known as Port S.S., is the finest on the market. Sallie Mae is expanding its loan-processing plant in Pennsylvania and is building a new one in Florida. It has additional processing plants in Texas, Kansas, and Virginia. Also, Sallie Mae makes warehousing advances to lenders in support of new loans. Since all student loans are guaranteed by the federal government and warehousing advances are fully collateralized, Sallie Mae does not have to contend with a loan loss reserve.

Sallie Mae assisted in the formation of a new corporation, The College Construction Loan Insurance Association, to underwrite both insurance and re-insurance on higher education and education health facilities.

Sallie Mae has paid consecutive cash dividends since 1977. Institutions control more than 85% of the common shares. Sallie Mae became public in 1983 and paid a 2 1/2-for-1 stock split in 1989.

Total assets: $41.1 billion
Common shares outstanding: 96.9 million

	1981	1982	1983	1984	1985	1986	1987	1988	1989	1990
REVENUES (MIL.)	641	772	860	1,160	1,216	1,300	1,582	2,172	3,169	3,503
NET INCOME (MIL.)	18	38	67	99	123	145	181	225	258	301
EARNINGS PER SHARE	.21	.43	.55	.76	.98	1.23	1.66	2.14	2.53	2.96
DIVIDEND PER SHARE	.016	.024	.033	.049	.073	.11	.16	.24	.41	.59
PRICES Hi	—	—	11.4	13.9	15.4	27.5	35.9	34.5	53.5	56.5
Lo	—	—	8.4	8.4	10.0	14.1	24.4	28.0	33.4	32.8

SunTrust Banks, Inc.

25 Park Place, N.E.
Atlanta, Georgia 30303
Tel. (404) 588-7711
Listed: NYSE
Investor contact: V.P., James C. Armstrong
Ticker symbol: STI
S&P rating: A+

SunTrust Banks is the product of the 1985 merger of Sun Banks of Florida and the Trust Co. of Georgia and the 1986 acquisition of Third National Corp., the second largest bank in Tennessee. At last count, SunTrust Banks had 21 banks with 323 branches in Florida, 10 banks with 190 branches in Georgia, and five banks with 110 branches in Tennessee.

SunTrust has over $25 billion of trust assets under management, the largest trust portfolio in the Southeast. SunTrust owns 12,066,624 shares of Coca-Cola, which has a market value of over $793 million but is carried on its books at $110,000. Also, SunTrust has a $3.7 billion mortgage servicing portfolio.

SunTrust is having some difficulty with its Tennessee operations because of a relatively soft real estate market. This factor has temporarily slowed the rate of growth.

In 1990, deposits of $25.1 billion were divided as follows: demand deposits, 25%; savings deposits, 22%; time deposits, 34%; short-term borrowings, 8%; long-term debt, 2%; equity, 7%; and other, 2%.

In 1990, loans outstanding were divided as follows: commercial, 34%; commercial real estate, 23%; residential real estate, 22%; and consumer loans, 21%.

In 1990, earnings assets of $27.7 billion were divided as follows: loans, 77%; investment securities, 20%; and money market assets, 3%.

Consecutive cash dividends for the holding company have been paid since 1985. Consecutive earnings and dividend increases on the predecessor companies go back many years. SunTrust paid a 100% stock dividend in 1986.

Total assets: $33.4 billion
Common shares outstanding: 126.8 million

		1981	1982	1983	1984	1985	1986	1987	1988	1989	1990
NET INCOME (MIL.)		—	—	—	—	167	245	283	309	337	350
EARNINGS PER SHARE		—	—	—	—	1.65	1.85	2.17	2.38	2.61	2.75
DIVIDEND PER SHARE		—	—	—	—	.57	.61	.65	.70	.78	.86
PRICES	Hi	—	—	—	—	20.4	27.3	27.8	24.5	26.9	24.3
	Lo	—	—	—	—	13.6	17.4	17.0	18.5	19.8	16.5

Super Food Services, Inc.

3223 Newmark Drive
Dayton, Ohio 45342
Tel. (513) 439-7500
Listed: NYSE
Investor contact: S.V.P. Finance and Treas., Robert F. Koogler
Ticker symbol: SFS
S&P rating: A+

As profiled in its 1990 Annual Report, "Super Foods is engaged in the wholesale grocery distribution business. As a full-line supplier to more than 950 affiliated retail stores in seven states, the Company is one of the leaders in the $96 billion wholesale food distribution industry.

"Generally, Super Food's business consists of the procurement, warehousing, order selection, and delivery of food and retail products.

Super Food Services, Inc.

The Company purchases from hundreds of processors, manufacturers, and growers. With careful attention to changing market conditions, products are ordered in large quantities and transported to Super Foods distribution centers.

"Each distribution center serves as a central source of supply for its customers within its operating area. Complete inventories of virtually every national brand grocery product sold in supermarkets are maintained, together with a number of high volume private label items. In addition, all distribution centers provide a full line of perishables including fresh meats and poultry, dairy, bakery, delicatessen products and frozen foods.

"Super Foods also offers a complete range of supporting services, which enables its affiliated retailers to compete effectively with all other types of food stores in their respective markets because of high volume, rapid turnover of inventories and operational efficiencies, the cost of the entire distribution and service system is maintained at a low level. As a result, retailers and consumers benefit from the overall productivity and efficiency of the operation and the Company is able to generate an equitable return on investment for its shareholders."

Super Foods distributes to approximately 335 IGA and 695 other independently-owned retail grocery stores, a number of chains (including Albertsons, which accounts for over 30% of sales), and convenience stores. It operates seven warehouses: three in Ohio, two in Michigan, and two in Florida. In 1991, Super Food acquired Kentucky Food Stores, Inc., which has headquarters in Lexington and serves 120 retail stores. Also in 1991, Super Food constructed a 100,000-square-foot perishable distribution center adjacent to its warehouse in Cincinnati, Ohio.

Super Foods has paid consecutive cash dividends since 1971. Institutions control more than 65% of the common shares. It paid 5% stock dividends from 1976 to 1982, a 50% stock dividend in June 1983, a 5% stock dividend in November 1983, a 5% stock dividend in 1984, a 100% stock dividend in 1985, and a 50% stock dividend in 1989.

Total assets: $304.2 million
Current ratio: 2.5
Common shares outstanding: 10.8 million

	1982	1983	1984	1985	1986	1987	1988	1989	1990	1991
REVENUES (MIL.)	1,129	1,225	1,291	1,397	1,422	1,532	1,569	1,697	1,772	1,826
NET INCOME (MIL.)	3.6	5.5	7.3	9.2	11	12	15	16	17	12
EARNINGS PER SHARE	.35	.62	.70	.88	.99	1.12	1.35	1.47	1.60	1.13
DIVIDEND PER SHARE	.086	.099	.13	.15	.17	.21	.25	.29	.32	.34
PRICES Hi	4.1	9.6	8.8	13.1	18.5	19.4	18.1	22.0	20.8	18.5
Lo	2.3	3.6	5.1	7.8	10.8	9.6	12.6	17.0	14.8	12.6

Super Valu Stores, Inc.

11840 Valley View Road
Eden Prairie, Minnesota 55344
Tel. (612) 828-4000
Listed: NYSE
Investor contact: V.P. Communications, Michael L. Mulligan
Ticker symbol: SVU
S&P rating: A+

Super Valu is the nation's largest food wholesaler. It functions more or less as a food broker to over 2,800 independently owned stores in 33 states with 20 distribution centers. Its operations are mostly in the Midwest, South, and West. In addition, the company has a majority interest in more than 100 retail grocery stores operating  under such names as Mornbacher's, Great Scot, Sunflower, and County Market. It both owns (19) and franchises (over 80) retail supermarket Cub stores and also franchises (over 90) retail grocery stores under the County Market and New Market logos.

Super Valu owns a chain of 104 ShopKo discount houseware and hardware stores. Also, Super Valu owns and operates two Twin Valu hypermarket stores, one in Cleveland and the other in Euclid, Ohio. The Twin Valu store combines in 180,000 square feet the groceries of a Cub Supermarket with the merchandise of a ShopKo store. It is expected that Super Valu will utilize the hypermarket concept to penetrate large cities such as Chicago.

Super Valu acquired the Food Giant Stores of Georgia in 1986 but to date has not followed up with any additional East Coast expansion.

In 1991, wholesale groceries accounted for 73% of sales and 69% of profits, retail foods accounted for 14% of sales and 2% of profits, and ShopKo for 13% of sales and 29% of profits.

Institutions own about 65% of Super Valu's outstanding shares. Super Valu has reported higher earnings in 16 of the last 17 years. It has paid consecutive cash dividends since 1936. It paid a 100% stock dividend in 1986.

Total assets: $2.6 billion
Current ratio: 1.1
Common shares outstanding: 75.2 million

		1982	1983	1984	1985	1986	1987	1988	1989	1990	1991
REVENUES (MIL.)		4,622	5,197	5,923	6,548	7,905	9,066	9,372	10,296	11,136	11,612
NET INCOME (MIL.)		65	68	77	83	91	89	112	135	148	155
EARNINGS PER SHARE		.89	.93	1.04	1.13	1.23	1.20	1.50	1.81	1.97	2.06
DIVIDEND PER SHARE		.23	.27	.30	.33	.37	.41	.44	.49	.59	.65
PRICES	Hi	14.1	18.5	16.9	23.9	27.9	30.4	26.4	30.1	29.0	30.3
	Lo	7.9	12.9	11.9	15.1	19.8	16.0	17.0	22.6	21.8	21.6

Synovus Financial Corp

901 Front Avenue
Columbus, Georgia 31902
Tel. (404) 649-2197
Listed: NYSE
Investor contact: Stephen L. Burts
Ticker symbol: SNV
S&P rating: A+

Synovus is a medium-sized bank and financial services holding company. Based in Columbus, Georgia, and formerly known as CB&T Bancshares, Synovus owns over 22 banks in Georgia, northwest Florida, and Alabama. In addition to its banking operations, Synovus owns and operates Synovus Securities, a full-service broker and owns 82% of Total Systems Service, a credit card processing subsidiary, which more recently became the issuer and processor of the AT&T Universal Card. Total Systems accounts for over 25% of Synovus's total income.

Columbus Bank & Trust of Georgia is Synovus's flagship bank. A conservative loan policy combined with an acquisition binge and a highly successful data processing operation have fueled Synovus's earnings.

Synovus Financial Corp.

In 1991, Synovus acquired the $135.6 million-asset Sea Island Bankshares of Statesboro, Georgia; the $22 million-asset First Coast Community Bank of Fernandina Beach, Florida; the $513 million-asset Athens Federal Savings Bank of Athens, Georgia; the $125 million-asset Citizens Federal Savings & Loan Association of Rome, Georgia; the $52 million-asset CB Bancshares of Fort Valley, Georgia; the $34 million-asset Citizens Bank of Cochran, Georgia; and the $30 million-asset Carroll National Bank of Carrollton, Georgia. Through the merging of many small banks, Synovus has been able to realize economies of scale and thus increase profitability.

In 1990, loans of $2.0 billion were apportioned as follows: commercial, financial, and agricultural, 36.1%; real estate construction, 6.9%; real estate mortgage, 32.2%; and consumer, 24.8%.

In 1990, income of $390.8 million was divided as follows: loans and fees, 57.4%; investment securities, 10.5%; other interest, 1.0%; and non-interest income, 31.1%.

Synovus and its predecessors had paid consecutive cash dividends since 1891. Institutions control about 5% of the common shares. Synovus paid a 100% stock dividend in 1984, a 50% stock dividend in 1985, a 50% stock dividend in 1986, and a 50% stock dividend in 1988.

Total assets: $2.9 billion
Common shares outstanding: 35.9 million

		1981	1982	1983	1984	1985	1986	1987	1988	1989	1990
NET INCOME (MIL.)		7.1	6.5	8.1	12	16	19	24	27	31	35
EARNINGS PER SHARE		.29	.27	.32	.44	.55	.63	.81	.87	1.01	1.05
DIVIDEND PER SHARE		.11	.11	.12	.14	.17	.21	.25	.28	.33	.37
PRICES	Hi	2.8	2.8	4.5	6.8	13.4	15.8	16.6	15.0	19.5	19.0
	Lo	1.8	1.8	2.6	4.4	5.4	10.5	9.6	11.6	11.3	12.5

Syntex Corporation

3401 Hillview Avenue
Palo Alto, California 94304
Tel. (415) 855-5050
Listed: NYSE
Investor contact: V.P. Public Affairs and Communications, Kathleen N. Gary
Ticker symbol: SYN
S&P rating: A

Syntex Corporation is a large manufacturer of ethical pharmaceuticals, but its success is largely attributed to its antiarthritic drugs Naprosyn and Anaprox. The chief competitive advantage of these two drugs is that they are nonsteroidal. These two drugs represent over 50% of Syntex's total sales.

However, Naprosyn loses patent protection in 1993. Syntex has plans for an over-the-counter Naprosyn product to be marketed through a joint venture with Procter & Gamble. Syntex will also wholesale Naprosyn to generic companies.

Additional human pharmaceuticals include Toradol for pain, Synarel for endometriosis, Cytovene for the treatment of AIDS-related eye infections, Cardene for cardiovascular ailments, Lidex, Norinyl and Femstat. Also, Syntex manufactures and distributes steroids used for dermatitis, oral contraceptives, and diagnostic products. In the animal health field, Syntex products include the dewormer Synanthic and the growth stimulant Synovex.

Syntex's future growth depends on the success of its newer pharmaceuticals. In the first quarter of 1991, sales advanced 16%, half of that from drugs introduced in the preceeding 20 months. Two new drugs with exceptional prospects are Toradol, a nonnarcotic analgesic, and Ticlid, to treat strokes.

In 1991, foreign sales accounted for 31% of sales and 62% of profits. Thus money exchange rates are a major factor in the earnings picture.

In 1991, pharmaceuticals accounted for 89% of sales and 95% of profits; diagnostics, 11% of sales and 5% of profits.

Syntex has paid consecutive cash dividends since 1963. Institutions control more than 50% of the outstanding shares. Syntex split two-for-one in 1982, 1985, 1987, and 1991.

Total assets: $2.3 billion
Current ratio: 1.5
Common shares outstanding: 240.9 million

		1982	1983	1984	1985	1986	1987	1988	1989	1990	1991
REVENUES (MIL.)		715	757	800	850	980	1,129	1,272	1,349	1,521	1,817
NET INCOME (MIL.)		134	149	135	150	199	249	297	303	342	424
EARNINGS PER SHARE		.50	.52	.50	.61	.81	1.03	1.25	1.33	1.53	1.89
DIVIDEND PER SHARE		.13	.16	.19	.22	.29	.43	.54	.68	.76	.83
PRICES	Hi	7.7	7.9	7.1	11.8	18.8	24.0	22.1	27.3	31.9	50.3
	Lo	3.6	5.6	4.8	5.9	10.2	11.5	16.1	18.3	23.4	26.8

SYSCO Corporation

1390 Enclave Parkway
Houston, Texas 77077-2027
Tel. (713) 584-1390
Listed: NYSE
Investor contact: Director Corporate Communications, Toni R. Spigelmyer
Ticker symbol: SYY
S&P rating: A+

SYSCO is the nation's largest marketer and distributor of food and related products to more than 230,000 restaurants, fast-food chains, hotels, motels, and institutions such as colleges, schools, hospitals, and nursing homes. Because of SYSCO's far-flung operation of 70-plus distribution centers in 36 states and Vancouver, British Columbia, it is an ideal distributor for widely franchised hotels and fast-food chains.

SYSCO distributes a broad range of food, including frozen food, produce, and related products. Its food items range from a complete line of frozen foods, fruits, vegetables, and desserts to canned foods and dry foods such as cereals and macaroni.

Related items sold include napkins, kitchen utensils, paperware such as cups, kitchen and restaurant equipment, and clean-up materials such as soaps and detergents.

SYSCO markets both national-brand products and its own private-labeled products. It also distributes to the retail food markets in New York. Its retail distribution consists primarily of consumer-sized frozen products.

In late 1988, SYSCO acquired Staley Continental's $2.5-billion food-service business for $725 million. It immediately sold Staley's manufacturing and processing operations, which resulted in a net investment of $475 million. It is gradually consolidating Staley's C.F.S. Continental's operations into its own and in 1989 and 1990 merged operations in Atlanta, Chicago, Los Angeles, Miami, Minneapolis, Orlando, Phoenix, and Pittsburgh. SYSCO expands primarily by increased market penetration and at a rate of five times the industry.

In 1991, SYSCO's food distribution and marketing was broken down as follows: restaurants, 60%; hospitals and nursing homes, 12%; schools and colleges, 8%;, hotels and motels, 7%; and other, 13%.

Officers and directors control about 6% and institutions about 55% of the outstanding common shares. SYSCO has paid consecutive cash dividends since 1970. In 1991, SYSCO completed its 16th consecutive year of higher earnings. SYSCO paid a 50% stock dividend in 1980, a 100% stock dividend in 1982, a 100% stock dividend in 1986, and a 100% stock dividend in 1989.

Total assets: $2.2 billion
Current ratio: 1.9
Common shares outstanding: 92.2 million

		1982	1983	1984	1985	1986	1987	1988	1989	1990	1991
REVENUES (MIL.)		1,700	1,950	2,312	2,628	3,172	3,656	4,385	6,851	7,591	8,150
NET INCOME (MIL.)		34	40	45	50	58	62	87	108	132	154
EARNINGS PER SHARE		.43	.48	.53	.59	.67	.70	.90	1.19	1.45	1.67
DIVIDEND PER SHARE		.055	.075	.085	.095	.10	.13	.15	.17	.20	.24
PRICES	Hi	10.5	11.2	9.7	11.7	17.0	20.8	19.5	33.5	38.4	47.4
	Lo	5.3	7.8	6.5	8.0	11.3	11.3	13.0	18.4	25.6	30.0

Tambrands Inc.

1 Marcus Avenue
Lake Success, New York 11042
Tel. (516) 358-8300
Listed: NYSE
Investor contact: S.V.P. P. E. Konney
Ticker symbol: TMB
S&P rating: A-

Tambrands, originally Tampax, is the largest manufacturer of tampons, with about a 60% market share. When women became concerned about toxic shock syndrome, during the 60s, Tampax, then a one-product company, suffered drastically. Subsequently, Tampax began to expand into related products.

> Tambrands, Inc.

In addition to Tampax tampons, Tambrands now manufactures and sells Maxithins, which are external pad and panty shields for feminine hygiene. It also makes and sells disposable diapers.

New management has made a number of changes for Tambrands and is contemplating more. In early 1990, it sold the unprofitable First Response, its diagnostic pregnancy and ovulation kit subsidiary, to Carter Wallace. Also, it sold another subsidiary, Physicians Formula, a manufacturer of hypoallergenic cosmetics, to Pierre Fabre, Inc.

Currently, management is selling to replenish inventory, rather than stocking up for sales promotions. On a positive note, Tambrands is beefing up its distribution system and targeting an increased market share for its personal hygiene products. Also, it is introducing a new odorless tampon.

Tambrands sells its products in 135 foreign countries and has subsidiaries in Brazil, Canada, England, Ireland, France, Spain, Mexico, Turkey, the Soviet Union, and China. Since 39% of sales are to foreign countries, currency exchange plays a major role in earnings.

In 1990, sales and income were geographically allocated as follows: United States, 55% of sales and 70% of income; Europe, 28% of sales and 22% of income; and other foreign, 17% of sales and 8% of income.

In February, 1991, the directors authorized the repurchase of up to 2.1 million common shares on the open market. Tambrands has no long-term debt and institutions hold about 80% of the outstanding common shares. It has paid consecutive cash dividends since 1942. It paid a 100% stock dividend in 1986 and another 100% stock dividend in 1990.

Total assets: $381.0 million
Current ratio: 2.1
Common shares outstanding: 41.4 million

	1981	1982	1983	1984	1985	1986	1987	1988	1989	1990
REVENUES (MIL.)	233	288	346	390	420	487	539	563	583	632
NET INCOME (MIL.)	42	43	51	57	62	69	77	85	1.7	98
EARNINGS PER SHARE	.94	.96	1.15	1.28	1.41	1.56	1.73	1.92	.04	2.20
DIVIDEND PER SHARE	.65	.66	.71	.76	.81	.86	.92	.98	1.04	1.11
PRICES Hi	8.9	13.3	15.5	15.5	22.9	30.5	35.6	31.6	38.3	45.5
Lo	6.9	7.8	11.3	11.7	14.2	21.8	22.4	25.3	26.3	33.8

Tootsie Roll Industries, Inc.

7401 South Cicero Avenue
Chicago, Illinois 60629
Tel. (312) 838-3400
Listed: NYSE
Investor contact: President, Ellen R. Gordon
Ticker symbol: TR
S&P rating: A

**Tootsie Roll
Industries, Inc.**

Tootsie Roll Industries is a leading candy manufacturer based in Chicago. The company's hallmark is the famous Tootsie Roll, which is chocolate of a chewey consistency. Also, Tootsie Roll Industries manufactures and markets Tootsie Pops, Tootsie Bubble Pops, Tootsie Pop Drops, Tootsie Flavor Rolls, Mason Dots, and Tootsie Gum Drops.

In 1985, Tootsie acquired Cella's Confections, Inc., a chocolate-covered-cherry manufacturer. In 1988, it acquired the Charms Company, a manufacturer of fruit-flavored hard candy and lollipops. Although purchased at a rather high cost (22 times 1987 earnings), Charms has consistently proven itself to be a very profitable acquisition for the company.

Tootsie Roll Industries has manufacturing plants in Chicago, New York, Tennessee, and Mexico City. Principal ingredients used in the manufacture of candy are sugar, corn syrup, vegetable oil, milk, and cocoa. Thus manufacturing costs are related to the highly volatile costs of commodities.

The candy items are widely distributed through retail outlets, vending machines, food brokers, and large grocery distributors. Foreign sales are to Canada, Mexico, the Philippines, and many other countries.

Tootsie Roll Industries has no long-term debt. It has both a regular and a Class B common stock issue. The Class B common stock is transferable on a one-to-one basis with regular common stock shares. However, the Class B common shares have ten votes per share as against one vote per share of the regular common stock. Chairman and Chief Executive Officer Melvin J. Gordon and his wife, President Ellen R. Gordon, control about 35% of the regular common shares and about 65% of the B shares. Tootsie Roll Industries has paid consecutive cash dividends since 1942. It has paid a 3% stock dividend in every year since 1964. It also paid a 50% stock dividend in 1986 and a 100% stock dividend in 1987.

Total assets: $160 million
Current ratio: 3.5
Common shares outstanding: 6.5 million
Class B 3.4 million

	1981	1982	1983	1984	1985	1986	1987	1988	1989	1990
REVENUES (MIL.)	76	76	78	93	107	111	115	129	179	194
NET INCOME (MIL.)	3.3	4.7	5.7	8.9	11	13	15	17	20	23
EARNINGS PER SHARE	.33	.48	.56	.87	1.11	1.29	1.46	1.67	2.04	2.27
DIVIDEND PER SHARE	.10	.10	.11	.11	.14	.16	.20	.21	.22	.22
PRICES Hi	3.2	4.1	5.3	9.6	17.4	23.3	30.2	32.5	36.3	48.5
Lo	2.1	2.3	3.5	2.8	7.0	14.4	18.3	24.5	22.9	30.1

261

Torchmark Corporation

2001 Third Avenue South
Birmingham, Alabama 35233
Tel. (205) 325-4200
Listed: NYSE
Investor contact: M. Klyce
Ticker symbol: TMK
S&P rating: A+

Torchmark (formerly known as Liberty National Insurance) is a large financial services conglomerate consisting of Liberty National Life, Liberty National Fire Insurance Co., American Life & Accident, Globe Life & Accident, United American Insurance Co., and United Investors Management Co. and its subsidiary, Waddell & Reed.

Liberty National Life is Torchmark's largest operation with over $20 billion of life insurance in force. Based primarily in the Southeast, it sells a full portfolio of life products, including accident, health, and annuity coverages.

American Life and Accident and Globe Life & Accident are both accident and health insurance carriers and operate through a network of agents and brokers.

United Investors Management is a financial planning company, which through its Waddell & Reed subsidiary distributes more than 16 types of mutual funds. United American Insurance Company writes life insurance for United Investors Management clientele.

Torchmark subsidiaries are very active in the sale and underwriting of Medicare supplemental policies.

In 1990, premium breakdown was as follows: individual life, 36%; individual health, 44%; and other, including property and casualty, 20%.

In early 1990, Torchmark made a failed bid ($50 a share, half in cash and half in Torchmark shares) for American General Corp., a large Houston-based life and health insurer.

Between 1986 and 1988, Torchmark purchased over 17.4 million of its common shares. There is some indication that Torchmark will continue to purchase sizable blocks of its shares on the open market. Torchmark has had 36 consecutive years of earnings and dividends increases. Institutions hold about 45% of the outstanding common shares. Torchmark paid a 100% stock dividend in 1985.

Total assets: $5.5 billion
Common shares outstanding: 51.4 million

		1981	1982	1983	1984	1985	1986	1987	1988	1989	1990
REVENUES (MIL.)		576	933	1,110	1,097	1,297	1,459	1,533	1,611	1,634	1,796
NET INCOME (MIL.)		70	75	98	130	165	205	189	185	211	229
EARNINGS PER SHARE		.94	1.06	1.32	1.62	2.20	2.73	2.86	3.11	3.88	4.28
DIVIDEND PER SHARE		.35	.38	.40	.45	.53	.80	1.00	1.10	1.25	1.40
PRICES	Hi	7.0	7.5	11.4	17.1	26.8	38.5	36.8	33.5	58.8	57.4
	Lo	5.0	5.5	6.5	9.3	14.6	21.3	21.8	23.8	30.0	38.0

America's GROWTH STOCKS

Tyco Laboratories, Inc.

One Tyco Park
Exeter, New Hampshire 03833
Tel. (603) 778-7900
Listed: NYSE
Investor contact: V.P. Irving Gutin
Ticker symbol: TYC
S&P rating: A-

Tyco Laboratories is a manufacturer of fire protection systems, flow control products, and electric and electronic components. Its Grinnell fire protection subsidiary is a very large designer, manufacturer, and installer of automatic sprinkler systems for new and existing buildings. Its Simplex subsidiary is a manufacturer of undersea cable and fibre-optic communications and power systems.

Also, Simplex manufactures and markets electrical supplies and electronic components. Its Mueller and Allied divisions manufacture and distribute flow systems, including pipes, pumps, and fittings used in the distribution of gas and water. The Wormald International Limited sub-

TYCO LABORATORIES

sidiary, acquired in 1990, is a large Australian manufacturer of fire protection alarms and other alarm devices. Through the Ludlow division, acquired in 1981, Tyco makes paper, polyethylene, and packaging products.

The Simplex subsidiary is experiencing record backlogs, with recent orders from AT&T and the U.S. Navy.

Earnings are being slightly restrained because of a combination of a cutback in construction and the issuance of a large number of shares for the acquisition of Wormald International.

In 1991, fire protection/flow control afforded 77% of revenues and 68% of income; electric and electronic components, 12% of revenues and 18% of income; and packaging, 11% of revenues and 14% of income.

Tyco has paid consecutive cash dividends since 1975. Institutions control more than 55% of the common shares. Tyco paid a 100% stock dividend in 1986 and a 100% stock dividend in 1987.

Total assets: $2.4 billion
Current ratio: 1.3
Common shares outstanding: 47.1 million

		1982	1983	1984	1985	1986	1987	1988	1989	1990	1991
REVENUES (MIL.)		552	574	650	674	796	1,062	1,575	1,971	2,103	3,108
NET INCOME (MIL.)		23	21	30	35	35	44	66	91	119	117
EARNINGS PER SHARE		.64	.62	.81	.94	1.02	1.27	1.93	2.31	2.90	2.57
DIVIDEND PER SHARE		.17	.18	.18	.20	.20	.20	.24	.27	.31	.35
PRICES	Hi	4.9	7.5	9.5	12.3	21.3	28.1	38.4	53.8	65.8	52.3
	Lo	2.5	4.4	6.5	8.3	11.6	15.8	21.0	32.3	37.1	28.0

Tyson Foods, Inc.

2210 W. Oaklawn Drive
Springdale, Arkansas 72764
Tel. (501) 756-4000
Listed: NASDAQ
Investor contact: Treas. Wayne Britt

Ticker symbol: TYSMA
S&P rating: A

Tyson, based in Arkansas, is one of the largest poultry processing plants in the United States. It has expanded both by acquisition and by extension of its product line. Tyson owns 24 hatcheries, 14 feed mills, and 29 processing plants. Some of Tyson's better known brand names include Chick 'N Quick, Tyson Chicken Entrees, Tyson Country Fresh Chicken Originals, and Weaver.

Tyson Foods, Inc.

Tyson acquired Valmac Industries in 1984 and Lane Processing and Heritage Valley in 1986. In 1989, Tyson entered into a bidding war with ConAgra for competitor Holly Farms Corp. Tyson won the war at $70 per share for Holly, a total cost of $1.29 billion. Tyson intends to divest itself of Holly's baking, flour, and by-products businesses. Near-term, the acquisition is dilutive; long-term, it should pay off.

Tyson markets both to the food service industry (55%) and to retail grocery distributors (45%). It markets fresh and frozen chicken, turkey, and Cornish hens. Also, it sells precooked poultry, breaded patties, marinated chicken breasts, nuggets, and other boned poultry. Likewise, Tyson has a pork, Crispito flour, and Mexican tortilla business.

Feed costs are a major component in the margin of profit of a poultry producer such as Tyson.

In 1990, sales were divided as follows: value-enhanced poultry, 69%; other poultry, 12%; pork products, 2%; Mexican food, 14%; and other, 3%.

Tyson has two common stock issues. The Class B shares have ten votes each and are 99.9% owned by the Tyson family, which maintains both financial control and management of the business. Consecutive cash dividends have been paid since 1972. Tyson paid a 100% stock dividend in 1983, a 150% stock dividend in 1985, a 100% stock dividend in 1986, a 50% stock dividend in 1987, and a 100% stock dividend in 1991.

Total assets: $2.6 billion
Current ratio: 1.2
Common shares outstanding: Class A 70.1 million
Class B 68.5 million

	1982	1983	1984	1985	1986	1987	1988	1989	1990	1991
REVENUES (MIL.)	559	604	750	1,136	1,504	1,786	1,936	2,538	3,825	3,922
NET INCOME (MIL.)	9.4	11	18	35	50	68	81	101	120	145
EARNINGS PER SHARE	.08	.09	.16	.29	.39	.53	.64	.78	.90	1.05
DIVIDEND PER SHARE	.005	.005	.005	.008	.012	.019	.02	.02	.02	.03
PRICES Hi	0.8	21.2	1.4	4.8	12.8	12.0	10.2	13.1	17.8	23.3
Lo	0.4	0.8	1.0	1.9	4.3	5.4	5.5	7.4	11.4	13.9

UST Corporation

40 Court Street
Boston, Massachusetts 02108
Tel (617) 726-7000
Listed: NASDAQ
Investor contact: Sheila Celata
Ticker symbol: USTB
S&P rating: A

UST Corporation is a Boston-based bank holding company with a lead bank, United States Trust Company, and three additional banking subsidiaries: U.S. Trust/Norfolk, U.S. Trust, and UST Merchant Bancorp, Inc. Also, UST Corporation has a data-processing subsidiary, a venture capital subsidiary, a leasing subsidiary, and a property research group.

UST Corp.

UST's focus is on small to medium-sized businesses. In addition to loans, UST has quite a number of fee services, such as safety deposit boxes, travelers' checks, letters of credit, foreign exchange, documentary collections, trade finance, and wire services as well as a sizable trust-management business.

UST Corporation has invested in a state-of-the-art computer system, which gives customers direct access to account information. It is now installing a second-phase computer system, which will enable customers to achieve on-line transfers between accounts.

During 1990, UST purchased from the Resolution Trust Corp., for

$6.1 million, the 17 Massachusetts branches of the failed Boston-based Homeowners Federal Savings Bank. The acquisition provided an addition of $960 million to UST's core deposit base and extended UST's banking operations to the South Shore and Metrowest suburbs of Boston.

At year-end 1990, loans of $1.86 billion were divided as follows: commercial, 55%; real estate construction, 8%; real estate commercial, 27%; real estate residential, 2%; and consumer, 8%.

In 1990, assets under management grew to $1.7 billion and noninterest income rose to $24.4 million.

UST Corporation has paid consecutive cash dividends since 1974. The Sidell family controls about 14% and institutional investors about 23% of the outstanding common shares. UST paid a 100% stock dividend in 1980, a 6% stock dividend in 1981, a 100% stock dividend in 1983, a 50% stock dividend in 1986, a 100% stock dividend in 1987, and a 5% stock dividend in 1991.

Total assets: $3.1 billion
Common shares outstanding: 12.9 million

		1981	1982	1983	1984	1985	1986	1987	1988	1989	1990
NET INCOME (MIL.)		5.4	6.3	7.3	9.3	13	19	24	28	28	1.9
EARNINGS PER SHARE		.64	.73	.85	1.00	1.24	1.60	1.84	2.11	2.10	0.13
DIVIDEND PER SHARE		.12	.16	.21	.27	.31	.37	.43	.51	.58	.60
PRICES	Hi	2.5	5.2	8.1	8.5	13.6	20.0	41.2	22.2	19.5	15.2
	Lo	2.4	2.4	5.1	5.6	7.5	12.3	17.6	15.7	13.8	5.2

UST, Inc.

100 West Putman Avenue
Greenwich, Connecticut 06830
Tel. (203) 661-1100
Listed: NYSE
Investor contact: Mgr. Investor Relations, Mark A. Rozelle
Ticker symbol: UST
S&P rating: A+

As described in its Investors Factsheet, "UST's roots go back to 1822, 40

UST

years before branded cigarettes were first marketed. Copenhagen, first sold that year, is one of the oldest brand names in American consumer products still in use. Skoal was introduced in 1934. Together, they are the best-selling brands of smokeless tobacco in the world. Over the last 20 years, moist smokeless tobacco has expanded its base among adult males who want to enjoy tobacco without lighting up. Its traditional customer base, rooted in factories, mines, and farms has grown to include active outdoor oriented adult males. The awareness of the Skoal name has allowed UST to broaden its appeal even further. Skoal Bandits, an innovative portion pack product, and Skoal Long Cut, are each available in four brands. Thus these two products of 1982 have grown into ten products in nine short years. This is testimony to both the effectiveness of UST's marketing and the receptivity of its adult audience." UST has a market share of more than 90% in moist smokeless tobacco.

"UST markets America's best selling imported pipe tobacco—Borkum Riff—and produces and markets Don Tomas premium handmade cigars from Honduras." Other products include Dr. Grabow Pre-smoked and Mastercraft imported pipes plus dry tobaccos such as Rooster, Red Seal, Bruton, and Devoe. Chewing tobacco is sold under the WB Cut name. Likewise, UST markets a number of smoker's accessories such as Dill pipe cleaners.

UST has expanded in recent years through its wholly owned subsidiary, International Wines and Spirits, Ltd. "UST's Washington State wine operation principally known for its Chareau Ste. Michelle and Columbia Crest premium wines, is one of the largest premium wine producers in the U.S. with 1990 sales of more than 17 million bottles. It also produces and markets premium wines from the Napa Valley under the Corn Creek and Villa Mt. Eden labels."

UST's 1991 Fortune 500 ranking (based on 1990 figures) were as follows: return on sales (29%), rank 3; return on assets (36%), rank 3; return on equity (47%), rank 13. In 1990, sales were divided as follows: tobacco, 86%; wine, 7%; and other, 7%.

UST has increased earnings for 30 consecutive years. It has paid consecutive cash dividends since 1912 and has increased cash dividends in each of the past 20 years. "Dividends and earnings per share have grown at 20% and 19% respectively, compounded annually over the last 10 years." Institutions control about 50% of the outstanding common shares. UST paid a 200% stock dividend in 1983, a 100% stock dividend in 1987, 1989, and 1992.

Total assets: $623 million
Current ratio: 3.9
Common shares outstanding: 212.1 million

	1981	1982	1983	1984	1985	1986	1987	1988	1989	1990
REVENUES (MIL.)	280	320	383	444	480	518	576	619	682	765
NET INCOME (MIL)	46	55	71	84	94	104	131	162	190	223
EARNINGS PER SHARE	.21	.26	.30	.36	.41	.46	.57	.71	.82	.98
DIVIDEND PER SHARE	.19	.12	.15	.18	.22	.25	.30	.37	.46	.55
PRICES Hi	2.1	3.1	5.1	5.4	5.0	5.7	8.1	10.6	15.4	18.3
Lo	1.5	1.8	2.6	3.9	3.8	3.8	4.9	6.1	9.8	12.4

UniFirst Corporation

68 Jonspin Road
Wilmington, Massachusetts 01887
Tel. (508) 658-8888
Listed: NYSE
Investor contact: V.P.–C.F.O. John B. Bartlett
Ticker symbol: UNF
S&P rating: A-

As profiled in its 1990 Annual Report, "UniFirst Corporation is a fifty-five year old leader in the growing garment service industry. Headquartered in Wilmington, Massachusetts, the Company serves more than one hundred thousand customer locations from facilities in twenty-eight states and Canada. Our forty-three hundred  employees provide superior quality occupational garments, career apparel, and imagewear programs to businesses of all kinds.

"The foundation of our business is manufacturing, cleaning, maintaining, and delivering at a competitive price, the work clothes our customers need. Therefore, we have a responsibility to make sure each of our facilities, from our very first laundry in Massachusetts to our newest manufacturing plant in Arkansas, is equipped with the most efficient and productive system available. In fiscal 1990, UniFirst invested over $22 million in enhancing existing facilities and undertaking new construction. The result will be measurable gains in cost-efficiency for years to come.

"UniFirst operates from one hundred locations in the United States and Canada including eighty Customer Service Centers, thirteen Nuclear Decontamination facilities, four Distribution Centers, and three Manufacturing plants."

In 1959, UniFirst became the first licensed vendor of garment decontamination services for nuclear facilities. Now, thirty years later, it remains the undisputed leader. The Nuclear Division now has 13 specialized plants across the United States. Garment decontamination for the nuclear industry is one of UniFirst's most rapidly growing and most profitable enterprises.

During 1990, UniFirst acquired plants in Arkansas and Los Angeles, the latter marks its first venture into the Pacific Coast area. UniFirst manufactures approximately 30% of the garments it services. Also in 1990 revenues were roughly divided among garment rental, 63%; non-garment rental, 29%; and other, 8%.

In late 1991, UniFirst Corporation acquired the uniform rental business of Rental Work Clothes, Inc. of Albuquerque, New Mexico, and the uniform rental business of Services Control Corp. of Phoenix, Arizona.

Consecutive cash dividends have been paid since 1979. Chairman and Chief Executive office Aldo A. Croatti controls more than 50% of the shares. UniFirst paid a 230% stock dividend in 1983 and a 100% stock dividend in 1989.

Total assets: $204.4 million
Current ratio: 1.7
Common shares outstanding: 10.2 million

		1982	1983	1984	1985	1986	1987	1988	1989	1990	1991
REVENUES (MIL.)		59	78	88	105	114	160	196	213	227	250
NET INCOME (MIL.)		4.6	5.5	6.4	6.1	8.3	7.8	8.7	12	14	13
EARNINGS PER SHARE		.46	.57	.64	.61	.83	.78	.86	1.14	1.40	1.29
DIVIDEND PER SHARE		.011	.037	.10	.10	.10	.10	.10	.10	.12	.12
PRICES	Hi	—	10.4	10.3	9.8	16.3	16.1	13.4	24.0	24.1	22.3
	Lo	—	7.0	6.6	6.5	8.4	8.8	10.9	12.9	13.5	14.5

Universal Corporation

Hamilton Street At Broad
Richmond, Virginia 23230
Tel. (804) 359-9311
Listed: NYSE
Investor contact: Treas. O. Kemp Dozier
Ticker symbol: UVV
S&P rating: A

Universal Corporation is the holding company for Universal Leaf Tobacco, the largest independent tobacco importer and exporter in the world. Universal's business also involves the buying and selling of building supplies, lumber, rubber, peanuts, sunflower seeds, and vegetable oils. In April, 1986, Universal acquired a Dutch commodities and lumber firm—Deli.

Universal's primary business is the purchasing, processing, and selling of tobacco to snuff, cigar, cigarette, and pipe tobacco manufacturers. Some years, Universal purchases 35% to 40% of the total domestic production of flue-cured and Burley tobacco. Universal derives more than 40% of its revenues from the sale of tobacco to Philip Morris.

In Europe, construction is picking up in anticipation of the Common Market's reduction of trade restrictions scheduled to take effect in 1992. With this in mind, Universal is in the process of expanding its Dutch building-products company. In August 1990, Universal acquired Gebrüeder Kulenkampff A.G. of Bremen, Germany, a large international leaf tobacco trading organization.

In 1991, tobacco provided 73% of revenues and 86% of profits; agricultural products provided 13% of revenues and 2% of profits; and lumber and building products provided 14% of revenues and 12% of profits.

In 1991, Universal spun off to shareholders Lawyers Title Insurance Company on the basis of one share of Lawyers Title for every four shares of Universal Corporation.

Universal has paid consecutive cash dividends since 1927. It paid a

100% stock dividend in 1984 and another 100% stock dividend in 1992.

Total assets: $1.3 billion
Current ratio: 1.3
Common shares outstanding: 16.4 million

		1982	1983	1984	1985	1986	1987	1988	1989	1990	1991
REVENUES (MIL.)		1,253	1,082	1,019	1,079	1,145	1,701	1,997	2,463	2,389	2,896
NET INCOME (MIL.)		34	37	38	46	47	56	61	54	45	20
EARNINGS PER SHARE		.99	1.06	1.11	1.33	1.37	1.63	1.78	1.60	1.35	.62
DIVIDEND PER SHARE		.40	.43	.45	.48	.53	.56	.63	.69	.73	.76
PRICES	Hi	8.5	10.6	11.0	12.3	15.5	18.4	16.9	19.5	18.1	34.0
	Lo	5.7	6.7	7.6	9.4	11.6	12.8	13.9	16.5	11.0	11.2

Valley National Bancorp

505 Allwood Road
Clifton, New Jersey 07012
Tel. (201) 305-8800
Listed: NASDAQ
Investor contact: Exec. V.P. Sam. P. Pinyuh
Ticker Symbol: VNBP
S&P rating: A

Valley National Bancorp.

As described in its 1990 Annual Report, "Valley National Bancorp, a $2.0 billion regional bank holding company headquartered in Clifton, New Jersey, was organized in 1983 and is registered with the Board of Governors of the Federal Reserve System under the Bank Holding Company Act of 1956. Valley's principal business activities are limited to those permissible for bank holding companies and include the management and control of the twenty-seven office $1.86 billion Valley National Bank, Passaic, New Jersey, Valley's commercial bank subsidiary.

"In addition on December 31st, 1990 Valley acquired all the issued and outstanding common shares of Mayflower Financial Corporation (Mayflower), a savings and loan holding company headquartered in Livingston, New Jersey, and as a result, acquired indirect control of the two office, $129.2 million Mayflower Savings Bank, S.L.A., Mayflower's savings and loan subsidiary."

Valley, situated in the Northeastern counties of Passaic, Hudson, Morris, Bergen, and Essex, New Jersey, through a combination of strict underwriting standards and expense control, is one of the most profitable banks in the nation. In 1990, return on assets was a high 1.47% and return on equity a strong 15.04%.

In 1990, loans of $1.45 billion were divided as follows: real estate mortgage, 43.5%; consumer, 28.2%; commercial, financial, and agricultural, 22.1%; and real estate construction, 6.2%.

In 1990, sources of $1.8 billion in revenues were interest on loans and fees, 79.4%; other interest, 1.0%; investment securities, 14.0%; fees and charges, 2.8%; and other income, 2.8%.

In 1990, deposits of $1.7 billion were divided as follows: time, 44.7%; savings, 40.0%; and non-interest bearing, 15.3%.

Valley National has paid consecutive cash dividends since 1936. It paid a 5% stock dividend in 1980, a 100% stock dividend in 1983, a 100% stock dividend in 1985, a 50% stock dividend in 1986, and a 50% stock dividend in 1988.

Total assets: $2.0 billion
Common shares outstanding: 12.7 million

		1981	1982	1983	1984	1985	1986	1987	1988	1989	1990
NET INCOME (MIL)		6.3	9.8	14	17	23	29	30	32	34	27
EARNINGS PER SHARE		.66	.93	1.00	1.50	1.83	2.25	2.39	2.54	2.67	2.14
DIVIDEND PER SHARE		.29	.32	.42	.55	.75	.90	1.12	1.19	1.32	1.36
PRICES	Hi	3.8	5.4	11.9	13.3	32.5	39.4	39.4	32.0	28.3	25.5
	Lo	2.8	3.8	5.6	11.9	12.0	26.0	23.8	24.5	24.0	14.3

America's GROWTH STOCKS

273

The Valspar Corporation

1101 Third Street South
Minneapolis, Minnesota 55415
Tel. (612) 332-7371
Listed: AMEX
Investor contact: V.P. Finance, P.C. Reyelts
Ticker symbol: VAL
S&P rating: A+

The Valspar
Corporation

Valspar, founded in 1806, got its early growth as a manufacturer of a superior varnish product. Today, it is one of the largest manufacturers of consumer paints and industrial coatings. Its operation may be divided into four segments: consumer coatings, industrial coatings, packaging coatings, and maintenance and marine coatings.

Consumer coatings is the largest segment, comprising 32% of sales. This segment manufactures and markets a complete line of latex and oil-based paints and varnishes, which are used by consumers such as painting contractors and do it yourselfers. It markets its products under such labels as Valspar, Majicolor, Minnesota Paints, and numerous private labels.

Industrial coatings make up 22% of sales and consist of decorative and protective coatings for wood, metal, and plastic. The furniture and wood panelling industries are major customers.

Packaging coatings comprise 21% of sales. Valspar is one of the major suppliers of coatings for beverage cans, aerosol cans, glass containers, and bottle crowns. It also makes coatings for flexible plastic materials, film, and foil.

Special products comprise 25% of sales and include resins, emulsions, marine coatings, and specialty sealers. Valspar is the second-largest manufacturer of colorants for tinting paints.

Valspar has 21 manufacturing plants in the United States and Canada and licensees worldwide.

In 1990, Valspar acquired the industrial coatings division of DeSoto, Inc., a major private-label paint manufacturer. During 1989, Valspar purchased McCloskey Corp., a producer of resins and wood coatings. McCloskey was only marginally profitable and will take some time for Valspar to digest.

Valspar has had 15 years of consecutive earnings increases. Consecutive cash dividends have been paid since 1964. It has raised its cash dividend in each of the past 11 years. Institutions hold about 57% of the outstanding shares. Valspar paid a 100% stock dividend in 1984, 1987, and 1992.

Total assets: $303 million
Current ratio: 1.5
Common shares outstanding: 21.8 million

		1982	1983	1984	1985	1986	1987	1988	1989	1990	1991
REVENUES (MIL.)		152	162	224	347	345	449	480	527	571	633
NET INCOME (MIL.)		7.1	10	11	12	15	18	18	23	27	28
EARNINGS PER SHARE		.33	.45	.48	.49	.63	.81	.82	1.04	1.23	1.27
DIVIDEND PER SHARE		.08	.09	.10	.11	.13	.16	.20	.22	.26	.30
PRICES	Hi	3.1	5.3	5.1	7.7	12.1	20.3	14.8	18.3	20.0	29.8
	Lo	1.3	2.9	3.8	4.8	7.4	10.7	10.6	11.9	14.7	17.9

Wachovia Corporation

301 North Main Street
Winston-Salem, North Carolina 27150
Tel. (919) 770-5000
Listed: NYSE
Investor contact: Comptroller Graham P. Dozier III
Ticker symbol: WB
S&P rating: A

Wachovia, formed in 1985 through the merger of Wachovia Corporation and First Atlanta Corporation, is one of the nation's premier high-quality growth banks. Wachovia has 218 North Carolina and 134 Georgia full-service banking offices. During 1990, Wachovia experienced moderate across-the-board loan growth.

Wachovia
Corporation

However, the bank has a most conservative loan policy, which it maintains in the strong competitive growth arena of the Southeast.

Wachovia's capital strength and profitability ratios are superb. Management style is strongly centralized with superior expense controls. The bank eliminated its loans to less-developed countries and avoids lending in any areas of above-average risk.

Other operations include mortgage, brokerage, leasing, insurance, and student loan services.

In 1990, earnings assets of $21.0 billion were apportioned as follows: commercial loans, 33%; investments, 25%; real estate loans, 24%; and retail loans, 18%.

In 1990, sources of funds were time deposits, 33%; savings and money market deposits, 19%; other deposits, 16%; borrowings, 21%; equity, 8%; and other, 3%.

In mid-1991, Wachovia Corp. acquired the $7.1 billion-asset South Carolina National Corp. for $800 million in stock.

Wachovia has paid consecutive cash dividends since 1936; First Atlanta, since 1886. Wachovia paid a 100% stock dividend in 1984 and a 20% stock dividend in 1989.

Total assets: $26.1 billion
Common shares outstanding: 70.0 million

	1981	1982	1983	1984	1985	1986	1987	1988	1989	1990
NET INCOME (MIL.)	52	53	85	100	188	194	177	244	269	297
EARNINGS PER SHARE	1.35	1.39	2.19	2.59	2.92	2.99	2.70	3.62	3.87	4.25
DIVIDEND PER SHARE	.44	.53	.62	.74	.82	.88	1.00	1.17	1.39	1.64
PRICES Hi	11.8	15.4	19.8	24.8	32.1	38.4	38.6	34.0	45.4	44.8
Lo	7.1	9.1	12.4	17.1	23.4	27.0	25.4	27.8	31.0	32.4

Walgreen Company
200 Wilmont Road
Deerfield, Illinois 60015
Tel. (708) 940-2500
Listed: NYSE
Investor contact: Asst. Treas. and Director of Finance, John M. Palizza

Ticker symbol: WAG
S&P rating: A

Charles R. Walgreen opened his first drugstore in 1901. Today Walgreen Co. is headed by his grandson Charles R. Walgreen III. As profiled in its 1991 Annual Report, "Walgreen Co. is the sales, profit, and technology leader of the U.S. chain drug store industry. Sales for 1991 topped $6.7 billion, produced by 1,646 drugstores located in 29 states and Puerto Rico. Nearly 75% of these stores have been opened or remodeled in the last five years.

Walgreens

"Founded in 1901, Walgreen celebrated its 90th anniversary this year. The company has 51,000 employees and 22,000 shareholders. Its drug stores serve more then 1.8 million customers daily and average $4.1 million in annual sales per unit. That's $425 per square foot, among the highest in the chain drug industry. Walgreen drugstores are served by eight distribution centers and five photo-processing plants.

"While guided by a conservative fiscal policy, Walgreen is dedicated to aggressive growth. Dividends, paid in every quarter since 1933, have been raised 16 times in the past 14 years."

Pharmacy comprises 35% of Walgreen's total sales. Walgreen fills 7% of all retail prescriptions in the United States, amounting to $2.4 billion in 1991 and an expected $2.8 billion in 1992.

Walgreen opened or acquired 160 retail drug stores in 1991, including six RxPress (pharmacy only) in Evansville, Indiana. Walgreen plans to open 110 stores (over half of which will be freestanding) in fiscal 1992. Walgreen has a goal of 3,000 stores by the year 2000. In 1991, Walgreen opened its eighth $43 million distribution center in Lehigh, Pennsylvania.

Walgreen operates five extended-care pharmacies, which provide unit-dose drugs for nursing homes. Walgreen has established Walgreen Pharmacy Mail Services to service an increasing number of prescriptions by mail. Walgreen is one of the top retailers of private label products, accounting for some 7% of the $2.5 billion private label market.

In 1991, sales were divided as follows: prescription drugs, 35%; non-prescription drugs, 14%; cosmetics and toiletries, 9%; general merchandise, 25%; tobacco products, 5%; liquor and beverages, 12%; and food service, 0%.

Earnings have increased in each of the past 17 years. Consecutive cash dividends have been paid since 1933. Institutions control about 47% of the outstanding shares. Walgreen split two-for-one in 1982, paid a 100% stock dividend in 1983 and 1985, and split two-for-one in 1991.

Total assets: $2.0 billion
Current ratio: 1.8
Common shares outstanding: 123.1 million

		1982	1983	1984	1985	1986	1987	1988	1989	1990	1991
REVENUES (MIL.)		2,039	2,361	2,745	3,162	3,661	4,282	4,884	5,380	6,047	6,733
NET INCOME (MIL.)		56	70	85	94	103	104	129	154	175	195
EARNINGS PER SHARE		.47	.57	.70	.77	.84	.84	1.05	1.25	1.41	1.58
DIVIDEND PER SHARE		.13	.15	.18	.22	.25	.27	.30	.34	.40	.46
PRICES	Hi	7.3	10.1	11.3	15.1	19.8	22.9	18.7	25.1	26.6	38.6
	Lo	2.8	6.5	7.2	10.8	12.1	12.4	13.6	15.6	19.9	24.6

Wallace Computer Services, Inc.

4600 West Roosevelt Road
Hillside, Illinois 60162
Tel. (312) 626-2000
Listed: NYSE
Investor contact: V.P.–Secy. Michael J. Halloran
Ticker symbol: WCS
S&P rating: A+

Wallace Computer Services, Inc.

Wallace Computer Services is an excellent way to profit from computers without getting hung up on hardware which can become obsolete. Based in Hillside, Illinois, Wallace is a major factor in computer services and supply. It produces a variety of standard and customized business forms. It ranks about fifth among forms producers and is noted for its continuous business forms. Also, Wallace markets computer labels, machine ribbons, software accessories, and office supplies. Its Barcode Asset Management is both a hardware and software system for barcoding inventory and asset control.

The Wallace Press segment prints a wide variety of directories, catalogs, and price guides by means of computerized type setting.

The label segment, acquired in 1988 through the purchase of Apollo Label, markets the CS Printware Label System, which gives the customer and the ability to print its own pressure-sensitive bar coded labels.

The direct mail segment, through its Visible Computer Supply Catalog, offers more than 8,000 items such as computer supplies, office supplies, software, and tax forms.

The Tops Business Forms division markets standard business forms to wholesalers, dealers, and mass-market merchandise chains.

In 1991, Wallace acquired Colorforms, a company that provides promotional graphics and mailing services to the direct mail advertising industry.

Through a network distribution system, Wallace services more than 100 major cities throughout the United States. Business forms account for 65% to 70% of yearly sales. Wallace has one of the highest pretax margins in the industry and accounts for 4% to 5% of market share.

Wallace Computer Services has increased earnings for the 30th consecutive year and dividends for the 18th consecutive year. Consecutive cash dividends have been paid since 1933. Wallace paid a 100% stock dividend in 1980, a 100% stock dividend in 1983, and a 100% stock dividend in 1989.

Total assets: $399 million
Current ratio: 4.3
Common shares outstanding: 21.5 million

		1982	1983	1984	1985	1986	1987	1988	1989	1990	1991
REVENUES (MIL.)		195	210	243	275	305	341	383	429	449	459
NET INCOME (MIL.)		14	16	19	22	24	26	32	37	40	35
EARNINGS PER SHARE		.76	.83	.95	1.10	1.20	1.27	1.53	1.76	1.86	1.63
DIVIDEND PER SHARE		.17	.18	.20	.23	.25	.30	.33	.40	.46	.50
PRICES	Hi	12.5	16.3	16.1	20.4	25.1	24.8	22.5	31.5	31.5	29.1
	Lo	6.8	11.4	11.9	15.1	18.5	15.8	17.3	21.0	15.9	19.0

Wal-Mart Stores, Inc.

702 Southwest 8th Street (P.O. Box 116)
Bentonville, Arkansas 72716
Tel. (501) 273-4000
Listed: NYSE
Investor contact: V.P. & Treas. C. Rateliff
Ticker symbol: WMT
S&P rating: A+

WAL-MART Wal-Mart is a chain of consistently profitable discount department stores located in rural areas of the Midwestern, Southern, and Southwestern states. Its stores are located away from large cities and strong competition. There are basically three chains operating under the Wal-Mart flagship. First, there are more than 1,250 Wal-Mart discount department stores (including five super-stores) in 35 states, operating under the name Wal-Mart Discount City Stores. Second, there is Sam's Wholesale Club, a membership-only club of more than 148 cash-and-carry stores in metropolitan areas. Third, there is Discount Drug, a chain of about a dozen drug and merchandise stores in the Midwest. In addition, Wal-Mart has four Hypermart U.S.A. stores, a combination of discount merchandise and grocery stores, operating in the Midwest.

There is a uniformity in size and merchandise among the typical Wal-Mart Discount City stores. Each store is about 70,000 square feet and divided into 36 departments. They include hardware, housewares, wearing apparel, jewelry, cosmetics, and automotive supplies. Wal-Mart features both national-brand and private-label items. Hard goods make up about 65% and soft goods about 28% of sales. Wal-Mart has 15 distribution centers operating within a 450-mile radius of its stores.

Wal-Mart has evolved into the largest American retailer. In 1991, Wal-Mart acquired Wholesale Club, operating 27 clubs in the midwest, and acquired the McLane Co., Inc., a distributor of grocery and general merchandise to over 25,000 retail stores in 11 states.

Wal-Mart has increased earnings for 27 consecutive years. It initiated cash dividends in 1973 and has increased its dividend every year since 1977. The Walton family controls about 40% and institutions about 30% of the outstanding common shares. Wal-Mart paid a 100% stock dividend in 1980, a 100% stock dividend in 1982, a 100% stock dividend in 1983, a 100% stock dividend in 1985, a 100% stock dividend in 1987, and a 100% stock dividend in 1990.

Total assets: $11.4 billion
Current ratio: 1.6
Common shares outstanding: 1.1 billion

		1982	1983	1984	1985	1986	1987	1988	1989	1990	1991
REVENUES (MIL.)		2,445	3,376	4,667	6,401	8,451	11,909	15,959	20,649	25,811	32,602
NET INCOME (MIL.)		83	124	196	271	327	450	628	837	1,076	1,291
EARNINGS PER SHARE		.08	.11	.17	.24	.29	.40	.55	.74	.95	1.14
DIVIDEND PER SHARE		.008	.011	.018	.026	.035	.043	.06	.08	.11	.14
PRICES	Hi	3.5	5.9	6.0	8.7	13.5	21.5	17.0	22.3	36.8	59.9
	Lo	1.3	2.8	3.8	4.8	7.3	10.0	12.2	15.0	20.1	28.0

The Washington Post Company

1150 15th Street NW
Washington, D.C. 20071
Tel. (202) 334-6600
Listed: NYSE
Investor contact: Mgr. Corporate Affairs, Rima Calderon
Ticker symbol: WPO
S&P rating: A

The Washington Post Company owns and operates the *Washington Post* newspaper, which has a strong grip on the Washington, D.C., metro newspaper market. A strong editorial policy has distanced it from regional competitors. It has a daily circulation of more than 838,000 and a Sunday circulation of more than 1,165,000. Also, the Washington Post Company owns the *Herald* of Everett, Washington, which has a daily circulation of more than 53,000 and a Sunday circulation of more than 64,000. In May, 1991, the *Herald* changed from an

281

evening to a morning paper. In addition, the Washington Post Company owns *Newsweek* magazine, four Post-Newsweek network affiliated television stations, Post-Newsweek Cable, the Stanley H. Kaplan Education Centers, Legi-Slate, Inc., and a 49% interest in the Bowater Mersey Paper Co., Ltd.

With clear writing, vivid photography, informative graphics, and an excellent editorial product, *Newsweek* has increased its circulation 10% in the past ten years. *Newsweek International* has three international editions: Atlantic, Asia, and Latin America.

Post-Newsweek Stations are WDIV/TV-4 Detroit, the highest-rated NBC affiliate in the country's top ten markets; WPLG/TV10-Miami, the top-rated South Florida television station; WFSB/TV3-Hartford; and WJTX/TV4-Jacksonville.

Post-Newsweek Cable (52 cable systems) subscribers grew to 435,896 at year-end 1990. The midyear acquisition of the Ada, Oklahoma, system added 6,600 subscribers. In 1990, Post-Newsweek Cable acquired franchises in Dundee, Perth, Leven, and Glenrothes, Scotland.

The Stanley H. Kaplan Educational Centers is the world's largest test preparation company. It has 146 permanent locations in the United States and Canada. Total revenue has doubled since the Washington Post Company acquired Kaplan six years ago.

The Legi-Slate, Inc., data base service, is the original and leading online information service covering Congress and the Federal Register.

In 1990, sales and profits were divided as follows: newspaper publishing, 48% of sales and 51% of profits; magazine publishing, 24% of sales and 10% of profits; broadcasting, 12% of sales and 24% of profits; cable television, 10% of sales and 10% of profits; and other businesses, 6% of sales and 5% of profits.

The Washington Post Company has two classes of common stock. The Graham family owns all of the Class A shares. The Class B shares, with limited voting rights, are about 17% owned by Berkshire Hathaway and about 49% owned by institutions. The Washington Post Company paid a 100% stock dividend in 1978.

Total assets: $1.5 billion
Current ratio: 1.6
Common shares outstanding: Class A 1.9 million
Class B 10.0 million

	1981	1982	1983	1984	1985	1986	1987	1988	1989	1990
REVENUES (MIL.)	753	801	878	984	1,079	1,215	1,315	1,368	1,444	1,439
NET INCOME (MIL.)	33	52	68	86	114	100	186	269	198	175
EARNINGS PER SHARE	2.32	3.70	4.82	6.11	8.66	7.80	14.52	20.91	15.50	14.45
DIVIDEND PER SHARE	.50	.56	.66	.80	.96	1.12	1.28	1.56	1.84	4.00
PRICES Hi	33.0	60.9	73.3	85.0	130.0	184.5	269.0	229.0	311.0	295.5
Lo	19.0	27.4	54.5	60.8	77.8	115.0	150.0	186.5	204.0	167.0

America's GROWTH STOCKS

Waste Management, Inc.

3003 Butterfield Road
Oak Brook, Illinois 60521
Tel (708) 572-8800
Listed: NYSE
Investor contact: Treas. James E. Koenig
Ticker symbol: WMX
S&P rating: A

Waste Management is one of America's premier growth companies. It is the largest and most comprehensive waste management firm in the world. Its operations encompass residential, commercial, industrial, chemical, nuclear, hazardous, solid, and liquid waste.

Its North American operations take place in 48 states, the District of Columbia, Puerto Rico, and five Canadian provinces. Waste Management serves over 800,000 industrial and commercial customers and over eight million residential customers. It operates over 125 landfills and has some 80 more under surveillance. It is increasingly involved in recycling paper, glass, plastics, and metal. Through 55%-owned Wheelabrator Technologies, Waste Management is engaged in the conversion of trash to energy (steam and electricity). It has a 1,000-ton waste-to-energy plant in Tampa, Florida, and is constructing another, which has twice the capacity, near Fort Lauderdale.

In 1990, Waste Management joined with Service-Master to form a new company, Service-Master Consumer Services L.P. The company merges Waste Management's pest control and Tru Green lawn care business with Service Master's consumer operation. Waste Management has a 19.9% interest in the new company.

Chemical Waste Management, 81% owned, offers hazardous waste disposal. It is rapidly gaining market share from related competitors, which do not have either the processing or landfill capacity of Chemical Waste. Its Chem-Nuclear Systems subsidiary provides radioactive waste management in the United States. Brand Companies, 49% owned by Chemical Waste, is the nation's largest asbestos removal firm.

In addition, Waste Management is involved in street sweeping services. Through its Envirotech Operating Services, it operates water and sewerage treatment plants for municipalities. Also, it sells Port-O-Let portable toilets. Waste Management has extended operations to Europe, Australia, New Zealand, Saudi Arabia, and Argentina.

Waste Management has increased earnings for 18 consecutive years and has increased dividends each year since their initiation in 1976. Institutions control about 50% of the outstanding shares. Waste Management paid a 200% stock dividend in 1981, a 100% stock dividend in 1985, a 100% stock dividend in 1987, and a 100% stock dividend in 1989.

Total assets: $10.5 billion
Current ratio: 1.0
Common shares outstanding: 490.1 million

	1981	1982	1983	1984	1985	1986	1987	1988	1989	1990
REVENUES (MIL.)	973	967	1,040	1,315	1,625	2,018	2,758	3,566	4,459	6,034
NET INCOME (MIL.)	84	107	120	143	172	371	327	464	562	709
EARNINGS PER SHARE	.25	.30	.32	.37	.43	.88	.73	1.03	1.22	1.49
DIVIDEND PER SHARE	.048	.063	.08	.098	.11	.14	.18	.23	.29	.35
PRICES Hi	5.3	7.0	7.8	6.0	9.5	15.0	24.3	21.4	35.9	45.5
Lo	3.3	3.3	4.8	3.5	5.5	8.6	13.9	15.8	20.4	28.6

Weis Markets, Inc.

1000 South Second Street
Sunbury, Pennsylvania 17801
Tel. (717) 286-4571

Listed: NYSE
Investor contact: V.P. Finance, Richard L. Wetzel
Ticker symbol: WMK
S&P rating: A+

Weis is a supermarket chain of about 120 retail markets with a home base in Sunbury, Pennsylvania, and additional markets in Pennsylvania, Maryland, Virginia, West Virginia, and New York. Its stores include

Weis Markets, Inc.

both the conventionally sized and super-centers. About a hundred of the stores are in central Pennsylvania. Weis owns about half of its store sites. Weis stocks both national-brand and private-label items. Its private label brands include Big Top, Carnival, and Weis Quality. Also, Weis operates five Amity House Ice Cream Shoppes. Its Weis Food Service distributes food to institutions such as schools and hospitals.

Weis manufactures ice cream, processes meat, processes milk and frozen foods, and has a delicatessen kitchen at its Sunbury location. It has two warehouses, one in Sunbury and the other in Milton, Pennsylvania. Its own tractor-trailer fleet transports merchandise to its retail stores.

Weis's strategy is to build supermarkets in less-competitive suburban areas. However, expansion into the Washington, D.C., area is bringing it into competition with Giant Stores. Also, Food Lion is about to expand into some of Weis's Pennsylvania locations.

In 1990, Weis acquired Allegheny Food's distribution operations in the Pocono Mountains and northern New Jersey. Weis plans to open ten new supermarkets during 1991.

In 1990, sales were divided as follows: grocery, 63%; meat, 15%; produce, 11%; and other, 11%.

Weis Markets is both cash rich and debt free. President Siegfried Weis controls about 30% and the Weis family controls over 75% of the common shares.

Weis Markets has paid consecutive cash dividends since 1940. It paid a 50% stock dividend in 1979, a 50% stock dividend in 1982, a 50% stock dividend in 1983, a 50% stock dividend in 1985, and a 50% stock dividend in 1987.

Total assets: $694 million
Current ratio: 7.0
Common shares outstanding: 44.7 million

	1981	1982	1983	1984	1985	1986	1987	1988	1989	1990
REVENUES (MIL.)	757	812	892	958	1,017	1,101	1,128	1,189	1,239	1,272
NET INCOME (MIL.)	38	43	50	55	60	65	76	83	86	87
EARNINGS PER SHARE	.82	.93	1.08	1.19	1.30	1.42	1.66	1.82	1.91	1.93
DIVIDEND PER SHARE	.20	.23	.25	.29	.32	.36	.43	.50	.56	.60
PRICES Hi	7.9	12.1	17.9	16.5	28.0	27.9	41.6	37.0	37.5	34.4
Lo	5.5	7.4	11.1	13.4	15.5	22.1	23.9	27.0	28.1	24.3

Westinghouse Electric Corporation

Gateway Center
Pittsburgh, Pennsylvania 15222
Tel. (412) 244-2000
Listed: NYSE
Investor contact: Asst. Director Investor Relations, J.R. White
Ticker symbol: WX
S&P rating: A

Founded by American investor George Westinghouse in 1886, Westinghouse Electric has evolved into one of the nation's largest and most diversified technology-driven companies.

Pittsburgh-based Westinghouse's operations are basically divided into seven categories: broadcasting, electronic systems, environmental systems, financial services, industries, furniture, and power systems.

Westinghouse owns five Group W television stations and 18 radio stations. It both produces and syndicates television programs.

Electronic Systems deals primarily with defense electronics and includes such military hardware as radar, infrared detection systems, missile-launching equipment, and aerospace electronic control systems. In addition, the company has begun applying its defense technology in nondefense applications such as air traffic control systems, security systems, and automated postal systems. This nondefense business has grown to be 30% of this unit's total business.

The Environmental Systems Group is involved in the managing, handling, and treatment of a wide variety of industrial, municipal, nuclear, hazardous, and toxic waste.

Westinghouse Financial Services, Inc., and its subsidiary Westinghouse Credit Corporation provide corporate lending, commercial and residential real estate financing, and leasing.

The Industries Group consists of four units: Thermo King Corporation, which is involved in the transport temperature control business; Distribution and Control, which markets electrical distribution products, circuit-protective devices, and control products; Westinghouse Electric Supply Company, which distributes electrical products made by 5,000 suppliers, including Westinghouse; and Westinghouse Communities, which is involved in Florida land and community development.

The Knoll Group is a global leader in the $16 billion office furnishings market.

The Power Systems Group manufactures such power generation systems as steam and combustion generators and nuclear reactors.

Consecutive cash dividends have been paid since 1935. Institutions control more than 50% of the common shares. Westinghouse had a 2 for 1 split in 1984 and another 2 for 1 split in 1990.

Total assets: $22.0 billion
Current ratio: 1.1
Common shares outstanding: 290.9 million

		1981	1982	1983	1984	1985	1986	1987	1988	1989	1990
REVENUES (MIL.)		9,368	9,745	9,533	10,265	10,700	10,731	10,679	12,500	12,844	12,915
NET INCOME (MIL.)		438	449	449	536	605	173	901	823	922	268
EARNINGS PER SHARE		1.28	1.29	1.27	1.52	1.76	.58	3.12	2.83	3.15	.91
DIVIDEND PER SHARE		.45	.45	.45	.49	.58	.67	.82	.96	1.15	1.35
PRICES	Hi	8.7	10.2	14.1	14.2	23.4	31.3	37.5	28.7	38.1	39.4
	Lo	5.8	5.5	9.3	9.9	12.7	21.0	20.0	22.2	25.6	24.3

America's GROWTH STOCKS

Wilmington Trust Company

Rodney Square North
Wilmington, Delaware 19890
Tel. (302) 651-1000

Listed: NASDAQ
Investor contact: Sr. V.P. Ted T. Cecala, Jr.
Ticker symbol: WILM
S&P rating: A+

Wilmington Trust Company

Wilmington Trust is a commercial and retail banking enterprise and the nation's eighth-largest personal trust institution with $6.5 billion in assets under management. Through its main office and six suburban branches with more than 34 offices, it is involved in a variety of banking operations. Its banking services include demand, savings, and time deposits. It makes mortgage, commercial, and consumer loans. Its large personal and institutional trust business is located in both Delaware and Florida.

In 1990, net interest income rose 8% to a record $125.5 million and noninterest revenues increased 11% to a record $90.4 million. Return on assets for 1990 registered a strong 1.87% and return on equity an improved 24.46%. These ratios, commonly used to evaluate the performance of banks, place Wilmington Trust among the best in the nation.

In 1990, Wilmington acquired Delaware Corporate Management (administrative and accounting services to more than 1,100 corporations), Wilmington Capital Management (investment management), Citibank's precious metals business, and the Peoples Bank of Harrington, a well managed bank in southern Delaware.

The Annual Report states that "In 1990, fees and commissions grew to a record $89.7 million and over the past five years grew at a 13% compound annual rate. The largest portion of fee and commission revenues is generated from a portfolio of more than $100 billion in trust, custody and investment management assets."

In 1990, loans of $2.6 billion were divided as follows: real estate mortgage, 41%; commercial, financial, and agricultural, 30%; installment, 24%; and real estate construction, 5%. Revenues of $427.9 million were divided as follows: interest on fees and loans, 62.9%; other interest, 1.3%; investment securities, 14.6%; trust management, 15.1%; service charges, 2.4%; and other income, 3.7%.

Wilmington Trust has paid consecutive cash dividends since 1914. Institutions hold about 44% of the shares. Wilmington paid a 100% stock dividend in 1983, a 100% stock dividend in 1985, and another 100% stock dividend in 1986.

288

Total assets: $3.8 billion
Common shares outstanding: 17.6 million

	1981	1982	1983	1984	1985	1986	1987	1988	1989	1990
NET INCOME (MIL.)	11	13	17	22	27	35	44	52	60	67
EARNINGS PER SHARE	.65	.79	.98	1.26	1.56	1.93	2.43	2.92	3.34	3.80
DIVIDEND PER SHARE	—	.36	.39	.44	.55	.63	.78	.92	1.18	1.44
PRICES Hi	—	5.5	7.9	11.0	19.0	25.5	36.0	31.5	46.3	45.0
Lo	—	3.3	5.0	7.8	11.0	18.3	20.0	23.0	26.5	30.3

Wisconsin Energy Corporation

231 West Michigan Street (P.O. Box 2949)
Milwaukee, Wisconsin 53201
Tel. (414) 221-2345
Listed: NYSE
Investor contact: Asst. Treas. Gordon A. Willis
Ticker symbol: WEC
S&P rating: A

Wisconsin Energy is one of the premier electric, gas, and steam utilities in the nation. It serves Milwaukee, northern Wisconsin, and upper Michigan. Its revenues are divided as follows: electricity, 84%; gas, 15%; and steam, 1%. Electricity revenues are divided as follows: residential, 26%; large commercial and industrial, 37%; small commercial and industrial, 25%; and other, 12%. Gas revenues are divided as follows: residential, 64%; commercial and industrial, 29%; and other, 7%.

> Wisconsin
> Energy
> Corporation

Wisconsin Energy's generating capacity is derived from the following sources: coal, 60%; nuclear, 29%; other utilities, 9%; and other, 2%. Wisconsin Energy's two-unit Point Beach nuclear station is ranked as one of the most efficient in the nation. Future energy needs will be satisfied by both combustion turbine units and purchased power.

Wisconsin Energy is rapidly expanding on the nonregulated front.

Its WISPARK Corporation subsidiary plans to develop large-scale industrial parks within Wisconsin Energy's utility subsidiaries' service territories. Currently it is developing Lakeview Corporate Park, a 13,500-acre landscaped commercial and industrial park near Kenosha, Wisconsin. Thirteen companies are now establishing operations at this site.

WISPARK has joined Midwest Harbor Development in the construction of GasLight Pointe, a $65 million residential and commercial waterfront complex on 12 acres along Lake Michigan in Racine, Wisconsin. The project includes a hotel, retail space, and boat slips. Also, WISPARK is developing Easte Pointe Commons, a housing development in Milwaukee.

Wisconsin Energy has paid consecutive cash dividends since 1939. Institutions control approximately 40% of the outstanding common shares. It paid a 50% stock dividend in 1982 and a 100% stock dividend in 1987.

Total assets: $1.4 billion
Common shares outstanding: 67.4 million

	1981	1982	1983	1984	1985	1986	1987	1988	1989	1990
REVENUES (MIL.)	1,152	1,303	1,418	1,435	1,441	1,411	1,365	1,541	1,493	1,442
NET INCOME (MIL.)	106	132	150	163	167	158	170	183	194	187
EARNINGS PER SHARE	1.47	1.80	1.99	2.18	2.38	2.37	2.55	2.73	2.88	2.77
DIVIDEND PER SHARE	.88	.95	1.03	1.12	1.22	1.32	1.42	1.52	1.63	1.74
PRICES Hi	9.9	12.9	14.4	16.9	20.4	32.4	28.9	27.9	32.1	32.5
Lo	6.9	8.9	11.0	12.9	15.5	19.3	21.0	22.5	25.1	26.6

Wm. Wrigley Jr. Company
410 North Michigan Avenue
Chicago, Illinois 60611
Tel. (312) 644-2121
Listed: NYSE
Investor contact: V.P. William M. Piet
Ticker symbol: WWY
S&P rating: A

Wm. Wrigley is the world's largest chewing-gum producer. It is presided over by William Wrigley, president and chief executive officer and grandson of the founder. Its products—Spearmint, Doublemint, Juicy Fruit, Freedent, Big Red, Orbit, Hubba Bubba (bubble gum), and Extra (sugar-free gum) are sold in more than 100 countries worldwide. Wrigley controls about 47% of the U.S. market and 37% of the international gum market. International sales are growing at a much stronger rate than domestic sales.

Wm. **WRIGLEY** *Jr. Company*

A subsidiary of Wrigley, Amurol Products, manufactures novelty gum products such as Bubble Tape and Big League Chew as well as hard candies and mints. Wrigley recently acquired the Reed Candy Company.

An associated company, L.A. Dreyfus Co. manufactures gum base for Wrigley and other gum-products companies. It also manufactures industrial coatings and adhesives. Another associated company, Northwestern Chemical Co., manufactures flavoring extracts and mint oil for Wrigley and other food-related companies. A third associated company, Wrico Packaging designs, manufactures and prints the various packaging and labels used by Wrigley.

For 1990, the geographic breakdown of sales and profits was as follows: the United States, 61% of sales and 59% of profits; Europe, 24% of sales and 27% of profits; and other, 15% of sales and 14% of profits.

Wrigley has no long-term debt. There are two classes of common stock. The Class B common stock has ten votes per share, in contrast to the Class A common, which has one. The Wrigley family controls 27% of the Class A common and 38% of the Class B common. Wrigley has paid consecutive cash dividends since 1913. It paid a 100% stock dividend in 1980, a 200% stock dividend in 1986, and a 100% stock dividend in 1988.

Total assets: $564 million
Current ratio: 2.8
Common shares outstanding: 29.6 million
Class B 9.6 million

		1981	1982	1983	1984	1985	1986	1987	1988	1989	1990
REVENUES (MIL.)		608	581	582	591	620	699	781	891	993	1,111
NET INCOME (MIL.)		28	36	39	40	43	54	70	87	106	117
EARNINGS PER SHARE		.60	.76	.85	.93	1.03	1.28	1.69	2.18	2.70	2.99
DIVIDEND PER SHARE		.38	.39	.42	.47	.52	.62	.85	1.09	1.36	1.48
PRICES	Hi	7.3	7.8	9.5	10.1	15.9	26.0	35.5	41.3	53.8	59.3
	Lo	5.4	4.9	6.6	7.5	9.6	13.9	19.5	32.0	35.5	43.8

BIBLIOGRAPHY

Babson-United Investment Advisors, Inc. *United & Babson Investment Report*. Babson-United Building, 101 Prescott Street, Wellesley Hills, Massachusetts 02181.

Growth Stock Outlook, Inc. *Growth Stock Outlook*. P.O. Box 15381, Chevy Chase, Maryland 20815.

Malkiel, Burton G. *A Random Walk Down Wall Street*, (1973). W.W. Norton Company, 500 Fifth Avenue, New York, New York 10110.

Merrill Lynch Advisory Publications. *Merrill Lynch Market Letter*. North Tower (20th Floor), World Financial Center, New York, New York 10281-1320.

Moody's Investors Service, Inc. *Moody's Bank & Finance Manual*, vols. 1 & 2. 99 Church Street, New York, New York 10077.

Moody's Investors Service, Inc. *Moody's Handbook of Common Stocks*. 99 Church Street, New York, New York 10007.

Moody's Investors Service, Inc. *Moody's Handbook of OTC Stocks*. 99 Church Street, New York, New York 10007.

Moody's Investors Service, Inc. *Moody's Industrial Manual*, vols. 1 & 2. 99 Church Street, New York, New York 10007.

Moody's Investors Service, Inc. *Moody's OTC Industrial Manual*. 99 Church Street, New York, New York 10007.

National Association of Investors Corporation. *Better Investing*. P.O. Box 220, Royal Oak, Michigan 48068.

OTC Review, Inc. *Equities*. 37 E. 28th Street, Suite 706, New York, New York 10016.

Standard & Poor's Corporation. *Standard & Poors Corporation Records*.

25 Broadway, New York, New York 10004.

Standard & Poor's Corporation. *Outlook.* 25 Broadway, New York, New York 10004.

Standard & Poor's Corporation. *Stock Guide.* 25 Broadway, New York, New York 10004.

Standard & Poor's Corporation. *Stock Reports.* 25 Broadway, New York, New York 10004.

Train, John. *Dance of the Money Bees* (1974). Harper & Row, Publishers, Inc. 10 East 53rd Street, New York, New York 10016.

Train, John. *Preserving Capital and Making It Grow* (1983). Clarkson N. Potter, Inc., Publishers, New York, New York 10016.

Walden, Gene. *The 100 Best Stocks to Own in America* (2nd edition, 1991). Dearborn Financial Publishing, Inc., 520 North Dearborn Street, Chicago, Illinois 60610-4975.

Wall Street Transcript Corporation. *Wall Street Transcript.* 99 Wall Street, New York, New York 10005.

About the Author

Thomas R. Drey is a retired instructor specializing in investment issues. He served as associate editor of *Stock Market* magazine and has had many articles on the stock market *published there and in the Commercial and Financial Chronicle.* Mr. Drey lives in Boston, Massachusetts.